THE LIGHT AFTER THE DARK

by
Alvin Abram

PUBLISHED WORKS:

MY SHTETL DROBIN:
The Story of Rabbi Abraham Feffer (Archive)

SHORT STORIES:
WHAT IT MEANS TO BE JEWISH
The Tribune

*

WHOSE THERE? A YID.
Canadian Jewish News

*

TA-TA-T-A-TA
A STORY IN TWO WORDS
GROWING OLD
Wordscape 4

*

I LOVE YOU DADDY
The Authors

POETRY
LOVE WITH RESPECT
JMW Anthology

MATERIAL USED BY OTHER AUTHORS:
AN ORDINARY WOMAN IN EXTRAORDINARY TIMES
Published by the Multicultural Society of Ontario (1990)
Excerpts from the Story of Ibolya Szalai
ESCAPE TO FREEDOM

THE BOYS
by Sir Martin Gilbert
Published by Douglas & McIntyre (1996)
Excerpts from the Story of Jehoszua Cygelfarb
THE GLASS FACTORY

THE LIGHT AFTER THE DARK

by
Alvin Abram

Abbeyfield Publishers
Scarborough Ontario Canada

"THE LIGHT AFTER THE DARK
Copyright © Alvin Abram, Toronto, Canada

All rights reserved.

No parts of this publication may be produced, stored in a retrieval system or transmitted in any form or by any means, electronic, mechanical, by photocopying, recording or otherwise for purposes of resale, without the prior written permission of the author or his assigns.

Although the people and the stories are true, the dialogue has been fictionalized to enhance the stories and created to assimilate the person's conception of what occurred. Fictionalized characters have been created to fill the void of a missing link in the story that the storyteller could not account for. The author and publisher welcome any information enabling them to rectify any reference in subsequent volumes.

Inconsistencies in spelling of personal geographical names are due to the various languages from which references were translated. The author is using the spelling that he found to be the most consistent.

Cataloguing in Publishing Data

Alvin Abram, 1936-
The Light After The Dark

Includes biographical references.
ISBN 0-9682274-0-6 (v. 1)

Published by Abbeyfield Publishers
33 Springbank Avenue
Scarborough, Ontario, Canada M1N 1G2

1. Holocaust, Jewish (1939-1945) – Personal narratives.
2. Holocaust Survivors – Canada – Interviews. I. Title.

D804'95.A27 1997   940.53'18'0922   C97-93138-1

Cover designed by Karen Petherick, Kadama Graphics, Markham, Ontario.

Edited by Bill Belfontaine, Abbeyfield Consultants, Scarborough, Ontario.

Page design and typesetting by Dennis Rowe.
Maps by AMA Graphics Incorporated, North York, Ontario.

Printed and bound in Canada

The author wishes to acknowledge the assistance of:

LEON KATZ

•

PRIMA CHROME FURNITURE COMPANY LIMITED
MARVIN MORTON

•

DATON METAL MFG. LTD.
ANTHONY ROSEMAN

•

AMD METAL INDUSTRIES LTD.
TONY QUINTIERI

STEPHEN CHESNEY
PARKER GARBER & CHESNEY

•

ONTARIO STORE FIXTURES INC.
MILTON SHIER

JS REPRODUCTIONS
DENNIS AND DIANE GOOD

•

SUN PRINTING/TOP BINDERY
WAN KIM

Table of Contents

THE LIGHT AFTER THE DARK

INTRODUCTION	viii
DEDICATIONS	x
ACKNOWLEDGEMENTS	xiii
FOREWORD: Professor Irving Abella	xv
CONTENTS	
1. AN EYE FOR AN EYE: Zalman Katz	1
2. THE PROMISES: Michael Kutz	41
3. WE WILL MEET AGAIN: Moishe Perlmutter	75
4. I HAVE A MISSION: Dubi Arie	129
5. I KNEW MY ENEMY: Marjan Rosenberg	167
6. DON'T WORRY – IT WILL BE GOOD: Batia and Feiga Schmidt	211
7. SKETCHES FROM THE DARKNESS	247
"WHY, ZAIDA?" *Fiction or is it Fact?*	259
DEFINITIONS	267
GLOSSARY	273
REFERENCES	277

Introduction

1. **AN EYE FOR AN EYE:** *Zalman Katz*
    (Dzisna, White Russia) A witness to the murder of most of his family. His brother is murdered by two farmers and the Chief of Police and Zalman swears revenge. He kills the two farmers, becomes a partisan and later joins the Russian army, earning a reputation for ruthlessness. Revenge or justice, it made no difference; to Zalman, it was an eye for an eye as he searched for the Chief of Police. As events developed, justice will play a solitary hand.

2. **THE PROMISES:** *Michael Kutz*
    (Nieswiez, Byelorussia) 12,000 Jews were executed and disposed in a pit. Buried alive, eleven-year-old Kutz escaped to become a partisan fighter in Russia. Before his mother was murdered, she asked that he keep two promises; never forget he was a Jew and if he survived, to go to Palestine. For forty-eight years after the war, he was able to fulfill one of the promises, but it was not until he arrived in Israel in 1990, did the meaning of the second promise become clear – and not because he planned it.

3. **WE WILL MEET AGAIN:** *Moishe Perlmutter*
    (Mulinsk, Ukraine) For three years, he lived in the forests like an animal, hiding from the Germans. After the war, he and his mother journeyed to Krakow, Poland to escape the backlash of Ukrainian anti-Semitism. Under the protection of Lena Kuchler (author of *My Hundred Children*), he, with the rest of the children fought off the pogrom that was mounted to burn them out of their temporary home in Zanopake, Poland. Forced to return to Krakow when he heard his mother was ill, he promised himself that one day he would meet his friends again.

Introduction

4. **I HAVE A MISSION:** *Dubi Arie*
(Warsaw, Poland) Born on the eve of Hitler's attack on Poland and carried by his young mother to Russia, Dubi learns of hunger and fear from the day he is born. After the war, his mother emigrates to Israel where she dies three years later. Orphaned, living in a kibbutz, Dubi learns to identify himself as a Jew. He fights in the Yom Kippur War, Sinai Campaign and the Six Day War, but it is not until he hears the shofar declaring that the Western Wall is in Israeli hands does he realize he has a mission. A mission that will take thirteen years to complete.

5. **I KNEW MY ENEMY:** *Marjan Rosenberg*
(Szydlowiec, Poland) Were they friends or enemies? One man knew he was a Jew – did the other? Forty-eight years after the war, Marjan received two letters; one from a priest and one from a farmer in Poland, requesting recognition for Yad Vashem for saving his life. How does someone respond to an episode from the past and can Marjan finally put everything into perspective? Did they save his life? It was a question he now had to answer.

6. **DON'T WORRY – IT WILL BE GOOD:**
Batia and Feiga Schmidt
(Kaunas, Lithuania) Survivors of the Kaunas ghetto where from 35,000 Jews, only 84 lived. For every move that should have spelled the death of herself and her daughter Feiga, Batia was able to make a counter move. Her intuition saved their lives more than once. Shipped to Stutthof, Poland where more from 30,000 women perished, they survived the death march. After the war, they would build a life in which thousands became the beneficiaries.

7. **SKETCHES FROM THE DARKNESS**
Hand-drawn sketches from prisoners in labour camps and from concentration camps, depicting the mood and background of a life deprived of liberties and the pursuit of religious beliefs.

Dedications

IN EACH OF OUR LIVES, THERE ARE PEOPLE WHO WILL HAVE MADE a difference. I would like to recognize two who played a major role in my life. They, more than any, moulded me into the person I am today.

From the age of fourteen, I found myself working long hours and attending school with little or no time to make lasting friendships. While in public school, I was disciplined for not paying attention, unaware that my problem was not inability but a short attention span. My mother, Roumanian-born and a citizen of Canada before the Holocaust, would tell me, "It is a gift to dream, when not asleep." That was her explanation for me not being able to focus on what I was being taught. In high school, I found myself in an open concept and my disability of not being able to focus proved to be less of a problem. My mother said, "It was all right to dream and that I should never lose that gift."

Over the next twenty-five years, I set aside that gift until one day she reminded me that I was never too old to dream and that I should put my dreams on paper. She was a remarkable, simple person who understood her son. Her ability to reduce a serious problem by simplifying it with a 'bubba' story, suggesting that with a little patience and some determination anything could be resolved. She was usually right.

Always proud of her Jewish heritage, she tried to ensure that her children never forget who and what they were and in what direction they should head. Her sharp mind passed away at 87 and the rest of her died when she was 92. Alzheimer's robbed her of her past and left it up to me to make sure that what she taught remained in focus. She said, "It was all right to dream" and I dream of a better world where the word Holocaust is no longer in the dictionary.

Dedications

* * *

SHE WAS FIFTEEN WHEN I MET HER AND IN ALMOST FOUR DECADES of marriage, she has been my inspiration. My first stories were of her as she developed into a role model that extolled her capabilities which accomplished far more than what she believed possible. As our lives careened from one crisis to another, she made me aware that fame and fortune were luxuries that were best pursued after reaching two primary goals in life – the love and respect of your family. It was only then that I realized that what I sought I already had and nothing else was as important.

While convalescing from a heart attack, I confessed to Marilyn that I wished I had pursued the vocation of my dreams. Without my knowledge, Marilyn enrolled me at York University and drove me to school, so that I would not miss my Creative Writing classes.

Without Marilyn's understanding, it would have been impossible to accomplish the writing and publishing of this book. The time required to research and interview meant she would spend many lonely hours in the same house, but separated from me by an invisible barrier that kept me in another dimension.

* * *

No one walks alone. We are the results of our environment and our relationship with other people. I was fortunate that my dream of wanting to write became reality because of the efforts of those who understood what it meant to dream.

ALVIN ABRAM
Toronto, Canada

Acknowledgements

I would like to acknowledge five people for their assistance in making this book possible. An undertaking of this size requires the cooperation of several "lay" people and I was fortunate to receive the support required to complete this project.

MATTHEW CORRIGAN, York University Professor who taught me how to make one page into three, then into ten and then into a book. He made me aware that I had stories in me I never knew existed.

TRUDY BODAK, Map Librarian at York University whose cooperation in locating old maps of the European cities made it easier to identify the communities in the stories. For her patience in finding me excerpts from a number of books that I built into my stories and to Joanne Halpert and Mary McDowell for their assistance in the library.

JANET PAGE who has the ability to criticize and still make it sound positive. She encouraged me with her positive outlook to continue when other commitments continually interfered with my time. Her advice and guidance was invaluable.

MURRAY ABRAMS, my older brother. Aware of my interest in this project, he appeared at my door with old books about the war which he had been collecting and gave them to me. I found in them rich background material.

TOM SHONFELD for allowing me to reproduce the original sketches, drawn by Holocaust survivors, in his possession.

Foreword

In April of 1942, just weeks before he was deported from the Warsaw Ghetto to the gas chambers and ovens of Treblinka, Chaim Kaplan wrote in his diary: *"When my life ends, what will become of my diary? Will they know about us and our experience? Will anyone remember or care?"*

It is precisely to ensure that we do remember and care that Alvin Abram has written this remarkable book. Here are the stories of six Holocaust survivors, who through dogged determination, staggering courage and sheer luck, withstood the dark years of Nazi barbarism and came to Canada to build new lives for themselves and their families. These are stories of horror and hope, of terror and triumph. *Above all, these are stories of inspiration*, of the indominability of the human spirit and of the refusal to surrender to the cruelties of that dreadful moment in human history. Rather, they fought back with vigour and creativity to preserve both their lives and their Jewishness.

It is a magnificent tribute to these men and women: to Zalman (Eugene) Katz, Michael Kutz, Moishe Perlmutter, Dubi Arie, Marjan (Michael) Rosenberg and Batia and Feiga Schmidt (Batia Malamud and Faigie Libman) – that they came forward to share their stories with Alvin Abram, and through him, the rest of us. These stories are difficult to read; how much more difficult they must have been to tell. And yet as these survivors know, it was imperative to give voice to their memories. Holocaust survivors are the living link to a history we can never recapture and recreate, and their stories are building blocks to a revitalized Jewish past. In the battle over the years to ensure Jewish survival and continuity, memory is the most important weapon in the Jewish arsenal.

Foreword

For the men and women whose experiences Alvin Abram describes, indeed for all survivors, silence would have been a tempting option, especially since language is inadequate to convey what they went through. Yet they chose to step out of the protective shadow of silence, even though it might have been the only adequate response to horror beyond comprehension, because they knew they had to tell the world what happened. Their continued silence, and the silence of other survivors would have merely consigned the six million victims to oblivion and their murders to ever greater meaninglessness. Only these memories can salvage some meaning from the ashes of Treblinka.

The trauma of the Holocaust is unparalleled in history. While generations to come may not remain as focused on it as we are today, it will always remain a central historical and religious point for Jews. Their understanding of this human disaster will depend largely on the testimony of the survivors of our generation. For them, indeed for all humanity, the most compelling requirement on us is not to forget, to refuse to bury the past and to encourage the survivor to speak loudly and publicly.

As well, the minority of the survivors will help defuse and uproot the hate-mongers and the Holocaust-deniers in our midst who are spreading their venom throughout society. Holocaust denial is to the anti-Semitism of the 1990's what Zionism was to the anti-Semitism of the 1970's and 1980's. It is the organizing metaphor of the new and frightening anti-Jewish movements of this decade. This is why books such as 'The Light After The Dark' are so profoundly important. The first-hand recollections and testimony of Holocaust survivors are the antidote to the poison of the previous Holocaust deniers. They will help undermine those malevolent polemicists who claim that there were no death camps, no deportation, no gas chambers, no crematoriums, no Anne Frank, no Holocaust.

Foreword

And since there were no war crimes, there were no war criminals, that the Holocaust was a hoax perpetrated on a gullish world by Jews anxious for monetary compensation and moral support to create the State of Israel.

The Nazis taught us one thing: that lies that go unchallenged become mistaken for truths; they become policies and ultimately they become murders. Of all the organs in the body, Jewish sages warned us, the tongue is by far, the most dangerous. But it can also be the most beneficial and illuminating, at least for those who use it to tell the truth. And that is what Alvin Abram and his collaborators have done. They have told the truth; they have vividly revealed their most painful secrets so that we might learn from them.

In commemorating the Holocaust, we should remember not only the too-familiar pictures of starving, skeletel Jews behind ghetto walls and barbed wire, photographs taken by murderers themselves, the Nazis, to demonstrate the helpless, sub-human quality of those they were killing. Of course we know the pictures are real; they are scored in our minds and our hearts. But we also know that they present only one part of what went on under the Nazis.

Before hunger, deprivation, terror and torture there was another part of life – life filled with meaning, spirituality, dignity, resistance and struggle, that even in the blackest moment in the history of the Jewish people, the enemy could not neither vanquish this spirit nor destroy it.

That is the message of this powerful, moving book, a message we must never forget.

PROFESSOR IRVING ABELLA
Co-author of:
None Is Too Many: Canada and the Jews of Europe 1933 - 1948
with Harold Troper

I AM A JEW

From the beginning of my life, I did learn,
    That I was a Jew and within me did burn,
The desire to know from where I came,
    And if my life would be filled with pain.

As the days and years passed – my questions grew.
    I searched through many books, looking for a clue.
There was much to read, but nothing I came upon,
    That gave me the feeling, that I did belong.

A Jew I was born – a Jew I can stay.
    But what is a Jew if he cannot live his way?
Only when I learned what made Israel a Jewish nation,
    Did I understand the need to continue with our creation.

I stood before the monument known as the Western Wall.
    My hands caressed the stones as to my knees I did fall.
My eyes filled with tears for the remorse and grief
    For those millions of Jews who died for their belief.

They will never stand in front of this place,
    And be filled with pride for the Jewish race.
The uniting of Jerusalem, the creating of a state,
    A country where Jews can live without hate.

Jerusalem, the city of David and Solomon the Wise.
    A city filled with tradition, of pain and cries.
A place where a Jew can find who he is at last,
    Where with every step, he can discover his past.

A home to stay after two thousand years away,
    To talk and walk and be able to pray.
I am a Jew, I can touch my past.
    I have returned, I am home at last.

There is pride in my step, my back is straight.
    I have found myself, I can now relate.
For no longer will I ask just who am I?
    I am a Jew until the day I die.

Alvin Abram

AN EYE FOR AN EYE

*"In spite of everything,
I still believe that people are good at heart."*

— ANNE FRANK'S DIARY

Zalman Katz: *"When I am awake, my memory does not let me forget and neither should those who were responsible."*

Map by **AMA**Graphics Incorporated

AN EYE FOR AN EYE

The Story of
ZALMAN KATZ

The industrial city of Bydgoszcz (Bromberg) is the capital of Bydgoszcz Province. Located on the Brda River in central Poland, it is served by a network of inland water carriers and railways at the eastern end of the Bydgoszcz Canal. It is a busy city. Heavily damaged during World War II, it was in the midst of a building boom on August 19, 1959, when the past and present came full circle and touched.

With a population of more than 250,000, it was divided into districts, each represented by political officials and a number of Chiefs of Police. Joseph Juszkevitz was one of the Chiefs of Police.

Inside his railway hut, the stationmaster was reading a newspaper when his telephone rang. A voice instructed him to write down a telegram to be given to Joseph Juszkevitz. The stationmaster rummaged in his desk looking for an official telegram form, found a stub of a pencil and laboriously wrote in his scrawl onto the form. It was a short telegram of twenty words. Painstakingly, he folded the sheet, inserted it into an envelope and sealed it. Unable to leave the station, he telephoned his brother-in-law to come right away and deliver the telegram for him. Several minutes passed before a middle-aged man entered the station and the stationmaster handed him the sealed envelope.

"Make sure Juszkevitz signs the receipt book that he received the telegram," the stationmaster told his brother-in-law. "He should be pleased; the telegram is good news."

His brother-in-law nodded, tucked the envelope into his shirt pocket and walked out of the station to his bicycle. He pedalled the short distance to Juszkevitz's office at the police station, but he was not pleased with the errand. Juszkevitz was not a likeable man. Rumour had it, during the war he was a collaborator and killed a lot of Jews. No big deal, but Juszkevitz was a mean son-of-a-bitch and everyone in Bydgoszcz was afraid of him. Given a choice, this was the last place he wanted to go. He parked his bicycle against the building and reluctantly entered.

An overweight police sergeant in an ill-fitting uniform sat behind a wooden desk busily writing. He looked up. "What's your business?" he growled.

Smiling to hide his fear, the brother-in-law answered, "Got a telegram for Police Chief Juszkevitz. It's good news." To prove what he said, he reached into his shirt pocket, removed the envelope and waved it at the police officer.

The officer's expression did not change. "Give it to me. I'll take it to him."

"Can't do that. The telegram's for him. He has to sign my book that he got it."

The policeman scowled, annoyed at having to get up. He walked to a door at the back of the room and waved for the brother-in-law to follow. After knocking on the door, the officer entered. Standing by the doorway, the brother-in-law's eyes were wide with fright and his hands shook as he peered inside.

"Telegram for you," the police officer said to the man sitting behind the desk. "He says it's good news."

The Chief of Police stared at the police officer and then turned his gaze to the terrified brother-in-law. Joseph Juszkevitz was a burly, heavy-set man with hard facial features and cold eyes. He had collaborated with the Germans, and willingly been involved in conduct that earned him a reputation for being ruthless. For the past fourteen years he had hidden his past by moving away from White Russia to Poland, but he could not hide the evil in his character.

Slowly Juszkevitz stood, his mouth turned into a scowl at being disturbed. He extended his arm to receive the telegram, and the brother-in-law scurried to him, placed the telegram in his hand and pushed the receipt book towards him. Juszkevitz turned the envelope over, his mouth twisted in disgust, his eyes glaring at the sealed container as if he could penetrate through the envelope's skin to its contents. He placed it on the desk and picked up his pen. With obvious disdain, he signed the book thrust into his hands by the brother-in-law and watched him quickly back out of the room. The two police officers laughed. The sergeant followed, closing the door behind him, still chuckling at the scare they had instilled in the messenger.

Juszkevitz sat, and tore the short side of the envelope open, removed the single sheet and unfolded it to read its contents. His face turned pale, drained of all colour in an instant, and his breathing quickened as he stared at the *words. Perspiration broke out on his forehead. He blinked several times, finally closing his eyes for an instant before returning his gaze to the words that leaped at him. Deliberately, he placed the telegram on the table, his eyes still fixed on the words staring back, mesmerized by their meaning.*

Slowly he rose from the chair, refolded the telegram, placing it into his back pocket. He opened the side drawer of his desk exposing his revolver. His cold eyes stared at the weapon before he picked it up and left his office by the back door, which opened onto an alley behind the building. Juszkevitz looked around for a brief moment before placing the revolver against his temple and pulled the trigger. The side of his head exploded, spraying brain tissue and bone onto the ground as his body collapsed against the building into a sitting position.

The police sergeant ran outside, and stopped short when he saw his superior slumped against the building with the revolver lying next to him. He leaned over and placed his hand over Juszkevitz's heart to confirm what was obvious. When he stepped back, the body slumped forward, face down on the ground, exposing the corner of the telegram sticking out of Juszkevitz's back pocket. He reached for it and read the twenty words. He shook his head in bewilderment. Why would Juszkevitz commit suicide after receiving such good news?

WHEN GERMANY INVADED POLAND ON SEPTEMBER 1, 1939, ALL territories east of the Vistula River fell into the sphere of Soviet influence. The Soviets maintained control of this vast domain until June 22, 1941, when Nazi Germany broke their mutual agreement and attacked the Soviet Union.

The code name for the invasion was 'Barbarossa'.
The objective: to acquire more land.
The obstacle: too many people.
The solution: get rid of the Jews.

The Soviet's fought well, but were slowly pushed back into Russia and eventually to the gates of Moscow. As Germany added huge amounts of new territories to its rule, they created four *Einsatzgruppe* (killing squad) areas.

The ultimate decision of the German high command in Operation Barbarossa was not to duplicate the death camps in Western Europe as the means of disposing of the Jews. Instead the mobile killing units became an integral part of the operation, covering a very wide area from the Baltic to the Ukraine. Once the conquered territory was in the killing squads' control, the disposal of the Jews commenced. It was presumed to be more efficient to dispose of the Jewish problem at its source than to transport them to the camps in the west. It had been calculated that over 1,300,000 Jews were executed, of which 446,484 were from Byelorussia.

Dzisna was located not far from the Russian border on the west side of the Dzisna River, south of the Dzvina River. An unassuming town of approximately six thousand people, of which about five thousand were Jewish. A close-knit community, whose inhabitants kept to themselves, having little to do with the so-called outside world. They allowed themselves to be isolated, concerned only with activities taking place within the town or with nearby communities.

Leib Katz owned a modest one bedroom house with a kitchen and dining room. As a controller of lumber, his income fell far short of meeting all of his family's needs. Poland's economy was struggling, with many people living on the charity of their families. Leib's work took him away from Dzisna, to the bushland of the Kruki swamps that surrounded the area, some fifteen kilometres from the town. He was responsible for authorizing the removal of trees without destroying the ecological balance of nature.

The land, although fertile for farming, had pockets of marshland and swamp containing a multitude of animal, fish and fauna life. As each generation of Polish families matured, the original farms were subdivided into smaller patches, with each expanded family undertaking to manage a smaller section. Gradually, the need for more land threatened both the swamps and the delicate balance of nature. The view from the top of the valley revealed quilted landscape divided into squares, occupied by a little house, generally near the road, a garden, and some livestock.

Malka, Leib's wife was a seamstress. Six days a week, ten to twelve hours a day she sewed at home, adding to Leib's income, making dresses to be sold privately or at the market. A large oven occupied the centre of the kitchen where Malka made her own bread and matzo from the potatoes she grew in the garden. As practising Jews, the Katzes maintained a kosher home, observed the Sabbath and attended synagogue.

Malka and Leib had five children, two girls and three boys. Efraim *(1918)*, Sophie *(1914)*, Ida *(1921)*, Moishe *(1923)*, and Zalman *(1925)*. While Ida, Moishe and Zalman went to the local school, Efraim worked at the local fire department and Sophie helped her mother at home. Tradition and harmony were combined into a lifestyle that promoted family closeness and faith. It was a simple life without unnecessary complications or political involvement. It was a past about to end.

Sophie   Ida   Malka   Moishe   Zalman   Efraim   Leib

The town of Dzisna was not a sophisticated or modern community even by 1939 standards. Most homes had no electricity or running water. The isolated environment preserved their Jewishness, preventing an erosion of their way of life. Without newspapers or radios, the residents became aware of the events in the world, from people passing through on their way to Russia. Since these events could never affect them, they were items of conversation only, having little impact on their lives. Their dreams were limited to their own experiences, never going beyond their own needs and ideals. Not too far away were other small towns and villages, such as Borkovichy, Vetrino and Polotsk whose way of life was identical to Dzisna. In a good number of instances, Dzisna families had relatives living in these communities through marriages arranged by the parents.

Eighty percent of Dzisna was Jewish; anti-Semitism was not an issue that occupied their thoughts. The community had six synagogues, where the children learned Hebrew six days a week, after attending a Polish government school five times a week. As in any community, some days had their moments of crisis and problems, but overall life was good. This was the way the Katz's grandparents lived, and their parents before them, and it would be the way Leib's children would live as well – or so it seemed.

On Sunday, September 17, 1939, the realities of the changing world reached Dzisna when the Soviet army crossed the Dzisna River. Two hundred Polish regulars attempted to defend Dzisna, but their efforts were wasted. The skirmish was quickly over when the Polish soldiers realized they could not withstand the whole advancing Soviet army, and retreated into the woods and marshes, leaving that portion of the country in Soviet hands.

The Soviet occupation created no immediate change for the citizens of Dzisna, since they had always lived only a stone's throw from the Russian border, and had gotten along well with their neighbours before the occupation.

Within a short time, they embraced the Soviets for the good they did while in Dzisna. Soviet Jewish soldiers told the citizens that life under the Soviets was better than under the Polish government. The stories they told excited them and when living conditions improved, the young were impressed.

The Soviets built a large brick factory and a clothing manufacturing plant in the area. People who had been unemployed all their life were working, and the local economy improved, bringing to Dzisna a sense of prosperity never known before. Although the workday was long, and the wages were small, everyone accepted the benefits without complaint, remembering how little they had before. The Soviets opened free schools, taught the local population the Russian language and about Russian culture. Seeing the results of this new ideology, the young Jews gradually moved away from their Jewishness. Within a short period, the traditional environment in their community changed, and the outside influence corrupted what used to be taken for granted.

Soon after the Soviets arrived, they identified all the Jewish communists and sent them to Siberia. When Jewish Polish refugees escaping from the Germans told of the beatings and ghettos, the elders of Dzisna did not believe them. Their stories were too outrageous to convince simple people that life outside Dzisna was not as simple. The Soviets sent them to Siberia in an attempt to silence their stories, inculcating a sense of false security in the unsuspecting citizens. The townspeople were glad to be rid of the troublemakers.

While life in Dzisna had improved with the Soviet occupation, elsewhere it did not fare as well. In cities away from the borders, the Soviets showed another side of their face. They closed down many Jewish schools and institutions, banned social, cultural and political activities and seized property and assets of Jews. Tens of thousands of Jews who fled the German occupied portion of Poland to

Bialystok were evacuated in large groups and shipped to Siberia. By trying to run away from one form of hell, the Jewish refugees were surprised to find they had reached a hell of a different kind.

The Soviets conscripted men into the army, and Efraim received notice on April 1940 that he was to join a unit. A product of his environment, he never had to leave the vicinity of his birth and now he was to be taken to places he could not even pronounce and fight a war on foreign soil. He bid his family farewell, slipping not only out of their sight, but out of their lives. *Years later, Zalman would learn that Efraim had been killed on the Russian Front on December 6, 1942 near Moscow and buried in an unknown grave.*

HITLER'S ATTACK ON THE SOVIET UNION CAUGHT THE SOVIETS unprepared. In the early morning of June 22, 1941, with the sky barely showing the light of the new day, thousands of German artillery opened fire across the Vistula River. No holds were to be barred in the taking of Soviet territory by Germany. Hitler insisted that his generals understand this very clearly when he said: *"The war against Russia will be such that it cannot be conducted in a knightly fashion. This struggle is one of ideologies and racial differences, and will have to be conducted with unprecedented, unmerciful and unrelenting harshness. All officers will have to rid themselves of obsolete ideologies. I know that the necessity for such means of waging war is beyond the comprehension of you generals, but . . . I insist absolutely that my orders be executed without contradiction . . . therefore the commissars will be liquidated. German soldiers guilty of breaking international law . . . will be excused. Russia has not participated in the Hague Convention and therefore has no rights under it."*

On July 4, 1941, the bridge crossing the Dzisna River was destroyed to prevent the Soviets from retreating, thereby splitting the whole front into three distinct strategic sectors. Valiantly, the Soviets continued to fight between the Dzisna and Dzvina Rivers for more than ten days, although the German main force had bypassed the area and had advanced 150 kilometres further to the east. The worried citizens of Dzisna watched and waited for the battle to end, unsuspecting and unprepared for what was going to happen. Soon they would find out that not only were the stories the refugees told true but were in fact much worse.

The German army advanced closer to Dzisna. Before reaching the city, the downtown core and outlining areas were bombed. Realizing their lives were in danger, the Katz family left Dzisna with as much of their belongings as they could carry, not sure they would ever return. They journeyed twelve kilometres to a farm belonging to Leib's non-Jewish friend, the Zurawski's, where they hid for two weeks. Before moving to Dzisna, Leib lived in a nearby village, and the father of the Zurawski family was Leib's good friend. Although of different faiths, the two men had always respected each other and that respect had grown into a meaningful friendship. The Zurawski's were Moskales, a Christian religion similar in nature to the Mormons.

Out of touch with the outside world, Leib naively believed that after the Germans took control of the territory, an acceptable way of life would again return as it had under the Soviets. The Katz family appeared safe, since the Germans had not expanded their territorial domination in the direction where the family were hiding, and their isolation left them unaware of the brutality taking place in Dzisna.

When the Germans entered Dzisna, they turned on the Jews. The commandant concluded the community needed 'order' and he conscripted the hoodlums and criminals to restore that order. Their first act was to enlist the police, who were now mainly fascists and hoodlums, to burn down one synagogue and desecrate all the others. Terror enveloped the Jews as unbridled killings and senseless violence became commonplace. Unaware, many Jews continued to venture onto the street, where they were accosted and robbed of their valuables and clothes. Hostages were taken and large sums of money extorted from their families, but the hostages were seldom released even after the ransom had been delivered. Everywhere the terror was aggravated by the sadism of the *Schutzstaffeln*, better known as the SS, representing the arrogance of Nazi ideology and the criminal nature of Hitler's regime. From harmony came disorder that reached the level of chaos, driving many Jewish families into hiding.

The Germans issued a decree that all Jews who had fled Dzisna must return. Those not complying with the order would be executed when found and those harbouring them would meet the same fate. Reluctantly, Leib and his family returned to Dzisna, but they left their clothes and belongings with the Zurawski's. Leib's friend assured him that his two sons, Constantine and Pavel, would protect their property as though it were their own, and for Leib, his friend's word was all the assurance he needed.

When the Katz family returned to Dzisna, they were confined in a Jewish ghetto. The ghetto occupied a small section of the town, an area barely large enough to support the number of people it held. Four and five families were forced to live in one room under conditions that proved almost too difficult to endure. The Germans confiscated Jewish businesses and sealed off Jewish retail stores for the exclusive use of the military occupiers or the SS. Sometimes Jewish shops were ordered to remain open so they could be plundered. Sanitary conditions could not be maintained in the ghetto, and disease and sickness spread. Although the ghetto was not surrounded by wire or gates with guards, the boundaries were clearly defined, and any Jew found beyond those boundaries was shot.

With the war moving further east, the bulk of the Germans left, leaving Dzisna in the control of the collaborators, and although the German presence was seen and felt, it was the local gentiles that the Jews had to contend with on a day-to-day basis. Escape was relatively easy. Capture was inevitable. The community leaders offered a reward for every Jew caught escaping – dead or alive, and many pursued those who tried to escape. The net worth of a Jew, man, woman or child had been reduced to three kilos of salt.

Without informing his family, Zalman Katz left the ghetto one night to make his way across the river into Russia. To live as they were living was senseless and he intended to escape. He reached the river and made his way to a hidden raft. As he was about to climb onto the raft, his sister Ida appeared, and pleaded with him not to go, to stay with the family. She feared his absence might mean reprisals against the rest of the family. Reluctantly, Zalman relented and returned to the ghetto.

And then they heard about what was happening in other communities with larger Jewish populations. On June 26, 1941, the Germans set fire to part of the Jewish quarter in Bialystok after locking over one thousand Jews in a synagogue. The synagogue was set ablaze with everyone inside. In Mogilev, more than three hundred Jews were shot; the stories coming out of Tatarsk, Krugloje, Starodub and Bobruisk were the same. The elders of Dzisna refused to believe what they heard. The stories were too gross to be believable.

Acts of resistance provoked savage reprisals. When the German soldiers returned, they collected one hundred men, women and children in Dzisna, and marched them to a wall. Standing side by side, every tenth person was ordered to step forward. Some men, a few women and two children did. The German officer strolled along the line. "Does anyone wish to change places with the ten?" he casually asked. They looked at each other, assuming what was being selected was a work detail. A man replaced a woman and a woman replaced a child. The ten were marched a few metres away and murdered. A mother ran screaming towards her dead child, and a soldier beat her to death.

The officer stated to the remaining prisoners, "We found a wire cut outside Dzisna. Whenever there are acts of sabotage, this will be how we will retaliate." No one knew if anyone from Dzisna had been responsible. The Germans didn't care.

On July 9, 1941, the Dzisna ghetto formed their own *Judenrat* (Jewish Council). A directive decreed all Jews in White Russia must register; wear two yellow Stars of David badges, one on the chest, the other on their backs; were not permitted to walk on the sidewalk, use public transportation, visit the parks, playgrounds, theatres, cinemas, libraries or museums or own a car or radio. All their property was confiscated. Food supplies were to be limited, and all able-bodied Jews, men, women or children were to be subjected to forced labour details. Gold, watches, jewellery, fur coats and clothes were to be turned over to the Gestapo. Those who hid their valuables were shot when the valuables were discovered.

The local Polish police became more brazen in their own acts of violence towards the Jews. Several arrived drunk at a ghetto school while the parents were on labour details, removed several pretty girls and raped them, leaving them in the street, half dead, to find their own way home. The Katzes grieved for the families, but that grief would become a preview for what they would feel.

Ida Katz had just turned twenty-one. While she was visiting a neighbour, the local police raided his house, beating the neighbour and dragged Ida outside. They forced her into the nearby woods, ripped off her clothes and raped her repeatedly. When they were finished, they left her on the ground bruised and bleeding with barely enough strength to drag her battered body home. Clutching her torn dress to cover her exposed body, she staggered into her house. She had been punched and abused so many times, that when her family saw her, they hardly recognized her. They hid her outside of Dzisna with a gentile farmer until she recovered, and then smuggled her to the town of Glubokoye where Leib's brother lived.

That winter, the Germans captured thousands of Russian prisoners. Before they marched them to a camp for internment, an SS detachment arrived, and executed all the commissars, Jews and Communists. Outside Dzisna, where the highway crossed the new bridge into Russia, the Germans went through a form of selection, looking for what they perceived were Jewish faces. Finally satisfied with their selection, they marched the prisoners into the woods and shot them. Many were not Jews.

At the age of sixteen, Zalman was pressed into the labour detail with the adults. Work gangs of 300 to 400 Jews – men, women and children – were forced to clean the roads with brooms and shovels. The temperature had dropped to 40 degrees below zero, snow created high mounds, swept by cold winds making the roads impassable, but the Jews were ordered outside without proper clothes to protect them from the sub-zero conditions. Many died from exposure. Any who collapsed in the snow were shot. Zalman watched the brutality of the Germans and became hardened to what he saw.

While shovelling snow, Zalman saw a couple of his close non-Jewish school friends walking towards him. He smiled at them since he was not allowed to speak, and to his surprise they spat on him and laughed as they passed. The saliva froze to his face immediately, a reminder for the rest of that day that he could not call any of his friends, friends any longer.

The cold winter, as well as the lack of food and heat took its toll on the community. It was impossible to stave off the inevitable – death became a welcome guest. Every day, the German police demanded more work or faster production from the starving Jews, but little food was made available to sustain them. When the Germans were not satisfied with someone's performance, they marched the exhausted Jew to the river and shot him, dumping his body into the water. Obedience was no longer the saviour to the living, only luck counted, if life was to continue and to some, being alive was no blessing.

As the Jews starved, local gentile farmers eager to profit from their misfortune, secretly arranged to barter jewellery for stale bread and vegetables. Families left the ghetto for the woods, where they traded whatever they had for food. What little they brought back, was hardly any help, but when hunger gnawed at the very fibre of the body, anything was better than nothing.

On February 8, 1942, the Katz family suffered their first casualty. Malka Katz died from starvation. Not long afterwards, word reached Leib, that on March 23, 1942, the Germans collected all of the Jews in Glubokoye including his brother and daughter Ida and executed them.

On June 1, 1942, two young boys escaping from the German atrocities in Poland arrived at Dzisna and informed the Judenrat that the Germans were systematically killing all the Jews in every community. They begged everyone to run and hide before it was too late. The Judenrat threatened to turn them over to the Germans if they continued to tell their "lies." The boys pleaded with the council, trying to convince them that they were telling the truth, but the Judenrat refused to believe the stories. Fearing for their own lives, the two boys left Dzisna and crossed the river into Russia.

On June 15, 1942, early in the morning, hidden in a blanket of swirling fog, German soldiers entered the Dzisna ghetto unnoticed. When the Jews became aware of their presence, they were not at first unduly alarmed because soldiers had come in before and had left without incident after roaming the streets.

This was not to be as before.

Armed with rifles and machine guns, the Germans broke down locked doors, screaming *"raus! raus!"* as they herded the families out into the streets. There was bedlam as they were gathered together and marched into a large house near the outskirts of the town and forced to sit on the floor, not knowing what to expect. Outside, Christian farmers were digging a pit.

Zalman Katz heard the rifle and machine gun fire. He leaped from his bed, yelled a warning to everyone in the room and jumped out the window. In all the confusion, hidden by the same blanket of fog that had concealed the Germans, he managed to escape. As he ran, sounds of explosions erupted and when he turned to look back, he could see the flames as the ghetto burned. The Germans converged on all four sides of the ghetto, shooting at everyone. The fog proved to be a weakness in their plan, preventing them from having a clear view of the streets, resulting in many escaping into the swamps. Some Jews had handguns and rifles hidden in their homes and killed several Germans before being shot or burned to death.

Many panicked and tried to run the gauntlet of Germans, leaving behind a bloody carnage of twisted bodies and torn limbs. Young children in flight were caught, and flung against the walls, their heads smashed to pulp. With systematic precision, the Germans shot and hacked at everyone, and then set fire to the homes in case there was someone hidden inside. The screams of terror was deafening as large groups were herded into the woods, forced to undress, shot and thrown into the pits dug by Christian farmers, some of the children were still alive.

The slaughter continued unabated until nine in the evening. When it was over almost all the Jews of Dzisna had been killed including, Leib and Sophie Katz. Their bodies were strewn in the streets in grotesque positions, a grim reminder of the ugliness of war and the insanity of hate. When all resistance finally ended, the Germans withdrew.

By some miracle about nine hundred Jews managed to escape the massacre including Moishe but he was unaware that Zalman had also survived and was hiding in the same swamp.

In time, most of the Dzisna refugees' flight from death was in vain. Almost all were killed while serving in the partisan units they joined. Some were caught by the White Russians, and traded to the Germans for eight kilos of salt, four packages of tobacco and their clothes.

The value of a Jew had risen.

ZALMAN HID IN THE KRUKI SWAMPS IN WATER UP TO HIS KNEES. He tied the loose limbs broken from trees with vines and built a raft to support his weight. For the next two weeks, he lived on the platform, leaving only to search for food, surviving on cranberries. Afraid of being seen by any of the local farmers, he approached nearby farms at night to scavenge for food, but the barking of the dogs inevitably chased him away before he could steal enough to satisfy his needs. He lost weight and was often disoriented and dizzy. Sometimes he saw someone in the distance and ran. Others seeing him ran away too. Everyone was starving and were forced to become bolder in their hunt for food resulting in their capture. A farmer Zalman knew named Zahorski came upon him and offered his help. He brought him food and clothes, telling him about the other Jews hiding in the swamp. For two weeks Zalman remained in hiding with Zahorski's help while local farmers and Germans roamed the area looking for runaway Jews. Zahorski brought him some unexpected good news. He had found his brother Moishe and arranged to bring him to hide with Zalman.

June, July, August and September of 1942 passed without any hope of getting away from the Germans. All the ghettos in the area had been destroyed. Occasionally, the two brothers would meet another Jew who told them stories of murder, rape and plundering done by the local citizens and the Germans. Moishe and Zalman stole clothing from the farmers and used it to buy food from other Poles who offered to help if rewarded.

Then they made a discovery that would change the course of their lives. They came upon Zahorski's sixteen-year-old son looking after the cows in the field, holding an empty machine gun he had found. They bartered a shirt for the gun.

"Now we were kings," Zalman remembers.

Zalman had a stronger personality than Moishe. He was innovative and more determined. Moishe moaned and cried over what had befallen them. Although Moishe was older, Zalman found himself making most of the decisions that controlled their lives. Zalman decided to rob a farmer. He burst into the farmer's house waving his empty machine gun, while Moishe stood at the door in view of the farmer's family. Zalman threatened to kill everyone, if they did not cooperate, pointing to Moishe by the door as one of twenty partisans waiting outside to burst in if the farmer gave them any trouble. He demanded food and got it. The machine gun made a decisive difference in their lives. Now they possessed the power of life and death over others and the means to carry out their demands. What they needed were bullets.

They heard of a band of armed resistance fighters in the neighbourhood and sought them out with the purpose of joining. No longer did Zalman want to hide. He wanted to fight the Germans and Moishe reluctantly agreed.

IN EASTERN EUROPE, MOST NOTABLY IN LITHUANIA, POLAND, THE Ukaine and Byelorussia, Jews frequently faced bigotry and animosity, not only from local inhabitants, but from anti-Nazi partisan groups who were infused with anti-Semitism. In Soviet White Russia, the residents of the Jewish ghettos were the prime movers behind the wide-ranging local partisan units. These units were mobile forces operating behind enemy lines in selected terrain, attacking the enemy through sabotage, sudden sorties or sporadic battles. No one knows the number of Jewish partisans in the total guerrilla movement, but they were significant and they proved their mettle in countless actions.

Jews were regarded as weak by most partisan groups and useless unless they joined with their own weapons and ammunition. Without weapons, they were made to perform menial chores. During October 1942, Zalman and Moishe joined a partisan brigade, commanded by a killer and anti-Semite by the name of Kanapelka. There were only three other Jews in Kanapelka's brigade of twenty-five, and Kanapelka never considered the Jews an integral part of his campaign at that time. Kanapelka loved to kill, undertaking sorties that were not always strategic, but offered opportunities to kill the Germans. After two months with Kanapelka, they became disenchanted with him, and when they heard of another partisan brigade that was more to their liking, with more Jews, they left Kanapelka's brigade, which had grown to more than 100 men.

Their new partisan brigade was a more disciplined band, run by a Russian commander called Polikov. His brigade of 125 men were primarily Jews from the surrounding ghettos, his sorties more strategic than random. They damaged and burned bridges and railways, dug wolf-pits in roads to destroy trucks, tore up railway tracks and cut telegraph lines. By avoiding direct confrontation, they managed to escape detection, engaging instead in sabotage and killing local police and Germans. Polikov and other partisans transformed areas that were sensitive and vital to the Nazi war effort into focal points of constant danger and instability. They evaded pursuit, moving rapidly from place to place, exploiting the surprise factor in essential combat. Their losses were very heavy, few partisan survived the years of struggle and the hardship of fugitive life in the forests. The Nazis, regarded the partisans as robbers and executed them without hesitation, both as a deterrent and to inflict fear in anyone considering joining. Often the Germans took reprisals against the townspeople for partisan actions in the area. Polikov understood this. Kanapelka didn't care who paid the price for his sorties.

By January, the weather turned nasty and Zalman and Moishe made arrangements to return to the Zurawski farm and retrieve their winter clothes. The night before leaving, Zalman found it difficult to sleep. He tossed and turned until he finally fell asleep, only to have a strange dream. In his dream, he was in a barn, lying on the hay with his hands tied behind his back when a poisonous viper appeared close to his throat. Before the viper could sting him, his father materialized and killed it.

When Zalman awoke, he thought his dream was a sign of some impending danger. He told Moishe of his dream. Moishe then told Zalman that he too had a strange dream that puzzled him. He found himself in the middle of a lake and tried to swim ashore. He couldn't remember how long he swam, but finally unable to keep himself afloat, he drowned.

They tried to interpret the meaning of their respective dreams, but could not reach an answer that satisfied them. They left for their date with destiny, unaware of the significance of their premonitions.

That day, January 6, 1943, they journeyed to the Zurawski farm with an officer from the brigade. Polikov's brigade operated a distance from where they were going and he gave the brothers an additional man for their protection. They knocked on the Zurawski's door to be greeted warmly by the two brothers. They were invited into the house, food, fruit and vodka placed on the table, and the three partisans ate and drank, grateful for the warmth of the Zurawski brothers' hospitality and a rare moment of relaxation and trust.

Too absorbed in eating and drinking, they were not aware when one of the Zurawski brother's left the house.

Once outside, he tied his dog inside the barn to prevent him from barking when he returned. Quietly he led a horse out of the barn, and away from the house before mounting. He rode to Dzisna to notify the Germans that three partisans were in his house. Constantine and Pavel Zurawski had decided after the Katz family left for Dzisna, that they were not going to return the Katzes belongings. If Leib returned, they would inform the Germans, so they could keep everything for themselves. Their father was unaware of their decision, and when Zalman and Moishe showed up, he was not at home.

German soldiers with the Chief of Police of Dzisna, Joseph Juszkevitz; a known collaborator and Jew-hater arrived to arrest the three partisans. Juszkevitz burst open the door and rushed in, followed by the soldiers, their weapons ready to shoot if the partisans gave them any trouble. Caught off guard, the three surrendered without a fight. Zalman stared at the two brothers, realizing their duplicity. Juszkevitz tied Zalman's right hand to Moishe's left hand, roughing them up at the same time. The soldiers tied the partisan officer's hands together, and pushed the three out the door to a horse and wagon supplied by the Zurawski brothers, laughing at the partisans for being caught so easily.

While the Germans and Juszkevitz were preoccupied with the partisan officer, Zalman untied the rope that joined Moishe to him. They made a break for freedom, running in different directions, Zalman to the right, Moishe to the left. Earlier, Zalman had complained of not feeling well and as he ran towards the woods, he felt disoriented and visually confused, finding himself hallucinating about being in a warm house, when he should have been concentrating on escaping. He had moments when he couldn't remember why he was running, his movements were erratic and jerky.

Juszkevitz focused his attention on both brothers in flight, but took aim at Moishe, who was running in a straight line. Juszkevitz shot him with his machine gun, striking him in the back repeatedly, even as Moishe's body lay on the ground. The partisan officer tried to escape in the confusion but was killed as well. This gave Zalman the time to escape into the swamp.

FEVERISH, ZALMAN REACHED A FRIEND'S HOME. LATER, STILL ILL, HE arrived at the partisan camp, where he told Polikov about the betrayal of the two Zurawski brothers. He requested permission to return with several men to punish the two brothers. Polikov agreed, but Zalman's fever became worse and he was too sick to leave immediately. He and twelve partisans were later diagnosed with typhus and confined to the camp.

Zalman pleaded with Polikov not to tell anyone he had survived the trap. If the two brothers discovered he still lived, they would seek the protection of the Germans in Dzisna, making their capture more difficult. Better the brothers think he was dead. After he recovered, the brothers would still be in their home, confident that no one was aware of what they had done. Polikov agreed.

Zalman now understood the meaning of their dreams. He would live, his brother would die, but not in vain. The three responsible for his brother's death would live only long enough to regret what they had done. He would punish them for their cowardly act. Their lives would be forfeited for the one they took. Their names were burned into his mind: Constantine Zurawski, Pavel Zurawski and Joseph Juszkevitz. By his hands they would all die.

When Zalman was well enough to travel, he and four partisans left for the Zurawski's home. After making sure there were no German soldiers about, they forced their way into the house. The Zurawski's thinking that Zalman was dead, were petrified to see him standing in the doorway with a machine gun pointing at them. Before they had a chance to say anything, Zalman spoke. *"What you didn't finish — I'll try to finish by myself."*

Zalman ordered the brothers outside. They begged for mercy, but Zalman had too much hate in him to consider anything but revenge. He pushed them against the wall of the house, moved back, turned and raised his machine gun in their direction. Cowering against the wall with the pain of their deed etched in his mind, he fired a short burst into their bodies. They slumped to the ground. Without looking at the bodies, he and the four partisans returned to the forest. There was no release of the pain in Zalman. The death of the brothers only opened the wound for further revenge. He needed to find Joseph Juszkevitz and remove him from this world. His revenge had to be complete.

At the burial of Constantine and Pavel, their father, a man of eighty, told more than 300 villagers that God had punished his sons for what they did. They had no right to steal from the Jews, who were his friends.

Zalman learned a price had been put on his head by Kanapelka for killing the Zurawski brothers. Kanapelka ordered David Pintzov, a Jewish partisan, to take several of the men and hunt Zalman down. Pavel Zurawski's young and good-looking wife had convinced Kanapelka that Zalman should die for what he did.

To avoid capture, Zalman returned to the Kruki swamps, sending the four partisans back to their camp. For the next three days, members of Kanapelka's band hunted him. Kanapelka declared publicly that Zalman would be caught, returned to the village where the Zurawski brothers died and hung. Zalman did not intend to have that happen.

One night, Zalman met a partisan from Kanapelka's brigade who did not know him, and engaged him in conversation, without revealing his identity.

"Have they found this fellow Katz, yet?" Zalman asked.

"Not yet," the partisan answered, "but Kanapelka will get the bastard!"

"He could be anywhere. He could be hundreds of kilometres from here. How can Kanapelka expect to find him?" Zalman probed the partisan, hoping to get information about the hunt.

"Have you not heard? Kanapelka went into Polikov's camp with eighteen men and took Polikov hostage. If Katz does not come in on his own, he will shoot Polikov instead."

"He won't! Polikov is a Soviet commander," Zalman replied, surprised by what he was being told.

"He will!" the partisan replied. "Kanapelka is mad," and with that statement he waved goodbye to Zalman to continue looking for the man he had just been talking with.

At the age of seventeen, Zalman had become a disciplined fighter. He was hardened to the inhumanities he had witnessed; death was something he had become accustomed to, even when those who were dying were the innocent ones. He had locked away his human emotions, not allowing them to emerge, for fear if they did, he would weaken and find himself a victim. If Polikov died it would be a tragedy of the war, for Zalman knew, if he turned himself in, he would be hanged within minutes. He believed Kanapelka was using him as an excuse to control the Jews. Polikov was an obstacle in the way of those plans, and by eliminating Polikov, Kanapelka could take over the brigade and the Jews. For Zalman to give himself up would only result in both Polikov and him dying, leaving Kanapelka the only victor.

The unexpected occurred. Zalman met David Pintzov alone in the swamp, hunting for him. Both were heavily armed on horses as they emerged into a large clearing from opposite sides. Recognizing each other, they approached slowly until they were only a few feet apart.

"Did you think you could get away from me?" Pintzov said. He smiled, his broken teeth and unshaven face, a grotesque mask. Pintzov enjoyed playing the game of the hunt and showed his pleasure at having caught the man he sought.

Zalman placed his hand on his belt, where he had special hand grenades that sprayed it contents when detonated. "Are you brave, David?" Zalman asked.

"What does bravery have to do with it? I have caught you and now you are mine." And as he spoke his hand moved to his holster, a look of satisfaction on his face.

"If you touch your gun, I will release the pin on this grenade. You are close enough to join me into eternity."

David Pintzov saw Zalman's fingers loop into the ring. The smile fell from his face, and a scowl appeared as the meanness of the man showed in his eyes. "You won't pull the pin," Pintzov said, but his voice lacked confidence.

"If you make any move for your gun, you will find out," Zalman answered. Zalman's face was expressionless. His eyes bore into Pintzov as the two stared at each other. Slowly Zalman backed his horse, keeping his eyes on Pintzov. The distance between them widened, but Pintzov made no move to reach for his gun, for he knew that Zalman could throw the grenade before he could clear his gun from the holster. Zalman reached the outer bushes and disappeared. The following day, Kanapelka executed Commander Polikov.

When Zalman discovered what Kanapelka had done, he knew his life was in jeopardy as long as Kanapelka had the power of life and death over him. That night, he undertook the dangerous journey to the partisan headquarters in the Kazian swamps, near Vilna, to inform them about what had happened. He rode until the horse could travel no more. At a farm, he stole another horse, and continued through the night at breakneck speed until once again his horse faltered. He stole another. By dawn, he had travelled eighty kilometres. At the camp he asked to see the commander-in-chief and told the partisan committee how Commander Polikov died.

After hearing Zalman, the commander-in-chief ordered Kanapelka's arrest. He was returned to the main camp, tried by his peers and removed from his command. As a result of his previous exploits, his life was spared, but he was demoted without rank to be a fighter and the brigade was given another commander.

After the war, Kanapelka was honoured by the Soviet government for his services as a partisan. He was given charge of a factory, but eventually ran afoul of the authorities, running away and hiding in the same swamps he controlled when he was a partisan, living off the land. He intimidated local farmers to feed him. One night, he left the swamp, and went to a farmer, demanding food and vodka. The farmer, fed up with threats of intimidation, filled him with so much vodka that Kanapelka collapsed into a drunken stupor. The farmer tied Kanapelka's hands and feet, put him into a large sack, and dragged him to the nearby railway tracks. He placed the sack in the middle of the rails, and waited for the next train to end Kanapelka's life – which it did.

Zalman stayed in the Minsk area and joined another brigade. He knew if he returned to Dzisna, even with Kanapelka not in charge, there were too many of Zurawski's relatives who thought as Kanapelka and would like nothing better than to kill Zalman.

It was also time to find Joseph Juszkevitz. What he did discover was that Juszkevitz had left Dzisna.

IT WAS DURING THE WINTER OF 1942, THAT THE PARTISAN movement was subjected to a severe test. Zalman joined the Suborov brigade, a large band of about 2,500 men, which was part of a larger group of 40,000 partisans. Constant harassment by the partisans resulted in the German forces having to withdraw operational men from the front line to support the local police who proved inadequate to safeguard the rear installations. During most nights, Zalman's group destroyed bridges, blocked roads and derailed trains. For almost two years, he learned the art of killing, showing no mercy, giving no ground and taking no prisoners. His reputation grew as a fighter who would not be compromised, and his ruthlessness became widely known, even to the gentiles of Dzisna.

In August 1943, the partisans were involved in a large-scale operation called the "War of the Rails" in the occupied areas of Leningrad, Smolensk and Byelorussia; a territory of more than one 1,000 kilometres long and 750 kilometres wide in which 95,000 partisans operated. Zalman and his group of four men would place dynamite on the tracks, wait for a train to reach the area of impact, pull a tripwire to detonate the dynamite under the train and blow it off the tracks. In the confusion they shot at anything that moved, running away before the Germans could regroup. Realizing what the partisans were doing, the Germans added another car in front of the engine to absorb the impact, causing only the empty flat car to be destroyed. The partisans wired the detonator after the train stopped, causing the dynamite to go off about twenty metres further back, destroying the cars behind the engine. To defeat this tactic, the Germans stationed guards to protect the rails every thousand metres for hundreds of kilometres, but without success.

With the collapse of the German invasion of Russia by late 1943, the Germans began retreating westward, leaving behind a scorched earth policy, driving the conquered population like cattle towards Germany. The partisan movement had become more widespread and better organized, creating mayhem at the German's rear. The swamps and forest were always better suited to partisan action and they used the terrain to their advantage. German military rule was shaky, restricted to the daylight hours because the partisans were the true masters of the night. The local population of Byelorussia and Ukraine who did not think of themselves as Russians were prepared to help the resistance because one effect of the German terror had been to turn many German sympathizers into supporters of the Soviet cause.

By March 1944, the Germans were destroying buildings and villages, pushing everything in front of them into a smaller pocket of defence until they reached Minsk. For six weeks, Zalman and more than 40,000 partisans were trapped near Minsk. The Germans concentrated their Stukas in the area, constantly bombing the men below, while more then 230,000 German soldiers converged into the area. Behind the partisans were the retreating German soldiers, and ahead of them were three lines of German defence with machine gunners located behind sandbags. The partisan commander told his men there was only one direction in which to go and that was ahead, even if it meant they all would die. They charged through a narrow opening in the German defence, and for more than three hours they fought, losing thousands of men as they inched through, eventually breaking the enemy line and surging to freedom. Behind them, the dead were stacked like cords of wood, one on top of the other.

From the beginning of April to May 4, 1944, their numbers shrank rapidly, with more than 25,000 partisans killed, many of them victims of mortar, bombs and gunfire from their own men. After the blockade was broken, the partisans who survived hid in the woods of Woropaivo, recovering from their near brush with death and preparing themselves for the next onslaught.

By the early days of June 1944, only 10,000 of the 40,000 partisans remained. When the Red Army liberated German-held territory, partisans were subjected to close scrutiny. Most of the able-bodied men were drafted into the army and often sent into the most vicious fighting areas. Partisans who had surrendered to the Germans were sent to labour camps or were shot. Only 25 percent were fully rehabilitated. To avoid being drafted and by majority consent, Zalman's group agreed to unite with the Soviet army and take future orders from Russian officers. Zalman joined the Uszachy brigade and wore a Soviet uniform. After nearly two years as a partisan, he now was a member of the Soviet regular army. His quest to find Juszkevitz was once again delayed, but the desire for revenge still burned within him.

The Soviets had promised to show their gratitude for what the partisans had done but were reluctant to be in their debt. Secretly, Joseph Stalin ordered that all partisans were expendable and should be sacrificed for the greater good of the war. As a result, during each battle, those who might some day be leaders were killed.

Zalman returned to the front line where his group seized important objectives, bridges, road junctions, fortified areas, towns and large villages, holding them until the advancing main Soviet army arrived. By late 1944, Zalman realized the Soviets were deliberately throwing the partisan survivors into one battle after another intent on killing them all.

In great numbers, the Soviet forces were squeezing the retreating Germans into pockets from which no escape was possible. More than 100,000 Germans were trapped in the Kurliandia pocket near the Baltic Sea, and being pounded by Soviet air and ground attacks. Clumps of Germans were annihilated in the thousands and buried in mass graves, identified with a marker on which was carved a single Russian soldier's name symbolizing what lay beneath. No German name would soil their land.

On the eve of an important offensive, Zalman, manning a machine gun, came under heavy mortar attack. A mortar exploded near him. The blast threw him into the air, slicing off the palm of one hand. He was taken out of the battle, and placed on a train with the wounded to go to the nearest field hospital. Later he learned, almost all of the 10,000 partisans committed to the battle had been killed.

As the train travelled southward, Zalman realized he was about 30 kilometres from Dzisna and decided to leave the train rather than be taken to a hospital from which he would be thrown into another impossible battle. The next time he might not be so lucky and he was not ready to die just yet. His quest had not been completed. Joseph Juszkevitz still lived, and for Zalman that was something he could not leave unfinished.

When the train slowed at a curve, Zalman threw himself off. He made his way to Dzisna, intending to locate some of the men he had fought with when he was a partisan. He recognized the faces of collaborators who had worked with the Germans before the Jews were massacred walking the streets of Dzisna. He wondered why they were free when they should be in prison or shot for their complicity.

He located several of his friends and he asked why the collaborators were still free. They told him that those who complained would be the ones killed. The collaborators were powerful people and had the ear of too many officials in high places. That night, Zalman documented what he remembered about each collaborator, and the next day he asked to see the head of the local KGB force, Major Suzdalcev. The KGB major heard Zalman's accusations and asked on what authority he had to make these accusations. Zalman produced a document given to him when he was a partisan, assigning him to find anyone who collaborated with the enemy and to have that person arrested. He had been given the responsibility of being an arresting officer and still retained the authority.

To Zalman's surprise, Major Suzdalcev arrested him, and had him imprisoned in the basement of the hospital to silence his accusations. While in confinement, Zalman's wound opened and he bled. He banged on his door demanding medical help. A doctor was brought to him and Zalman learned he was being sent from Dzisna to the front line to prevent him from exposing the influential people whose dubious background they wanted hidden. Later that day, an inspection committee arrived at the hospital from Moscow and Zalman managed to get word to them about what was happening in Dzisna. They released him and arrested Major Suzdalcev and all the names on Zalman's list. When Zalman's accusations were confirmed, the accused were sent to the front line. An attempt was made on Zalman's life, and those responsible were also arrested and sent to the front line. The head of the inspection committee asked Zalman to stay in Dzisna, to locate other collaborators, but he declined. For declining, he was ordered to the front line as well.

Before leaving, Zalman heard of a woman named Fanta confined in a small crawl space, having paid a gentile to hide her from the Germans. The farmer had threatened to hand her to the Germans because she had run out of money. Locked in her self-made prison, Fania was not aware that the Germans were no longer a threat. Upset about what he had heard, Zalman journeyed to the area looking for the house, found the woman and removed her from her prison. She had not been outside of the tiny space for two years, and when Zalman brought her into the light, she was blind and unable to stand. Her body had become bent from crouching during her imprisonment and could not straighten.

Afterwards, Zalman went to the swamp, to the place where he was told his brother had been buried. He searched the grounds until he found a mound of earth that looked as if it might contain a body and carefully dug into the mound. He uncovered his brother's remains, placed them into a coffin, and took the coffin to Dzisna, to where the Jews from the ghetto massacre were buried. On one of the corners of the huge grave, Zalman dug another grave for his brother so he would be close to his father and sister.

Zalman returned to the front line. To his surprise, he found himself in the same squad as the KGB major from Dzisna. Major Suzdalcev promised to kill Zalman, but during the ensuing battle, the major was shot from behind by an unknown soldier.

Zalman served in the Soviet army until May 8, 1945, when Germany unconditionally surrendered. The war in Europe had finally come to an end. Now Zalman prepared himself for his own private war – hunting for his brother's murder – Joseph Juszkevitz.

But that was not to be.

A division of 6,000 men were sent to fight against Japan, when it was learned that Japan and Germany had made a secret agreement to become allies against Russia in the event the Soviet army's crossed the Volga River near Stalingrad, which it did on September 28, 1942. With the defeat of Germany, Stalin decided to support the Americans against Japan although Japan had reneged on its agreement.

Zalman was bound for another war.

One day from the coast of Japan on August 28, 1945, Zalman learned that Japan had surrendered two weeks before, ending the Second World War.

Zalman's division was sent to Kazakhstan to be used against civilian unrest, and while there, the Soviet government offered release from active duty to any soldier who had been wounded at least three times or had served in the army for five years. Zalman had served for two years with the partisans, and three years with the army, so he applied for his discharge and it was granted.

NOT WANTING TO RETURN TO THE MEMORIES OF THE PAIN AND death that took place in Dzisna, Zalman moved to Riga, Lithuania in 1946; he was twenty-one years old. His first quest was to find Joseph Juszkevitz. The trail had grown cold. His own inquiries had returned without anyone knowing what had happened to Juszkevitz. He notified the International Red Cross that he was looking for his lost cousin, Joseph Juszkevitz, who used to be the Chief of Police of Dzisna. Could they help find the only remaining member of his family? They promised to send out notices throughout Europe in an attempt to locate him.

Zalman married Mara in 1949, and in 1952 they had a son, Leon. In 1957, the Soviet Union allowed those who were born in Poland to return to the country of their birth and under the political geography of 1939, Byelorussia was Polish territory. Zalman applied for repatriation and was granted permission to return to Poland, to the city of Stetin, finding employment as a taxi driver. Resigned to the fact that Juszkevitz was either dead or hiding somewhere beyond his reach, Zalman tried to put the past behind him although he still burned with anger and hate for the man who killed his brother.

In 1959, Zalman returned to Riga to visit with his relatives. When he returned to Stetin, he was told the Polish Secret Police were looking for him. He was wanted for questioning. He appeared at the local headquarters feeling uneasy about his summons. When he gave his name, and asked why he was summoned, they would not say. He wondered if the many enemies he had made during the war had decided to get their revenge. Zalman was escorted into a small room in which a private and a colonel were waiting for him with a stenographer to record their conversation. The concern on Zalman's face was obvious, and the stern faces of the police officers did not suggest that this was a friendly visit.

They interrogated him about Dzisna for four hours – what he did during the war and if he had proof of his statements. He produced documents and showed the medals given to him by the Soviet government. Finally satisfied, they asked him a question that jolted him upright in his chair.

"Do you know someone named Joseph Juszkevitz?"

Zalman nodded. "Yes. I am looking for him."

"Why?" the colonel asked.

Zalman told them about his brother's death and Juszkevitz's role in his murder. When he was finished there was silence.

The colonel reached into the desk and removed a photograph. "Would you know Juszkevitz if you saw him again?"

"Know him? If I only saw his bleached bones, I would know they were his," Zalman answered.

The colonel placed the picture in front of Zalman, saying, "He's dead." Zalman gazed at the photograph of his enemy laying on the ground with part of his skull shattered. He waited for the colonel to explain.

"Juszkevitz was the Chief of Police in a district in the city of Bydgoszcz. Are you familiar with the city?"

Zalman nodded.

"He received a telegram, read it, and then went outside and shot himself in the head. When his body was discovered the telegram was found in his pocket. It was from the International Red Cross and it read, 'A RELATIVE OF YOURS, ZALMAN KATZ IS TRYING TO GET IN TOUCH WITH YOU. WE HAVE GIVEN HIM YOUR ADDRESS.' It listed your name and address."

Zalman smiled. "The chase ended as it should – by Juszkevitz's own hand." How strange, he thought, that Juszkevitz took his own life because he feared I would kill him. How poetic. He shook his head in wonder, the smile growing ever wider. How bizarre. The International Red Cross could never have notified him after they found Juszkevitz because they didn't know where he lived. When he left the country, he never notified them of a forwarding address. He had thought the matter was dead. Now it was.

He hoped Moishe could rest in peace.

THE MEMORY OF ZALMAN KATZ'S EXPERIENCE OCCUPIES A permanent place in his mind. Each date, each death, each tragedy is an open sore that continues to fester without let up. He remains unforgiving. There is no remorse for what he has done, nor does he feel that any is needed. Millions of people have died, and generations of Jewish unborn have never had a chance to enjoy life, while many who were responsible are still alive and free from punishment.

With the birth of Israel, Zalman Katz is proud that the Jews are a nation and not a tribe aimlessly wandering the world. There is now a place for every Jew, no matter where he or she lives. Canada has been good to him, and his family. He feels blessed that when his first choice was denied him, he chose this country instead.

But hate is here as well, and it must never be allowed to grow as it did in Europe. Jews should never walk to their deaths quietly, but resist with every fibre of their being. With tears in his eyes, he ends with, *"when I am awake, my memory does not let me forget; nor should those who were responsible."*

Leon Katz, Zalman Katz and the only Jew left in Dzisna at the memorial monument to Jews in the Dzisna cemetery.

Zalman Katz

THE PROMISES

*"First they came for the socialist
and I did not speak out – because I was not a socialist.
Then they came for the trade unionist
and I did not speak out – because I was not a trade unionist.
Then they came for the Jews
and I did not speak out – because I was not a Jew.
Then they came for me – and there was no one left to speak for me."*
— Reverend MARTIN NIEMOLLER

Michael Kutz: *"Of what purpose was there to forget. Who benefits more by the forgetting? When living with hate, what is beyond acceptability becomes acceptable. To perform the acts of brutal inhumanity done to the Jews was interpreted not as an act of atrocity by the fascists but as a service necessary for the cleansing of a race. Hate begets hate and wrong becomes right. To forget and forgive is not an answer. Remembering is. This way, the guilty are constantly reminded of their guilt."*

Map by **AMA***Graphics* Incorporated

THE PROMISES

The Story of
MICHAEL KUTZ

The forty passengers in the bus were excited, expressing sounds of joy, laughing at funny and not so funny comments with their eyes fixed on the scenery flashing by their windows. Michael Kutz was one of the passengers. Every square inch of space he gazed upon, smelled or could touch, if the bus were to stop, were scenes from Jewish history and he was filled with pride that at last he was in Israel.

Fifty years had passed since he promised his father he would go to Palestine and he had finally arrived. It should have been a happy time for him, but his thoughts were emotionally tangled in his purpose for being in Israel, and of the realization he had finally fulfilled the last of his parents dreams; both of whom were dead. His father killed fighting the Germans and his mother, murdered by the Ukrainians. They were victims of a war of atrocity that interrupted their beautiful lives and destroyed their dream of making aliyah to the promised land. He also lost a brother and two sisters to the same madmen that murdered six million Jews.

Michael closed his eyes, trying to shut the memories that filled his thoughts, but he quickly opened them again. To have waited this long to come to Israel, it would be a shame if he didn't gaze upon the sights that only he was able to see. He had made himself a promise, he would let his eyes be the sight for his dead family and let them see the glory that belonged to the Jews of the diaspora. The bus entered the outskirts of Jerusalem and everyone became excited, shouting at each other as the historical landmarks appeared.

Soon . . . Michael thought, soon he will see the Western Wall. For more than three thousand years, the Wall has stood as a monument to the everlasting strength of Jewish presence. It was revered as the holiest of places for Jews all over the world. From the time he decided to take this trip, he knew he had to come to the Wall, and say a prayer for his father and mother, his brother and his sisters. After the war, he had prayed for them, and hoped that in death they were able to find the peace which had eluded him.

He was fifty-nine, and had devoted his adult life to bringing yiddishkite to Jewish children denied the opportunity of learning the marvels of their faith because of economic reasons. His had been a good life, rich in the personal rewards of having accomplished a mitzvah without having asked for anything in return, except the satisfaction of fulfilling his promise to his mother. He regretted his parents could not know how he had tried to do what he promised, but at least he was aware, and from that he took his comfort.

The bus stopped at the top of the hill overlooking the Western Wall, and Michael saw hundreds of people praying. Soon it would be his turn. With seven hundred people on this Mission, they were told to wait until their bus number was called before proceeding to the Wall. The Israeli guide asked everyone to leave the bus and wait by the door. From where they stood, at the top of the hill, the panoramic view was breathtaking as all eyes feasted on the scene.

Suddenly, Michael felt two pairs of hands grip both his arms, physically lifting him from the ground. He tried to free himself, but was suspended in their grip, being carried towards the Wall. "Stop!" he yelled to his friends. "It's not our turn."

"That's where you are wrong, Michael," one of them replied. "This is long overdue." Michael turned his head, and was amazed to see the more than seven hundred others following.

EARLY IN THE TWELFTH CENTURY, MANY JEWS FLED GERMANY TO Poland and Russia. Some journeyed to the old city of Nieswiez, located in Byelorussia, southwest of Minsk and as close to Russia as it was to Poland. The Jews became an important part of the local community, representing a large portion of the population. Over the years, the abuse by the government resulted in the Jewish community growing within themselves instead of integrating with the general population.

As a result of the Russo-Polish War of 1920-1921, Poland acquired immense territories, of which Byelorussia was a part, and governed the territories as an extension of Poland. Nieswiez became a typical Polish city with narrow cobbled streets, picturesque buildings, long walkways and tall majestic Roman Catholic churches, offering the appearance of a quiet, friendly and peaceful city. In 1941, Nieswiez had a population of 25,000 of which 10,000 were Jewish.

As a result of the Nazi-Soviet Pact of 1939, all territories east of the Narew, Vistula and San Rivers would be under Soviet influence. After the German army invaded Poland on September 1, 1939, Byelorussia reverted to Russia and Nieswiez became a Soviet city once again. With the German occupation of Poland (west of the Vistula River), being a Jew was tantamount to being sentenced to death. The status of a Jew was designated by the invaders as an inferior being; someone less than human, to be treated with contempt and loathing. Plans were implemented for their removal from the Nazi conquered lands. Jews located east of the Vistula River were not affected until June 22, 1941, when Germany broke the pact it signed with Russia and invaded their territory.

Michael Kutz was then ten years old. At his age, his life should have been very simple; in school preparing for his bar mitzvah and looking forward to the day when he would take his place in the Jewish community. Instead he was taught more stringent values – how to survive. He had no concern for politics, local or global, nor did he understand the meaning of being hated. A very large Jewish population conveyed to Michael the impression he lived in a Jewish city, since all of his neighbours and fellow students shared his faith. He had little contact with gentiles except when he accompanied his father to see a non-Jew outside the city. It was the nature of Joseph Kutz's occupation to do business with everyone.

Joseph Kutz had originally come to Nieswiez as part of the Russian army during the First World War. When the war ended and his army unit returned home, he chose to remain and marry Aida, the woman he met as a soldier. Joseph was a forestry assessor, responsible for deciding what part of a forest could be designated for commercial use and what could be allocated for park use. He was active in local city politics, a community volunteer and respected by everyone, no matter the nationality or their religious convictions. He was a hard worker, a devoted husband and a good father.

He and Aida were Zionists, committed to the belief that Palestine should be the home for all Jews and it was this they taught to their children.

Aida kept a traditional kosher home, and raised the children to be proud of their Jewish heritage and to respect the rights of others. Tzalia, the older brother, two sisters, Hanna and Nahama, and Michael, the youngest were being prepared for the day they would leave Poland and make aliyah to Palestine. Aida's mother shared their home and was the only living grandparent.

Always inquisitive, always a seeker of answers, Michael approached his father with his confusion. "Poppa," he asked, "why do you want us to go to Palestine? My friends say that Poland is now the home of the Jews."

Joseph thought a minute. "No, Michael," he answered, "at one time, Poland was a haven for the Jews. Palestine is our real home. It was the home of our people thousands of years ago, and God willing, someday it will be yours and mine. Your mother and I believe that every Jew should return to Palestine, and when they do, the Jews will once again have their homeland. Your brother Tzalia will be the first to go to Palestine. That is why he is attending a training camp where he is being taught how to live on a kibbutz. Life in Palestine will not be easy. It will require hard work and sacrifice, but at least the effort will be for ourselves. After he is established, we will follow."

Michael continued to argue. "But Poppa, why can't we make a home in Poland? Everyone here is Jewish, and if we don't bother with those outside of here, why should they bother with us?"

Joseph smiled, a sad smile. "Many years ago," he answered, "Poland was the home of many Jews, but no more. A Jew is always an unwanted guest when things go bad. It is always the Jews who are blamed for all the wrongs which befall the Christian community. When you listen to the radio, you will hear the Germans using hatred of the

Jews as an excuse to further their own ambition. Many bad things are happening. Someday, you and your brother may have to be the men in our house. If there is a war, I must leave, but I pray that may not be. Meanwhile, we will continue to make plans to go to Palestine and hope that all will be well."

But all was not to be well.

Adolf Hitler attacked the Soviet Union and expanded his territorial domain to include Byelorussia, the Ukraine and parts of the Balkans. Joseph left one night to join the main Russian forces to fight not only the enemy of his country, but the enemy of his beliefs. With the onslaught of the German invasion, anti-Semitic rhetoric increased and became more physical. The German army advanced rapidly, and throughout their advance, they advocated the indiscriminate killings and beatings of anyone thought to be a Jew. It became apparent that the murder of a Jew was not a crime by German law, and all the Jews feared for their lives.

The non-Jewish residents of Nieswiez fell into step with Hitler's philosophy, venting their hatred and envy, releasing emotions of hate buried for many years. They were made to wear a yellow star of David on their outer garments, forced to walk in the middle of the street along with the cars and animals, clean the gutters, chop wood and look after army horses. As a display of their inferior status, they were made to bow when confronting anyone other than another Jew. They were treated as less than a chattel, with no consideration as an inferior species and subjected to every physical and mental abuse possible.

The *Judenrat* (Jewish-led committee) was created by the German authority for the government to speak to the Jewish population. Prominent local Jewish leaders and rabbis were coerced into becoming the Jewish Council for the area surrounding Nieswiez. They had the responsibility of obtaining men and boys for labour-oriented work for the Germans or the Jewish community would suffer for the shortcomings. To enforce their demands, they periodically arrested up to ten Jews almost every week and held them hostage. They ordered the Judenrat to collect contributions for the German coffers, such as gold, silver or other items deemed essential. If the quota was not collected by the deadline, the hostages were executed.

After Joseph left Nieswiez, the situation deteriorated and Aida found herself almost helpless to protect her children. As the months passed and living conditions worsened, she had difficulty finding enough food. Secretly she sold textiles to non-Jewish friends using Michael as a runner. Late at night, Michael would take the cloth to a rendezvous outside Nieswiez, and exchange what he had for food from gentiles sympathetic to their plight. One farmer was especially helpful as Michael used his knowledge of the back roads to reach his farm and was always given as much food as he could carry. He would make his way back, careful to avoid being caught by a German patrol, which would mean his death and the death of his family. At the age of ten, his was an onerous responsibility. One that he had to accept – or die.

The radio reported defeat after defeat and the high casualties of the Russian army. Aida sensed her beloved husband would never return. Intoxicated with their many victories, the Germans behind the battle lines turned their attention to the Jews and Aida prepared her family for the worse.

The random killings of Jews increased, with the tension in the streets being so thick with fear, that it was almost possible to cut it with a knife. After several were killed without warning, Aida called her children together. "The news on the radio is not good," she told them. "The war goes badly for the soldiers fighting the Germans and I fear your father will not return."

The children cried.

"Listen well to what I say to you. Above all, I want you to remember that you are Jews and you have a right to be proud of who you are. If your father were here, he would tell you not to forget Palestine. It is there you will find peace and a home. That is where we Jews should live and please God someday we will. Some of you must survive and tell the world what the Germans are doing. I want you to promise me, never forget who you are and what you have been taught. You are Jewish and have no reason to be ashamed. Always be proud of your heritage. Remember your father's words and go to Palestine. It is our home."

Michael was no longer the child of a few months ago and he realized from what he had seen, that his mother could not protect them from the Germans. He was frightened and confused. He didn't understand why they were being treated by the Germans in this way, but realized from the way his mother spoke that evil things were taking place and something worse was about to still happen.

Aida took Michael aside and talked to him. "Remember your father's words and never forget who you are. I want you to promise me that you will survive and you will never forget what you have seen."

For his mother's sake he promised he would never forget. He would do all in his power to honour her request and tell the world everything he witnessed. And someday, he promised her, he would also go to Palestine.

Aida prayed for a miracle. She hoped her family would not be harmed. There were conflicting rumours circulating that all the Jews would be taken to a labour camp, but word also reached the community that two large pits had been dug outside the city by Christian labourers. There was confusion about the news; the fear of being uprooted and the purpose of the two pits. Whatever was about to happen, did not bode well for the Jewish community.

On October 29, 1941, the Judenrat informed the population that every Jew, no matter the age or health, had to assemble in the main city square. Each person was to bring their papers identifying who and what each did for a living and they could take with them only the clothes they wore. Without exception, the edict had to be obeyed. The Commandant told the Judenrat that it needed 500 craftsmen, and submitted a list of preferred occupations, especially textile workers, who would remain behind. Those selected would be sent to a Jewish ghetto to be set aside in Nieswiez. There they would use their skills for the benefit of the Third Reich. The rest to be sent to a labour camp.

The next morning, most were dressed in their best clothes, and wearing more than one layer, intending to use the extra garments for bartering. They also hid items of value on themselves to be used to bribe officials. Unable to bring suitcases, they contrived to carry what they could under the different layers of clothes they wore or had sewn into the hem of their garments.

Aida's mother was ill and could not leave her bed. Aida left her, even though the orders were explicit that everyone had to assemble at the city square. She refused to believe the Germans would do harm to an old and sick woman. She naively expected they would send her later to wherever they were being taken when her health improved. From all over the city, the Jewish population converged onto the city square for their appointment with death. Hanna and Nahama walked hand in hand with their mother while Tzalia held Michael's hand.

As they approached the square, they passed local and German auxiliary police along the perimeter holding rifles. The square soon filled with more than 12,000 Jews as there were over 2,000 additional Jews who had fled from other cities and were hiding with friends or relatives. As a result of the German ultimatum, they were forced to leave their hiding places and join the residents in the square. The air was cool and there was a sprinkling of snow on the ground. Before long, the cold held their attention. The very young and the old soon found the cold air penetrated through their multi-layers of clothes. They tried to keep warm and their spirits positive, not wanting to face any negative implications. A premonition of an impending disaster hovered over them and an undercurrent of fear prevailed.

After the Jews left their homes, German soldiers entered the houses, searching for anyone that had not complied with the orders; when found, they were shot. Those in the city square heard the shots, but were unaware of what was happening. Aida's mother was murdered in her bed as an object lesson for her disobedience.

The Commandant arrived. Using a loudspeaker, he read the names of the craftsmen supplied to him by the Judenrat. His instructions were brief and concise. The craftsmen were to assemble in another section of the square, and be taken away. While the Commandant issued his orders, more German troops appeared and surrounded the entire area.

A wave of panic swept the crowd.

They began to mill about.

Those whose names were not read became alarmed and raised their voices begging to be taken as well. Those who heard their names, moved through the swaying crowd to where they were instructed, attempting to take their families, too. The Commandant allowed a few, but most of the wives and children were denied access to where the craftsmen waited. Members of the families pushed against the German barrier, trying to join their husbands, but the soldiers used their rifle butts to control the unruly crowd. Soldiers surrounded the elite group and marched them out of the square.

A terrible wail tore from the throats of the people, while confused and frightened children hugged their parents and cried. Portions of the crowd surged forward, but the German soldiers liberally used the butts of their rifles to quell the crowds unruliness. All the while, the Commandant intimidated the crazed Jews with threats that if they did not stop their pushing and shoving, they would all be shot. The threats quieted the hysteria and the people remained where they stood.

The Commandant ordered the people to form smaller groups. Soldiers moved among them, counting and shoving them into pockets of 200 without concern for families. The people surged in all directions in an effort to rejoin their families. In the confusion, Michael lost his hold on Tzalia's hand and was pushed behind several adults that he did not know. A German soldier was counting nearby Michael, who was now lost in a sea of bodies and legs that towered over him. As the people milled about, Michael was grabbed by the soldier and pushed into another group. Amid all the pushing and shoving, he tried vainly to catch sight of his mother, but was prevented from moving out of his group. He was bumped and stepped on by the milling people and hemmed in by legs and bodies. He called his mother's and Tzalia's name, but his small, weak voice was lost in the melee and hysteria that enclosed him. They were hidden in the swaying crowd – never to be seen again.

After the Germans created pockets of 200, the groups were force-marched from the city square. The soldiers and local police kept a tight control over the almost 12,000 Jews, preventing anyone from escaping. As they were herded towards the unknown, everyone was talking; The words trembled with fear. A morbid dread that their lives were threatened and there was nothing they could do about it. Many cried or wailed their grief. Occasionally, a machine gun chattered, followed by screams from the people. Those who tried to escape were shot within a few feet of their attempt.

At an intersection in the road, the long lines were broken into two distinct sections and marched in separate directions. Michael was positioned further back and saw one column heading towards the small community of Snow.

Michael's section was escorted onto the grounds of Radziwil Park, where a fifteenth century palace, that Michael had visited often with his father was located. They passed the castle with its more than 500 rooms, beautifully blending into the winter scene, striking a picturesque appearance of their winter surroundings. Michael shivered with fear, realizing the road they were on went no where, but back to where it started.

As the Jews in front crested a hill, they began to wail at what they saw and the sound became a wave as it flowed back to the last person in the line. Before them was an enormous pit, and standing around the pit were Lithuanian and Ukrainian soldiers, whose uniforms were splattered in blood. The German soldiers lined the pit area, forcing the Jews to move closer. When they could go no further without falling in, they were stopped.

Michael was unable to see beyond the men and women that surrounded him. Another gasp of horror escaped from everyone's lips. The voices of the men could be heard begging God to help them, while small children screamed and the women wailed their terror into the air like sirens pleading for help. The crowd tried to move back, but the German soldiers forced the Jews to stand their ground. Machine guns chattered, and again the crowd screamed, drowning out the cries of those who were shot. Grenades erupted amid the screams of terror and pain. Everyone swayed in different directions trying to run away from the horror confronting them, but the soldiers had created a tight inescapable pocket around the section, and the crowd was glued to their places, no matter how hard they tried to move back.

There was movement ahead and Michael's group was pushed forward. He watched 200 Jews pushed to the edge of the huge pit.

Men disrobed.

Children removed their clothes.

Women stood naked.

They shivered at the edge of the black cavern while the soldiers laughed, and pointed at the comical sight of the embarrassed and frightened. Those watching cried and wailed. Most of the men continued to pray; others tried to comfort their families. The children buried their faces in their father or mother's body, sensing what was about to take place, not wishing to see.

Michael could not see anyone familiar. He was alone and terrified. His short height made it awkward to see beyond the press of bodies surrounding him. He heard an explosion and then more explosions mingled with screams from the pit area. Machine guns chattered and the people nearest to the pit screamed again. The sounds were captured in the winter air, resounding over the snow covered hills, to those still unable to see, caught up in the hysteria, screamed as well, spreading their fear like a contagious disease throughout the milling throng. The crowd tried to move back again, but the German soldiers pointed their rifles and bayonets at them, and continued to keep them contained. Michael was almost trampled between the milling adults.

Another group moved forward. Michael was now able to see everything. People stood at the edge of the pit trying to hide their naked bodies. He watched them jump over the lip, disappearing in seconds. Soldiers threw grenades after them, while others shot bursts from their machine guns into the dark, gaping hole.

He could hear the cries from the wounded in the pit, as the voices of the terrified people around him screamed insanely. He continued to watch as one group after another was forced to follow each other. By the time he was ushered to the edge of the pit, the soldiers had tired of their sport. It was a matter of expediency, and their throwing of the grenades and the shooting was less accurate and more mechanical. Michael removed all his clothes and stepped forward to the lip of the pit. Someone brushed hard against him, knocking him over the ledge. He landed on top of a body swimming in blood. Someone fell on him, wedging him between two bodies. He heard the explosions and the bullets striking the bodies beside and above him. A blow to his head caused him to black out.

When he regained consciousness, at first he was confused as to where he was, followed instantly with the knowledge that he was alive. He could feel something sticky running down his head and the weight pressing on top of him was making it difficult to breathe. The shooting had stopped, he could not hear any guns or grenades, but he could hear the muffled moans of the wounded crying out for help between the press of dead bodies. It was blacker than night. The utter blackness disoriented him, unable to determine which direction was up.

Michael extended his arms forward, touching the naked bodies that surrounded him. He pushed his skinny shoulders between the two bodies above him and began burrowing through them; grabbing at arms and legs, squirming and squeezing towards what he perceived as the surface, clutching and pushing in the direction of his escape from the nightmare that had engulfed him. His fingers grabbed at the faces of the dead, a hand brushed his body as his feet stepped on the backs of those he passed, no longer caring at the injustice of their death. His breathing was laboured, and he was afraid that he was going to lose consciousness. Panic gripped him, afraid he was crawling in the wrong direction, when suddenly he pushed his way through the last row of bodies, and peered out into the cold, unforgiving night.

All was deadly quiet. Cautiously, he listened for any movement from the police or soldiers in case they were still standing on the lip of the pit. He peered from among the bodies trying to see over the edge, but there didn't appear to be anyone about. The air was frigid, causing Michael to shiver. He realized that for him to climb out, he would have to use the bodies as a ladder. As quietly as he could, he crawled on his stomach over the dead, and pulled some of them against the wall, creating a small pyramid. When he was finished, he stepped onto their backs and pulled himself out. He lay on the snow, trying to remember where exactly he was and in which direction the main gate was located. The cold air on his naked body made him tremble. He rose to his knees, and with all the energy he could muster, he ran into the darkness. Behind him the cold air blanketed the dead and dying. The howl of the wind was the only *kaddish* that could be heard for their passing.

THE FRIGID AIR CUT INTO MICHAEL'S NAKED BODY, SUCKING OUT his strength, depleting his energy and robbing him of his breath. His feet flew over the ground, as if they were wings, running with the knowledge that if he wanted to live, he had to put as much distance between the pit and himself before the sun rose. Driven by fear, desperate to survive, Michael ran through the dark and forbidding forest, generating heat from his exertion that temporarily warmed him. Whenever he was forced to slow his pace to catch his breath, the cold air penetrated into his exposed pores, jabbing at his heart. His feet were cut and bleeding from slipping on rocks, Michael pushed his exhausted body to its limit.

As he ran, he looked for shelter, his skin was turning blue, but desperate for warmth, he was unable to see anything that could shield him from the cutting wind. His chest hurt and his breathing became laboured. In the distance, he made out the outline of a large building and recognized it as a convent. Michael ran towards it, remembering that the women in black clothes were the ones who took care of the poor and sick people on the streets of Nieswiez. Desperate for the warmth of a room, he pushed himself to the front gate, hoping they would help him escape from the Germans.

His body had lost its ability to absorb its own heat and he could not stop shivering. The world around him was spinning in unnatural motions, causing him to grope with trembling hands for the bell cord by the gate; his breathing came in short gasps as he huddled against the convent door trying to shield himself from the biting cold. When the door opened, with his last ounce of energy, Michael lunged inside and around the person blocking the entrance.

He turned to face a woman dressed in black. She appeared ageless, small, slightly bent in posture from the years of homage and she looked fragile. Surprise swept across her face, seeing a naked boy appear out of the night. She removed her cape and covered Michael with it. With quiet dignity, her voice soft and filled with kindness, she asked, "Who are you, my child? Where did you come from?"

Michael could not speak.

"Why are you here?"

Michael cried.

"I am the Mother Superior of this convent. How can I help you?"

With his tears flooding down his cheeks, Michael explained what had happened in Nieswiez and begged the Mother Superior for her help. Listening intently, she nodded her head a few times as Michael related what his tired and confused mind could remember. She led him into the inner recesses of the convent, along darkened, cold and forbidding corridors into the kitchen. In a locker by the door, she found clothes belonging to the janitor and gave them to Michael. Though much too big, he put them on, and cleaned himself by the sink, while the Mother Superior prepared hot food and administered to his cuts and bruises and doctored his head wound. After he had eaten, she sat across from him.

"You cannot stay."

"Why?"

"It is not safe for you here nor is it safe for those who cannot leave."

"Hide me. I will not be in anyone's way."

"It is not that. The risk is too great. If they find you, we will all suffer. Our lives are in danger if you stay."

"I have nowhere to go."

"I can direct you to those who may help you. I can do no more."

The fear of returning to the darkness overwhelmed him, but he was given no choice. The Mother Superior prepared a bag of food, and gave him directions to a neighbouring village. Quickly the Mother Superior ushered him out the convent gate, wishing him God's protection and locked the door after him. Alone, eleven-year-old Michael, once again had to face the unknown and the fears of his thoughts.

Outside, the evening had turned colder. Michael began his trek through the dark forest, apprehensive and with extreme caution, alert for sounds that might cause him to hide. The moonlight barely penetrated through the trees, offering him little comfort as he made his way in the darkness towards the village. When he had almost reached his destination, Michael remembered the gentile farmer who showed his kindness when the family was in need of food. Aware he was near his farm, he decided to change directions, and seek out his help.

Upon reaching the farmer's home, Michael knocked on the door. When the surprised farmer saw Michael, he swept him into his arms crying with joy, that he had survived the massacre and was safe. He was ushered into the house, where his wife brought Michael hot soup and food as she attended to the bruises and cuts that the Mother Superior had covered. Michael related his story, and when he was finished the farmer recounted to Michael what he knew.

"The Germans ordered several local farmers to the two sites days ago, he among them and had them dig the pits," he said. "They would return each day, and make the hole bigger until finally ordered to stop and leave the site. Before they left, Ukrainian and Lithuanian soldiers arrived in trucks filled with gypsies and cripples and killed them all. Their bodies were thrown into the pit as one would dispose of a worthless carcass. The farmers were unprepared for what they saw and some screamed hysterically. Others went into shock, their minds unable to accept the barbarism of what they had witnessed. One went mad. The Ukrainian and Lithuanian soldiers had blood on their uniforms, and appeared indifferent to their act. It was a horrible sight that will haunt him for the rest of his life." There was silence after he finished speaking, as the pictures in their minds revealed the terrible events that both had suffered through.

The farmer offered to hide Michael in the stable until Spring. Since it was obvious he was not part of the family, it was imperative he not be discovered or all were doomed. Michael stayed hidden from October 1941 until April 1942, coming outside only at night when no one was around. For six months, his world was always in sight of the barn, filled with fear of being discovered. There was no room for error, as the farmer's family lived two lives. They were committed to saving Michael, aware of the risk they had undertaken. They shared their food and took care of his immediate needs; maintaining an appearance of a normal life to their neighbours, warning him of any impending danger in time for him to move into the woods until it was safe.

The farmer made discreet enquiries if there was a partisan group nearby with Jewish fighters. Although concerned for Michael's safety, he exposed himself and his family by asking questions that if asked to the wrong person would jeopardize all their lives, but fortunately he aroused no suspicion. In April 1942, the farmer finally established contact with several Jews from a partisan group operating in Russia. They took Michael with them to live in the forest.

On July 17, 1942, a few months after Michael joined the partisans, Nieswiez was to again find itself the scene of martyrdom. The leaders of the ghetto received news of the massacre of Jews from Horodzei, only eight miles away. From the original 500 craftsmen, the ghetto had swollen to 5,000 by the influx from other communities.

On July 18, the German authorities ordered the Jews to assemble at the marketplace, but many people hid themselves in cellars and bunkers instead. An emergency meeting was held in the ghetto shule. Members of the Council appealed to the people not to run away, leaving behind the unprotected elderly people, the children, and the sick, but to remain and fight and die with dignity.

They agreed.

The Germans entered the ghetto on July 21, not expecting any resistance and were surprised to be met by a barrage of small gunfire and a machine gun. The main weapons were gasoline and kerosene bombs, which they showered onto the unsuspecting Germans.

Every Jew was ordered to provide himself with some means of defence, whether it be an axe, a hammer, a knife or even a stout piece of wood. Each house became a fort, with the occupants prepared to give their lives to fight their enemy. Jews barricaded in the shule returned the Germans fire. When the Germans crashed through the ghetto gate, the Jews drew their knives and irons; reached for their pile of stones and charged into them. The Germans increased their firing, but the Jews engaged in hand-to-hand combat, shooting at the Germans and the police at close quarters or clubbing at them in a blind fury. Soon the ghetto was filled with the dead and dying. Bodies were strewn throughout the streets like discarded puppets. The Jews set fire to their homes, which quickly spread towards the centre of the city. A horde of local peasants from the outlying area, swarmed into the burning ghetto, plundering the homes before they were devoured by the flames. People ran, screaming, crying as the madness of the pillaging, and the fury of the Germans intent on killing the Jews was matched only by the frenzy of every Jewish man, woman and child trying to flee the burning ghetto.

Small groups of Jews burst from the ghetto gates. Once outside, they were beaten by zealous peasants. Others were killed in flight. A small group succeeded in reaching the forest. That day, 5,000 Jews perished, but the Germans paid the price with their own lives. Expecting to find a cowering and submissive enemy, they learned the lesson of arrogance and over confidence.

THERE WERE 125 PARTISANS OPERATING FROM THE BRIGADE THAT Michael joined. Few were Jewish, because the partisans did not trust Jews. They did not have enough weapons for their own fighters and even less ammunition and what little they had, they refused to share. Anti-Jewish hatred was still prevalent although they fought a common enemy. As the Jewish fighters proved themselves more than capable, their presence was then tolerated. Not too long after Michael joined, the brigade planned an operation to blow up a building in White Russia that was the District Headquarters for suspected Polish collaborators. He volunteered, but many of the partisans were reluctant to include an in-experienced small boy, especially one as young as Michael.

The mission consisted of only Jewish partisans, who had to hike 25 kilometres into White Russia; destroy the building and kill as many of the police as they could. The Commander of the partisans listened to his men's objections, but he argued that Michael was essential to the mission's success. Several non-Jewish fighters were apprehensive about Michael being captured and forced to reveal the location of their camp, but the Commander wanted Michael to go because he could crawl closer to the ground, avoiding detection, wire the explosives and home-made bombs and return to the camp with less risk. Reluctantly it was agreed and Michael became part of the mission.

Six men and Michael left at midnight and reached their destination in five hours. Everyone had knapsacks of dynamite on their backs, a rifle and a gun. At 5:50 in the morning, Michael camouflaged with ferns, slowly crawled through the open ground to the barbed wire, removed his cutter and snapped a few strands to squeeze through the small opening.

He reached the back of the building and buried the explosives near the door. The remaining members of the team had separated into two groups. One group was watching Michael in case he needed help while the other stationed itself ready for the police and collaborators to come out the front door.

Michael finished burying the explosives and crawled away from the building. The two groups were ready. Five minutes later the back of the building exploded. Three policemen ran out half naked and were shot. Fire erupted causing other explosions. Men ran out the doors or jumped from the windows as the Jews picked their targets and killed those running out. Sirens wailed and German troops from the surrounding area arrived. The partisans slipped unnoticed back into the forest and hid. The following night, they returned to their camp, where they learned that fourteen police were dead and five were wounded and the building was thoroughly destroyed.

Jewish partisans gained respect as fighters and showed amazing bravery and were instrumental in the success of many operations in which Michael always took part. They equipped themselves with the booty of those they killed, and for the next two years, Michael became an integral part of any campaign in which Jews were involved. By now, the Russians who had been skeptical of the fighting ability of the Jews, accepted them fully. The partisans were always mobile, never staying in one place too long, fearing detection from wandering collaborators intent on capturing them or a Jew for the reward. In the winter months, they used other tactics. The snow became their enemy in that it left evidence of their presence, and they avoided the forest, keeping to more open ground, but always hidden from view. From a young boy of ten, Michael had grown to be a man of thirteen – without the formality of a bar mitzvah.

In the Fall of 1943, the combined partisan groups and the underground were involved in a large-scale mobile campaign called the War of the Rails. More than 120,000 lengths of railway line would be torn up and 836 enemy supply and armoured trains were derailed as well as 186 railway bridges destroyed. Partisans entered into enemy territories, motivating the local underground into destroying enemy garrisons and different lines of communications. The thirteen year-old Michael turned fourteen and then fifteen, a skilled, veteran fighter.

In the summer of 1944, the war still waged, but the front line had moved passed Nieswiez. The German retreat was constant and the fighting blazed in Poland. Michael asked permission to leave the partisans, to return to the place of his birth and see if there were other survivors of that terrible massacre. Dressed in his Russian uniform, a pistol on his hip and carrying his rifle, he entered Nieswiez. With the confidence of someone who knows what he is capable, he marched the war-torn streets to where he once lived. When the local residents recognized him, they could not believe their eyes. Some crossed themselves fearing they were seeing someone from the dead. Everyone avoided contact with him by leaving the sidewalk and moving between the carts and horses. Three years before, he was not allowed to use the walk, now his presence forced the residents to step onto the road out of fear for what he might do.

Michael found only fourteen Jews hiding in the Nieswiez. Few had escaped before the march to the pits; the rest had been in hiding. He was the only survivor of that terrible day – the only bloody witness to the massacre. For protection, they moved into an empty house. Because of Michael's status with the local partisans, he was given access to whatever food or clothing he needed and used this privilege to help the others. He was the youngest survivor of all of them, but he had the most experience and the others looked to him for leadership.

Soon after his arrival, Michael went to Radziwil Park, to the pit he had miraculously escaped and gazed over the area. It had been smothered in lime to dissolve the bodies laying beneath the surface and was covered over with earth. He did not know if his mother, brother or sisters were where he stood or at the other pit outside the community of Snow. It did not matter where they lay – only that they never be forgotten.

Staring at the mass grave, Michael's reverently trembling voice spoke to his mother, tears flowed from his cheeks, his voice shaking with emotion.

"Momma. It's Michael. I pray you have found peace. I have kept my promise to you, Momma. I have survived to bear witness against those who have done this evil. I will never forget you. I will devote my life so no one forgets what has happened here. I will be a living testimony of that terrible day. As long as I live, I will be a reminder to those who were responsible, it will never happen again. Go with God, Momma." Unashamed, he slowly dropped to his knees and cried, releasing the pain stored in his soul, sobbing and longing of a family that was no more.

To honour the Jews murdered in the massacre of Nieswiez, the fourteen survivors erected two plaques and placed one at each pit. Afterwards, the Russian authorities ordered them removed and replaced them with their own that declared the victims were Soviet citizens without acknowledging they were Jews.

Later, Michael and his friends became aware of a farmer using the headstones from the Jewish cemetery for foundation material at his farm. They commandeered a truck, and went to the farm carrying picks, axes and shovels and ordered the farmer to return the headstones. When he refused, they dug up the stones, cleaned them with care and placed them in the truck. They were unable to recognize all the names, but among them, Michael found his grandfather's stone. The authorities arrived, the farmer having gone to the city to report what was happening on his farm. They tried to stop the small band of Jews but Michael warned them to stay back as they were returning the stones to the Jewish cemetery. If they were removed again, they would be punished. Small in height, young, revolver in his belt, defiantly Michael stared into the eyes of the authorities, his face showed no fear – just anger and his own hate. They backed away, leaving Michael and his comrades to finish their labour of love.

They returned to the Jewish cemetery with the grave stones in the truck, placing them behind the main wall. They searched the grounds to identify Michael's grandfather's grave, finally discovering a wooden marker placed by the stonemaker to identify a site before he'd erected the stone. Michael placed the headstone over the grave and said a prayer. When he left the site, he knew at least for the present, the cemetery was protected by their vigilance.

With the end of the war, Michael journeyed to Moscow to find his father's family. Once located, they tried to make him forget what he had experienced, but he was unable to find peace within himself. He returned to Nieswiez.

"I had nobody . . . not one in my own family survived and there was no future for me staying in Nieswiez. The memories of what lay over the hill was too painful to see, day in and day out. I decided to go to Warsaw." Because he did not have proper documents to leave Byelorussia, he hid from the authorities by day and travelled by night until he arrived in Warsaw. But Warsaw was a wasteland, entirely devastated by the Germans in their relentless efforts to eradicate the Jews. The Jewish district had been razed to the ground, not a single building remaining intact. From more than a half-million Jews, there remained only a handful and they were not staying. Restless and unable to start a new life in Warsaw, he continued to Lodz, always looking for relatives. When he found other members of his family, they tried to persuade him to forget his experience, but he could not.

"Of what purpose was there to forget. Who benefits more by the forgetting? When living with hate, what is beyond acceptability becomes acceptable. To perform the acts of brutal inhumanity done to the Jews was interpreted not as an act of atrocity by the fascists but as a service necessary for the cleansing of a race. Hate begets hate and wrong becomes right. To forget and forgive is not an answer. Remembering is. This way, the guilty are constantly reminded of their guilt."

For three years, Michael Kutz travelled throughout Europe looking for that place he could call home; a place where he could live for the future instead of in the past. A law was passed by the Communists preventing anyone from leaving the country of their birth, but Michael refused to remain in Poland, witnessing the postwar hatred that was surfacing against the Jews. He wanted to emigrate to Israel to honour his father's last wish, but failed to obtain the proper documents. Frustrated and disappointed, Michael travelled from one country to another, searching for a place to live. He crossed the borders of Italy, Czechoslovakia, Austria, and eventually arrived in Geneva, Switzerland. In 1948, he applied to emigrate to Canada and was accepted with 500 other war orphans.

MICHAEL KUTZ IS MARRIED WITH TWO CHILDREN. HE HAS NEVER forgotten what his parents requested . . . to be proud of his heritage and to go to Palestine. To accomplish the first, Michael immersed himself in the Canadian Jewish Congress, Jewish community organizations and the Zionist movement. He discovered young boys who were unable to have bar mitzvahs for financial reasons or the indifference of the parents and it bothered him. So many had died to preserve a heritage that had lasted thousands of years and still many new generations were being denied the opportunity to understand the meaning of being Jewish. To be born a Jew, did not mean they knew what it was they had inherited.

With his help, many boys attended Hebrew Schools. In some cases, it meant him paying for the tuition. He found Jewish children from broken homes, and encouraged their parent to give their child the bar mitzvah lessons so necessary to understand their faith. When Jews from the Soviet Union came, he arranged that they, too, be given the blessing of having their own bar mitzvah.

He hoped they would understand the importance of being Jewish and to be proud of their birthright. He wanted them to make aliyah into their past and understand who they were. He unselfishly devoted his life to bring Judaism to those who needed it the most; the future generation – Jewish children. He did it knowing that what he was doing would have pleased his parents.

The unexpected occurred. Michael learned of an uncle living in Netanya, Israel (near Tel Aviv). In February 1990, he decided to visit him, hoping that by talking to him, he would find the peace of mind which had eluded him all these years. Having lived through the Holocaust, he could never understand how the world could look the other way and let it happen. Michael never forgot what his father said before the German horde invaded. "We are Jews. Palestine is our home." The time had come to see this land that his father had hoped would be their home someday.

Michael contacted his uncle and told him of his plans to visit Israel. He flew with the Jewish National Fund's Tu B'Shevat Mega Mission. Unknown to him, the Jewish community in Montreal had other plans for Michael. Plans that would culminate a lifetime of dedication to a promise. There were 750 Canadian's in two 747 El Al airplanes that arrived at the Ben Gurion Airport. Sixteen buses waited to take the passengers to their first sight – the Western Wall.

As the buses wound their way along the outskirts of the East Bank, the guide described the passing scenes. "The road into Jerusalem was a strategic link in the battle for the new State of Israel. On this highway, trucks came with many life-saving cargoes to feed and transport the people and bring food to Jerusalem in 1948."

Michael recalled the memories of other highways in his own country and understood the pain and tragedy the fighters of Israel must have endured. Beneath the wheels of the bus was asphalt, put there by Holocaust survivors, who, having survived the war in Europe, gave their lives for Israel. They passed English-built fortifications located on top of hills, travelled through huge forests of new trees rising from the sand and earth, placed by the hands of children. Michael marvelled at the beauty of the country of his father's dreams.

The bus travelled into valleys and over hills, peaking on a high crest that opened a panoramic view of the city of Jerusalem. The occupants fell quiet as they gazed at the wonders of their past. The buses weaved through twisting, narrow streets, stopping outside the grounds of the Western Wall. They had arrived. This was where time began; where history began its lengthy march; where the Jewish civilization matured and where Michael would finally face his past. Instead he was to undergo an experience that would bring a new meaning to the many years of tortured memories and unselfish deeds.

Eager to see one of the wonders of the past, the 750 passengers poured from the buses. Unexpectedly, passengers from Michael's bus formed a wedge with Michael in the centre. Two men held both his arms and propelled him toward the sacred grounds. Confusion marked his face as he was unaware of why he was forcibly directed to the Wall before his turn. As they led him, the men began to sing in Hebrew.

Near the centre of the Western Wall, a rabbi was waiting for them at a large wooden desk; a look of welcome shining from his face. Many tourists and residents standing nearby became aware of the wedge of men approaching. Attracted by the sight of the yellow hats worn by the passengers from Michael's bus, they watched the men holding Michael stop in front of the rabbi, saw him open the desk to expose several scrolls and carefully open one to a prearranged place. Everyone's eyes were upon him as he began to chant. Michael Kutz, at the age of fifty-nine was having the bar mitzvah that the war had denied him.

One by one, men from his bus stepped forward and read from the scroll. Tears flowed from everyone's eyes. Michael read his portion of the scriptures with his voice breaking, hands shaking, and tears freely flowing down his cheeks. When the reading was over, everyone formed a circle and danced. Men from all over the grounds ran to join the celebration. Chassidim, tourists and soldiers held hands, raised their combined voices in spontaneous joy, singing Hebrew songs around a crying Michael Kutz. With his hands clasped in front of him, tears running down his cheeks, Michael finally understood his father's prophetic words.

Michael Kutz

Now he knew why Palestine had meant so much to his father.

It is here, that he feels Jewish.

It is here, where all Jews belong if not in body then at least in spirit.

It is here, that a Jew knows he is a Jew.

"Poppa, I have come home," he cried out loud. "I have kept my promises."

MICHAEL KUTZ

On Sunday, June 6, 1993, Michael Kutz was the recipient of the Commemorative Medal for the 125th Anniversary of Canadian Confederation from his Excellency The Right Honourable Ramon Hnatyshyn. It was given to him for his work with the Knights of Pythias and the Canadian Jewish Congress.

3

WE WILL MEET AGAIN

"It is a fantastic commentary on the inhumanity of our times that for thousands and thousands of people, a piece of paper with a stamp on it is the difference between life and death."

— DOROTHY THOMPSON
American Journalist

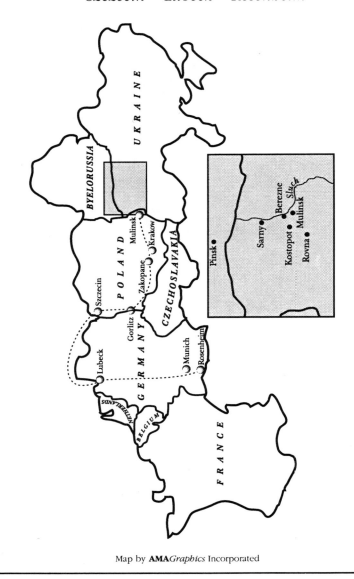

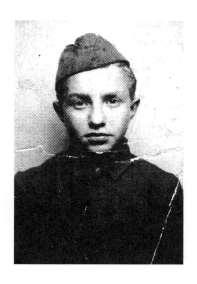

WE WILL MEET AGAIN

The Story of
MOISHE PERLMUTTER

Moishe Perlmutter raced across the street to the flat shared with his mother; face flushed, breathing rapid, eyes shining with the excitement of a decision he had just made. He rushed up the narrow, stairs, barged through the door, frantically calling to his mother. Sara emerged from her bedroom, a look of fear on her face from the tone of her only surviving son.

"What is the matter, Moishe?" she asked. "Is something wrong?"

"I can't go with you to Canada, Momma. I'm going with my friends to Palestine. They are waiting for me. They are leaving any minute. There is a man at Rosenheim sent by the Brikha (underground) to smuggle them out of Germany to France. I want to go with them."

Sara's eyes opened wide. Her hands trembled when she covered her mouth in shock from the unexpected request. "Moishe. You are only sixteen. Do you realize what you are asking? If you go to Palestine, we may never see each other again. I don't want to lose you now. Not after we have survived the Germans." She began to cry.

"No, Momma! Don't cry. You have sisters in Canada. There is no one waiting for me. My friends are going to Palestine and I want to go with them. I have never had any friends and now they will go without me. Please! I want to be with my friends."

"How will I know if you are all right? How will I know if you are safe? Your poppa is dead. Gershon is dead. We are the only ones left. If not for you, I too, would be dead and now you want to leave me."

"I want to live in Palestine. I want to be a Jew in my own country. Nothing will happen to me . . . not after what we have been through. Let me go, Momma. I will visit you. I promise. Let me go to Palestine with my friends."

Sara gazed lovingly at her son, knowing the hardships and pain he had endured. So young to have experienced so much. From an innocent child before the Germans came, to an animal living in the forests of the Ukraine and back to being human because of friends he made in Krakow and Zakopane. She reluctantly understood with a heavy heart. It pained her as a mother to realize he needed his friends as much as she needed him. She clenched his hands. "You won't change your mind?"

Moishe slowly shook his head. The tough kid from Mulinsk, who had robbed and stolen, cheated and starved was crying. He could not speak, only shake his head.

"I will miss you," she whispered. "Go with your friends and be safe."

Moishe kissed his mother, his face beaming from her words of release. He wiped the tears away with the back of his hand and waved goodbye, racing out of the room and through the door.

"Your clothes, you didn't take any clothes," his mother shouted after him, but he was gone.

With lungs bursting, he raced his small body through the streets and alleys towards Rosenheim, the DP camp where his friends were quartered. He had to hurry because they told him they would be leaving anytime and they couldn't wait for him if he was not there when they had to leave. It was only a few years ago in 1945, when he was in Krakow, that for the first time in his life he had finally made close friends. Afterwards, when Lena Kuchler had taken all the children to Zakopane, he and his friends had fought off the Polish anti-Semitic parasites who were trying to burn them out. With his machine gun and his friend's rifles, their shouts and shooting had frightened the Poles who turned tail and ran faster than they had come.

Moishe entered the converted army base and charged toward the barrack housing more than forty orphaned boys. With the words of happy greetings on his lips he banged open the door only to stop suddenly. The barrack was empty. Never since coming to Rosenheim had the barrack ever been without someone inside. He peered about the empty room in panic. There were no traces of any personal belongings and he realized his friends had all gone – he was too late. They could not wait. They had gone to Palestine and he had been left behind. He stared at the empty barrack for a few more minutes before he left deeply depressed. He made a promise – we will meet again.

THE REPUBLIC OF UKRAINE BORDERED POLAND, CZECHOSLOVAKIA, Hungary, Roumania and the Black Sea. A good portion of the northern country was covered in forests; the central known for its steppes and the western section, for the Carpathian mountains. It was a country rich in mineral resources and had an abundance of agricultural land. The Ukraine was the most densely populated of all the Soviet republics, three-fourths being of Ukrainian descent, with the balance being Russian or Jewish. The Jews numbered over one million.

Front row:
Sara, Moishe, Gershon and Godle Perlmutter

Surrounded by trees and lakes in a picturesque valley in western Ukraine, secluded by distance but connected by a dirt road, was the tiny village of Mulinsk. The village consisted of 250 people of which sixty were Jewish. It had only two mud-packed streets, both of which were unnamed. Tiny Mulinsk, shaped like the capital letter 'T', was a typical, basic rural Ukrainian community without in-door plumbing and with water hand-drawn from artesian wells. The houses occupied a square of land in which residents grew their own vegetables and some raised livestock and chickens. At night, it was necessary to carry a kerosene lamp to follow the paths that connected the different places or rely on the moon for guidance.

Were it not for its location, Mulinsk would be considered just a cluster of houses in the wilderness, for its singular importance far overshadowed its size; it was a train depot. Trains stopped at the village and passengers disembarked for Berezne, Sarny or any number of communities, for Mulinsk was on the crossroads that led elsewhere. Not far away were the cities of Rovno, Zhitomir and Tarnopol with access to the Ukraine, Soviet Union or Poland.

Most residents of Mulinsk spoke Yiddish, Polish and Ukrainian. The tolerance of the Ukrainians towards the Jews was always strained, fuelled by myths and distortions taught from birth. It was believed that Jews used human blood for sacrifices and they were responsible for the death of their Christian saviour almost two thousand years ago. Anti-Semitism was an open sore, resulting in verbal abuses and taunts from those who found it convenient to use the Jews as an excuse for their own deficiencies. The word pogrom struck fear into all the local Jews, wary of any times when hostilities from the non-Jewish population could rear up and strike them.

The Ukraine became an independent republic between 1917 and 1921, but after a long struggle for recognition, lost its independence under the Stalinist regime and became part of Russia. Between 1932 and 1933, Stalin engineered a famine in this richest of wheat growing countries, which caused an estimated seven million deaths.

GODLE PERLMUTTER WAS THE COMMUNITY BAKER. HIS WIFE SARA worked with him and cared for their two sons, Moishe, and Gershon. Behind their house they grew enough produce to satisfy their needs. They owned a cow which gave them milk, and a horse that pulled the wagon used to sell bread every day in the nearby communities.

Godle fought against Japan in 1903 and served in the Russian army in World War I. He was wounded in 1915, and rewarded with a piece of land in Mulinsk. A religious man, devoted to his faith, he permitted his home to be used for *minyans* (quorum) and religious services.

Being Jewish, particularly in 1941, meant devotion to a way of life that had survived thousands of years. Each community was a pocket of Jewish culture that rarely differed from another. There were enough Jewish men in Mulinsk and the surrounding areas to conduct daily minyans at Godle's house and they dreamed of building their own synagogue. Godle offered part of his land for the building and in 1937, material was purchased for the auspicious day their synagogue would rise. But the war would prevent that from ever happening.

Moishe attended school in Mulinsk. It would be here he would experience his first taste of anti-Semitism at the age of seven. His teacher never called him by name, only "Jew". "Come to the blackboard, Jew! Pick up the books, Jew!" The tone and implication were obvious and he used his position to degrade and humiliate. There were only three Jews in Moishe's class, and he felt the barbs of his teacher's tongue bite into him often.

The gentile children talked down to the Jewish children and one day Moishe was threatened with a beating by a bully the next time they met. Small in stature, scrawny, but tough, Moishe had his share of fights and knew how to take care of himself. He waited for the bully to appear. In anticipation, Moishe broke a branch from a tree and hid it under his coat. He would rather not have to use it, but at his young age he had already learned that what he preferred was not what he would be able to do. Confronted by the bigger boy, Moishe tried to avoid the fight, but the bully made it clear he intended to whip him and whip him well. Finding himself alone in a crowd of gentiles, Moishe pulled out the branch and struck the bully's face, marking his cheek and nose. The bully dropped to the ground – the fight was quickly over. At seven years, Moishe was aware that being Jewish was far different from being Ukrainian.

IN CONCERT WITH THE GERMANS, THE RUSSIAN ARMY ANNEXED land east of the Bug and San River on November 1, 1939 to the Ukrainian border. Some 25,000 Ukrainian refugees fled Soviet-held territory to Poland, preferring to be allied with the Germans than with the Russians. They joined nearly half-a-million Ukrainians already living in Lemko, southern Podlachia and the Chelm regions.

The Russian occupation brought improvements to the little community of Mulinsk. Electricity created an economic mini-boom and their living conditions improved. Although the community baker, Godle was better known as a glazier. Godle's tool in trade as a glazier was a steady hand and his prize possession – a little diamond. With the diamond held at a proper angle, he was capable of cutting all kinds of glass to any size. It would be because of this service, that the Ukrainians would protect him and his family from meeting the same fate as his neighbours. Realizing that being paid with money for his glazier services was almost impossible, he bartered his labour for produce and material, always giving value. His reputation as a fair person grew among the gentiles and they called him a *mentsch*; fair, honest and someone who could be trusted.

One day, a gentile neighbour's house burned to the ground and almost everything he possessed was lost. Penniless and without any shelter, he asked for Godle's help. Not that Godle was wealthy, but he was someone who was known to help when his neighbours. Godle offered him a temporary solution. He went to the man's property, dug a large trench, lined it with straw and boards, and then made a roof across from wood that had survived the fire. When finished, he had created a temporary shelter for the man. The man placed whatever furniture he had inside the makeshift structure, allowing him a place to sleep on his own property. What Godle had done for his neighbour would become another reason why his family had a better chance at surviving after the Russians left.

Being an independent businessman was not allowed in occupied Russian territory, and Godle learned early that capitalism and communism were at opposite ends of a spectrum. A relative brought Godle bad news. "I come to warn you the Russians will come here soon and take your bakery away."

"Take it away! Why? I am the best baker in the area. My bread is better than those that make their own."

"It has nothing to do with quality, Godle. This is the way the Communists operate."

"If they take it away from me, who will operate it?"

"You!"

"Me! So why take it away?"

"Because that's the way they do things. You should go to them and offer the government man your bakery. Better that you offer than they should take. This way they will make you the manager of your own bakery and you can continue what you have been doing."

"But the bakery will be theirs – not mine."

"Yes."

Godle thought over what was asked of him and with a great deal of reluctance agreed. He notified the authorities he wished to give his bakery to the people, and was thanked for thinking more of the people than of himself and offered the position of manager. Godle accepted. Once the government was involved in the bakery business, procedure at the bakery changed – for the worse. He was informed he had a quota to attain. It would be his responsibility to produce a fixed number of loaves per pound of dough and to do that, he would have to add more water to extend the bread and reduce the dough. Godle was not happy to produce volume at the price of quality, but he submitted.

No longer an independent businessman, he sold his horse and wagon. With the garden, the cow and the small income from the bakery, they managed to tolerate the political changes. When Godle was forced to increase the quota of bread without increasing the ingredients, he became frustrated and angry. Tired of trying to accomplish the impossible, threatened by the government for not cooperating, Godle resigned and walked away from the bakery. Still his life did not change appreciably. Godle could obtain whatever he needed by bartering and hiring himself out as a glass cutter.

With the coming of the Russians, the Ukrainians altered their attitude towards the Jews, especially Moishe's teacher. Afraid for his life because of his anti-Semitic comments, he begged the forgiveness of the children for the things he had said. The Russian occupation had swung social acceptance in favour of the Jew as long as they were there to protect them.

THE RUSSIANS CONSOLIDATED THEIR CONTROL OVER THE COUNTRY through a reign of terror. When they retreated before the German army, more than 400,000 Ukrainians would become their victims. Members of the intelligentsia, clergymen, important political figures and nationalists were killed or dispatched to the Gulags in Siberia. With the German invasion on June 22, 1941, additional deaths and destruction was unleashed by the retreating Russians as tens of thousands of political prisoners were massacred and buried in unmarked graves. A scorched earth policy by the Russians dismantled factories, and moved more than ten million people to the Urals, while destroying whatever they could not take. By the time the Germans occupied the Ukraine, more damage to the country was done by the Russians leaving, than by the invading German army.

Word spread of the advancing Germans and many Jewish families fled. Godle refused to leave. No amount of pleading by his friends could convince him to abandon his house and property. After the Russians retreated, anti-Semitism once again surfaced. Although not completely immune from the abuse and degradation heaped on the

Jews, Godle and his family were protected by gentiles who had been the beneficiaries of his glass cutting.

When the Germans were in Mulinsk, they confiscated part of Godle's house to accommodate officers. One of them did not share the same views of contempt of the Jews as did his fellow companions. He asked Godle, "Why did you stay?"

Godle was unable to give him an answer.

The Germans organized Polish and Ukrainian policemen as the guardians of the German empire, responsible for the control of the Jews – but not to kill them. All the Jews were ordered to turn over their valuables on penalty of death, and were forbidden from going to school or owning property. As a result of the brutal and irrational policies in Ukraine, it became one of the great German wartime blunders. The Nazi leadership held a racist conception of Eastern Europe in which the Ukraine was nothing more than a colonial *Lebensraum* (living space) fated to be ruled over by an Aryan captor. All livestock was confiscated but Jews were allowed to keep their gardens for food. Godle was devastated by what he witnessed and his health suffered.

One Saturday, a policeman appeared at his house. Godle was *davening* (praying) when the policeman ordered him to come outside. Godle left his house, followed by his dog, who jumped around and barked, showing his displeasure at the policeman. Annoyed, the policeman shot the dog.

"That will teach you for having a dog," the policeman said. "Bury him," he ordered.

Godle looked at his dead dog, anger on his face. He replied, "Not on the Sabbath."

"I said to bury him – now," the policeman demanded, angry at the lack of respect Godle was giving him.

"No!" answered Godle. "Not on the Sabbath. I'll bury him tonight after sunset."

"You will bury him now or I will shoot you as well." He pointed his revolver at Godle.

"If you want him buried now – bury him yourself," Godle answered angrily, daring the policeman to shoot him.

The policeman's face was red with his anger. He had never allowed a Jew to talk to him this way. He wanted to kill the impudent Jew, but he had been told that Godle was untouchable. He struck Godle across the face and lumbered away. Godle returned to the house to continue his praying.

As long as Godle and his family remained in Mulinsk, he was untouchable. Someone always protected him and his defiance was not dealt with as it might if displayed by any other Jew. That protection did not last much longer. All the Jews were forced to leave their homes, and were transported to the Berezne ghetto, north of Mulinsk in Volhynia on the western banks of the Sluch River. The only possessions they were allowed to take was what they could carry.

Within the ghetto were thousands of Jews confined by a high wire fence with guards continually patrolling the perimeter. The ghetto was small with all occupants forced to wear a yellow patch on their outer garment signifying they were Jews. As many as fifty people were confined in a room making living and sleeping conditions almost impossible. Berezne was larger than Mulinsk, and had its own synagogue and Judenrat Council. This Jewish Council was not an instrument of the German authorities as much as they were unscrupulous thieves who used their position for personal gain. They did not distribute the bread the Germans allocated to them, but sold it, pocketing the money. Since all the Jews would be killed, they reasoned, there would be no one to testify against them.

There was little food, forcing the people to eat grass and leaves. Some left the ghetto, searching the countryside for anything edible such as potatoes and vegetables. Once they found something, the difficulty was bringing it back. To be caught carrying food meant death, but to starve meant death as well, and so the risk of being caught was not a factor, only the success of bringing the food back safely.

Not wearing the yellow patch was also punishable by death, yet Moishe at the young age of thirteen defied the order and moved about without it. Ukrainians stood outside the fence, shouting insults at the Jews, offering foul words and gestures to show their contempt. The Jews ignored them and this only offended the Ukrainians more, who took to shooting at the yellow patches as targets, killing the wearer without warning. Until Jewish police were organized to protect them, the Jews kept away from the fences.

There were few Germans in Berezne. Their captors were the Ukrainians whose function was to maintain order. To help the Germans in guarding the Jews, the Ukrainians organized a Jewish police force who did not bear arms. They recruited men who were not motivated by a sense of communal responsibility but by self-preservation. They were callous, ruthless and tenacious in their will to engage in the duties imposed on them.

(Jewish police regulated the flow of pedestrian and vehicular traffic inside the ghetto's and maintained law and order. Later, the more reputable ones came to serve dual and compatible purposes: to protect the Jewish community while it enforced German orders in the least oppressive way.)

The Judenrat accepted large sums of money as bribes from those that depended on them for fairness and understanding. To be on a work detail offered a better sense of security that many opted for, but the price was a pay-off in textiles and cash or gold.

Moishe was an obstinate young boy who showed no fear towards his capturers. As an act of defiance, he had made his way out of the ghetto on many a night, dug for potatoes and smuggled them back inside. He ate them raw. More often, they were rotten, and had been left by the farmer as unfit to eat, but when hungry, everything was edible. When the farmers complained that the Jews were raiding their vegetables, the Jewish police were instructed to punish the perpetrators. Moishe was caught.

The Jewish police were waiting as he squeezed through the fence. They pounced on him, beating him and threatened his life if he ever left the ghetto again. The bruises only hardened Moishe. His defiance of the Ukrainians and the Jewish police was to challenge them to try and catch him again, for he was not intimated by their presence, but catch him again they did. They beat him with rubber truncheons on his back and shoulders until they were satisfied he would never leave the ghetto again. Moishe was not discouraged, he left – and often.

The Germans came for Godle. They needed a glass cutter to fix the many broken windows in a German base near Mulinsk, established by the Polish Army before the Russians arrived. Godle received better living conditions than in Berezne, and although not in good health, he could perform the work without too much difficulty.

However, his son Moishe did not fare as well.

He was sent to a labour group with over fifty men to cut squares of peat moss for fuel. They were guarded by Ukrainians, who baited and hit them when they didn't work hard enough. A few times, when it appeared Moishe might be singled out for execution, someone would intervene. "Don't touch that one. That's Godle's son," and Moishe would be spared.

When they returned to Berezne, most of the Jews were gone, sent to Kostopol. Moishe and his mother were shipped to a camp called Mulnishka. Life once again became an ordeal of hard work and little food. By July 1942, there was a sense of an impending disaster, as word reached them that the Jews from the ghettos were being killed.

The final liquidation occurred simultaneously in the summer of 1942 as many Aktionen (SS round-up of prisoners) were organized by the Germans to cleanse it of all the Jews. This was the second phase in the systematic extermination to be carried out by the Sipo, largely made up of personnel from the Einsatzgruppen.

As the oldest male in the family at fourteen, Moishe told his mother and brother they were going to escape before it was too late. That afternoon, they left the compound as if on an errand and when out of sight of the guard – ran in desperation and fright.

When they heard the barking of dogs they thought the Ukrainians had discovered their escape. What Moishe was not aware, was that others had come to the same conclusion and taken the initiative to flee as well.

Hour after relentless hour, the three raced through the forests, across rivers and around farms, putting as much distance between them and the camp. When it was dark they still did not stop. They continued on, crashing into trees and falling into ditches, afraid they would be overtaken and captured. The dogs were silent, telling them they had succeeded in their escape. When they stopped, it was to drink water from a stream before continuing on their flight to freedom, and with each step supposedly taking them further away from their prison. When the sun rose, they were confident they were many kilometres from the labour camp, but still they pushed on, cresting hill after hill, pushing their tired bodies onward. At the top of one such hill, they stood frozen in shock. Before them was a sight they could not believe. The unthinkable had happened and their exhausted bodies rebelled at their mishap. They had run all afternoon and all night in a circle only to return to Mulnishka. Quickly they retreated, running in the direction they had just come.

Tired and hungry, they returned to Mulinsk to find Godle because he was familiar with the countryside and with his help they had a better chance of eluding their jailers. After reaching the base, Moishe stole inside and found his father. The number of Jews at the base had been getting smaller, and it was obvious to Godle that when they took someone away, it was not back to any labour camp, but to a hole in the ground. With only three Jews left, Godle needed no other excuse to join his family. That night, they hid in the forest.

THE FOUR WERE CONSTANTLY ON THE MOVE. BY DAY THEY HID IN small forests, giving them a view of anyone approaching and by night they moved to a more desolate location. They ate what they could find or steal, always on the move, afraid to be seen. With the coming of harsher weather, the cold bit into their unprotected bodies, creating unbelievable hardships, but they continued to improvise, desperate to stay alive. When they could not steal food, they pushed the snow away from the ground hoping to expose something edible or they begged for bread from a sympathetic farmer. Once they were blessed when a farmer gave them four full loaves of bread with some wild blueberries. What a treasure! They were able to live on it for more than a week.

The Germans had a standing reward of three kilos of salt for any Jew captured dead or alive and most farmers actively sought them to obtain the precious ingredient being offered. *(In some communities, a reward of 1 kilo of salt was offered for every head of a Jew, and it was not unusual to see someone returning from a hunt to collect his reward carrying the decapitated head in a bag.)*

The freezing weather took its toll. During the night, they huddled together, trying to reduce the effect of the wind and cold behind a natural barrier. Between the inclement weather and the lack of food, whatever life they had became harder to endure. During one freezing night, desperate for some warmth, they made a fire. Moishe dug a cave into a hill, scooping out the earth with his hands and a branch from a tree. When the hole was big enough for the four, Godle made a fire, throwing branches onto it. The warm air enveloped them, and for the first time in days, they were not freezing – but not for long. The fire threatened to ignite their clothes. Panicstricken, they fled the cave before they became victims of their folly.

To their misfortune, a Ukrainian who knew Godle stumbled upon them. He demanded the diamond Godle used to cut his glass, threatening to shoot him if he did not cooperate. Stubbornly Godle refused. The Ukrainian beat Godle and took the diamond. Unable to understand the technique on how to hold the precious stone, the Ukrainian returned to their hiding place and gave Godle back the diamond.

The weather turned colder. Desperate for warmth, they came upon a barn and ignored the risk of being caught and entered. Godle heard a sound that was out of place and warned everyone to be quiet. He gazed into the semi-darkness trying to detect from where the sound was coming, fearing someone else was inside. Cautiously he moved across the straw covered ground, peering into the darkened corners, trying to pick out a shadow that was out of place. He saw a human form and called, "whose there?" There was only silence. "We are friends," he added.

From out of the shadows a man appeared. It was Mottle from Mulinsk. He was alone. He told Godle he had left his family wanting to hide alone. Godle took his family to the safety of the loft where they spent the night. The next morning Mottle was gone. *(He survived the war and moved to Haifa.)* For the next few days, the family stayed in the barn until the weather improved, but Godle's health continued to deteriorate.

They took to hiding in larger forests in hopes of finding a natural shelter. It was there, they came upon Yitzhak, a young boy, crawling on the ground, his face and clothes covered in blood. They washed him as best they could, and were surprised to find he had no wounds, the blood that covered him from head to foot was not his. He told them, he and others were marched to a large pit and forced into it. The Germans machine-gunned everyone. He was struck by a falling body and knocked unconscious. Several bodies fell on top of him, shielding him from the bullets. When he regained consciousness, he escaped. *(When the war ended, he emigrated to Palestine only to be killed in the War of Independence in 1948.)*

With his health steadily deteriorating, Godle realized he was becoming a burden to his family. He told his wife and sons he was going to seek out a Ukrainian friend and ask him to hide him until he was better. He did not know if his decision was wise, but if he didn't receive help soon, he would die from the cold weather and insufficient food. It was now Moishe's responsibility to keep his mother and brother alive.

During the spring of 1943, Moishe came upon many of their neighbours while hiding. The stories they told were always tragic and painful. They learned about the 17,000 Jews murdered in Rovno, of 2,200 killed in Koritz, 30,000 buried in Kiev – some alive. Large or small, it made little difference, every community was affected. Ukrainians helped the Germans and were rewarded with the clothes of the Jews who were murdered.

Periodically, Godle would reappear, afraid his presence was proving a danger to himself and the person who hid him. He always found someone he had befriended before the war willing to hide him for a short time. Inevitably his presence became a risk, and he would be forced to leave and fend for himself. On many of the roads that crisscross the country were small kneeling huts; a place to pray while on a journey. Often, the Ukrainians would leave food or wine as a gesture of Christian benevolence inside the hut for the weary traveller. Godle would avail himself of what he found. In time, he was seen as a ghost or a holy man and many Ukrainians left him food.

During this same period, Gershon would also disappear for weeks at a time, preferring to be on his own. To identify another person as a Jew, the word 'Amchod', (my nation) became the password. They met Dobra, who had been hiding in the bush with her two sons for two years. She told how one of her sons had been killed by a Ukrainian while he was begging for food. *(Her other son Sevik became one of the 100 children that Lena Kuchler saved.)* Not long afterwards, Moishe lived such a horror. He and another boy approached a farm house intent on begging for a piece of bread. The other boy knocked on the door while Moishe stood a few feet behind him. The door opened, a farmer stepped out with an axe and decapitated the boy. Moishe ran as he had never run before, escaping from the Ukrainian who chased him with the axe swinging over his head, shouting foul words after him.

In the forest, they met Monyac, a boy from Chelm. He had walked hundreds of kilometres to hide from the Germans and by cunning and stealth had been able to survive for over a year. *(He later returned to Chelm after the war to find his mother and was killed by Ukrainians in an anti-Semitic pogrom.)*

Godle's health continued to deteriorate. In the early months of 1943, the weather took a turn for the worse. Godle and Moishe dug a cave inside a hill to be out of the path of the wind and the snow. Without a fire, they huddled together in the tunnel trying to keep warm. The next morning, at the age of 65; Godle's tired body no longer suffered and no longer cared, for he no longer lived. Moishe buried him in the cave without a marker to identify his final resting place.

As the winter months became harsher, and the inclement weather increased in intensity, Moishe and his frail mother trekked from one refuge to another, hiding in the forests, a victim of the freezing cold. Sara begged Moishe to build a fire after a terrible day, aware that to do so would be suicidal if the smoke was detected. He nevertheless dug a hole into a hill, made a small cave and they squeezed themselves inside. With branches and leaves, he built a small fire, containing the smoke within the cave. The warm air was a momentary blessing that was to leave a longer dismal effect. In the morning, when Moishe opened the front of the cave, his mother found she was blind, helplessly, totally blind. For the next thirty days, Moishe hid his mother while he foraged for food, bringing back what he stole or found. Fortunately, with time, her eyes regained their sight.

A group of Jewish families called "The Tenth" possessed guns and boldly raided Ukrainian farmers for food and clothes, dividing the loot among themselves. To be a part of their group became a privilege with many benefits. Gershon wanted to join them, but Moishe did not. As chance would have it, Gershon found a gun without bullets. Ignoring Moishe's advice, Gershon approached the leader of The Tenth, asking to join.

They turned him down.

The Tenth became a power to be reckoned. Originally thought of as an elite group of Jews, it was discovered that their acts of force were motivated by their own selfish needs and gratification. It was while hundreds of Jews were hiding in an area known as Abluva, that the true character of the Tenth was realized. The Tenth became aware that the Germans had discovered where the Jews were hiding. Instead of informing everyone of the intended raid, they left unannounced for Russia, leaving the others unprepared for the assault that followed.

The area was surrounded by German and Hungarian soldiers. Moishe, Gershon and Sara were hiding in the bush when the attack took place. People emerged from their hiding places, running in every direction. Shots were fired and several fell to the ground dead or wounded. There was mayhem and panic as the volume of screams from the running Jews echoed into the night, while the Hungarian and German rifles destroyed the lives of those whose only thoughts were to survive. A bullet entered Moishe's right calf and came out the other side. Holding onto his mother, they continued to run away from the massacre. Gershon screamed in pain as a bullet entered his back and came out his stomach. In the ensuing confusion, they became separated.

When Moishe and his mother were safe, he tied a cloth around his wound to stop the bleeding. Gershon also managed to escape and he used his shirt to tie around his stomach and back to stop the bleeding. Gershon did not know how badly he was injured, but his immediate priority was to elude capture, and for the next three days, he hid without getting any medical care.

In time, they were united. Although both had suffered bullet wounds, they still could move about. During the summer of 1943, word reached them about a deserted village that had been partially destroyed. In the fields surrounding the village were unpicked food, but the area around the village had also been burned to the ground, with no place to hide. The need for food over-shadowed the risks of capture, and the three journeyed to the village, finding many others in hiding.

They lived close to the deserted village. By crawling on their stomachs through the field, and keeping their heads below the height of the vegetables, they were able to pick what they needed; always wary about raising their heads above the short stalks. Because of the risk of detection from low flying airplanes, they were careful to cover their tracks, making sure there were no signs of their presence. Although the risk of discovery was high, they avoided detection until the winter months. When the season changed, they left and returned to hide in the forest again, knowing if they stayed, the snow would reveal their presence.

Moishe's wound healed, but Gershon went through periods of extreme pain. His body healed, but the internal damage needed attention and he had no one to help him.

By November 1943, the war had changed directions from east to west with the Russians on the offensive. The

Germans retreated and were met by armed resistance from Ukrainian insurgents as well as the advancing Russian army. As the war pushed westward, the fighting neared to where the Perlmutter's were hiding. Their clothes had been reduced to dirty rags, patched together with assorted fabrics and Moishe's shoes were slabs of wood, tied by a rope.

THE RETURN OF THE RUSSIANS TO WESTERN UKRAINE IN 1944 DID not stop the fighting. The independence movement that had been suppressed during the war years once again surfaced. Over seven million Ukrainians, more than one-sixth of the prewar population had been killed. Out of a population in 1941 of 41.9 million only 27.4 remained. The balance were dead, deported or evacuated. Hatred for their rescuers was still higher than for the Germans.

Moishe, Gershon and Sara returned to Mulinsk to find their home had been confiscated again, this time as a hospital and they were confined to a single room until the authorities were convinced they were who they claimed. When Moishe informed the authorities that others were still hiding in the bush, he was told to bring them to Mulinsk. To assure his return, his mother was held as a hostage.

With their house converted into a hospital, Moishe and Gershon had their bullet wounds attended. Moishe's wound had healed on its own, the bullet having passed through the fleshy part of his calf. Unfortunately, Gershon continued to suffer from his stomach wound and the doctor's were unable to help, for although they attended to his surface wound, it was the damages inside that continued to plague him.

For the next fourteen months the Perlmutter's resumed their lives. Moishe had become hardened by the war, resenting the hardships his family had endured, the death of his father, and the pain he and his brother Gershon suffered. It altered his perception of people and the world. Distrust became his outlook, anger instead of respect. If he feared anything, he kept his emotions bottled up inside of him, displaying no outward signs of his anger, but he exhibited a resourcefulness for survival.

The Ukrainians were again more cooperative with the Jews, fearing when the Russians returned the Jews would again be protected citizens, and did not want to antagonize their own position. With the Russian army moving westward, the Ukrainian militia patrolled the area, trying to appear like professional soldiers. Most were illiterate, and incapable of deciding which was their left from their right foot. An enterprising individual conceived the hay-straw drill. On their left foot, the militia attached a sprig of hay, on their right, a sprig of straw. With all the pomp and arrogance of their position, they marched down the street in unison as their leader repeated over and over: hay – straw, hay – straw.

Moishe didn't trust the Ukrainians and as he watched the confusion that prevailed after the war, he realized there were opportunities for those who were not afraid to take chances – and Moishe was afraid of nothing and no one. He went to the flour mill where he manipulated the workers into giving him scoops of flour until he had about three kilo's. With the flour, he had his mother make bread; the type of bread that made his father well-known. With the bread, he bartered for eggs and butter. His mother boiled the butter, adding a sweetener to it and cut them into cubes. He travelled by train to Sarny and bartered his contraband at the market for salt and yeast. Moishe returned to Mulinsk carrying his booty in a sack and bartered for meat and flour and the cycle repeated itself.

He had no documents allowing him to sell any products and to travel anywhere without proper credentials meant, if caught he could go to jail. He purchased forged travelling papers that were reasonably good copies but could not stand close scrutiny. As long as he wasn't caught he could profit from his scheme. On one of his trips, Yitzhak *(the boy who had escaped the pit)* and Moishe were on their way to Sarny when Yitzhak overheard two Ukrainian men say they were going to kill the boy with the eggs. Frightened, Yitzhak jumped off the moving train. When he returned to Mulinsk, he told Sara what he overheard and feared Moishe was dead.

Realizing he was being observed, Moishe left the train. Instead of going to the market. He decided to sell his wares at the rail station, purchased a pot and filled it with water. He boiled the sixty eggs he had and sold his contraband to the passengers entering the city and immediately afterwards returned to Mulinsk. It was his biggest sale.

On another trip, after finishing his sale, he boarded the train for Mulinsk, tucking his bag containing twenty kilos of salt and four kilos of yeast under his seat, hiding it with his body and his feet. A policeman approached and accused him of black market activities.

"Where are you going?" he demanded.

Moishe mumbled the name of a village beyond Mulinsk.

"Why were you in Sarny?"

"Visiting," he answered.

"Lies! I think you were selling on the black market. Let me see your documents."

Moishe handed him his paper.

"I don't like these," the policeman said waving the papers in Moishe's face. "I think they're forgeries. You're under arrest. I'm taking you to jail when we reach Mulinsk." When the train arrived at Mulinsk, the policeman motioned Moishe to follow, but Moishe ran in the opposite direction and hid. The policeman stayed on the train when it left.

On May 1, 1945, the Russian government offered free transportation to anyone wishing to be repatriated to Poland. Moishe had enough of the Ukraine and did not want to stay in Mulinsk any longer. He convinced his mother they should go to Poland, having heard that land owned by German civilians was being given to Polish citizens and he proposed to apply for some of it. They were unable to persuade Gershon to leave, choosing to remain behind with people he knew, than to go somewhere different. Moishe, Sara and twenty-five Jews from Mulinsk boarded the freight train and travelled west to Poland – to a new life.

As they neared Krakow, Moishe overheard Polish gentiles planning to teach the Jews on the train a lesson after they passed Krakow. When the train stopped, he urged his mother off and let the train continue without them. Everyone from Mulinsk also left the train when they became aware of the threat. The journey to a new life had ended before it started.

WITH HARDLY ANYTHING OF VALUE OTHER THAN WHAT THEY were wearing, Moishe and Sara left the railway station. A Jew approached them and asked if they needed help. He told them of a house at Dluga Street 38, run by a Jewish Committee looking after survivors and he urged them to go there. With no other place to go, they went to Dluga Street.

On a long, dark street, opposite the tram station they saw the house. There were many Jews milling about the steps of the front door; going in, coming out, congregating in small groups, arguing loudly, listening, dispersing and then creating another gathering. A cluster of men and women were staring, some groping at sheets of paper attached to a board and crying. Moishe approached a man with a shaven head.

"What are they doing?" Moishe asked.

The man looked at him curiously before answering. "The Jewish committee is bringing out the names of those who have died in the different concentration camps." He pointed to the bulletin board. "That list of names is from Auschwitz, sometimes it is Mauthausen, Buchenwald, or Treblinka."

"What are those places?"

The man looked puzzled. "From where do you come?"

"Mulinsk."

"Where?"

"From the Ukraine," Moishe added when he realized the man did not know where Mulinsk was located.

The man nodded his head in understanding. "They were death camps."

Moishe didn't know what that meant.

"Have you come here for help?" the man asked.

Moishe nodded his head.

"They are filled to the roof with refugees. I doubt if there is room for more. We wait out here for food. They promised to give us chits for clothes and blankets, but so far we have received nothing. Those people," and he pointed to the crowd around the bulletin board, "are here to find if anyone in their families survived but all they see are lists of deaths. Go inside and try to get help, but don't expect much, they have so little."

Moishe and Sara entered the house, threading their way past people standing or sitting on the floor. They climbed a dark and dingy stairwell, filled with more people. Some were withdrawn and morose, many were skeleton-thin with barely anything covering their bodies. The steps were wet and slippery from spilled food, walking on them was dangerous. Carefully they manoeuvred their way between the sitting people and approached a desk where others were waiting their turn to be interviewed.

The line moved forward until Moishe was in front of a man with papers scattered over the surface of his desk. "Your name?" he asked, his voice exhausted, his thin body and tired face showing the ordeal he was enduring.

"Moishe Perlmutter and my mother Sara. We're from Mulinsk and have nowhere to go." He leaned on the table and stared intently at the man, challenging him to ignore them.

The man wrote each name on a different sheet of paper. "Are either of you sick? Do you need immediate medical care?" he asked. His voice was mechanical, without feeling, yet his appearance suggested that he too was a survivor. He looked at Sara and offered a tired smile, "Are you all right, Mrs. Perlmutter?"

Sara found strength to smile back, "I had a large boil on my neck that a doctor in Mulinsk operated on and it has become infected." She pointed to the back of her neck.

He replied with more feeling. "Go to the second floor. There is a hospital room where they will look after you." To Moishe, he said, "Go to the third floor. All the children are on the third floor," and he waved his hand at them to leave so that he could attend to those who waited in line.

Moishe saw his mother to the hospital room and climbed to the third floor, entering a large, dimly lit room filled with children of all ages. There were about fifty, perhaps more, but it was impossible to count them, for they were running around wildly. Some were pushing and shoving each other or pulling one another's hair. A few sat in the corners, trying to hide. The only furniture was a long table and a few rickety benches, several dirty blankets were piled in the corner.

Most of the children were small and younger than Moishe. Standing in a separate group, Moishe saw older boys. He approached them with caution as they watched him with suspicion. "My name is Moishe. I'm from Mulinsk," he said. No one responded. "When do we eat?"

A few laughed.

"Have you killed Germans?" asked a tough-acting boy with long hair falling into his eyes.

Moishe shook his head.

"I have! My name is Yonik. I'm fourteen. How old are you?"

"Sixteen," Moishe answered.

"Sixteen! And you haven't killed any Germans? I was a partisan," he bragged as he pushed out his chest. "I used to carry two revolvers, one in each hand and I would hold the reins of my horse in my mouth when I attacked."

Moishe looked skeptical.

Unperturbed, Yonik continued. "We moved like lightning, shooting Germans on both sides of us as we rode into them. Sometimes I threw grenades. Ever use dynamite?"

Moishe shook his head.

"The best was the dynamite. We crept on all fours to the rail tracks where the Germans pass. We'd wire the dynamite and bury them, then hide in the bushes or behind the trees and wait for the train. Sometimes they let me light the fuse. You had to time it right, so that the whole train would explode and then hundreds of Germans would fly through the air. I loved to see the Germans go right up in the air and then fall back, like dead pigeons. It was wonderful!"

"Don't let him fool you," a boy with a kerchief over his right eye interrupted. "He's really a pussy cat. He just acts tough. I'm Naiten. Welcome to our home," and he swept his arms out to indicate the dirty, squalid room.

Moishe pointed to the kerchief. "What are you hiding?"

Naiten smiled. "Grenade. It went off too close to me and I lost an eye. The doctor told me there are twenty-one pieces of shrapnel still in my body."

"Don't ask him to show you," another boy interrupted. "They come to the surface and he picks them off. My name is Stefan. That's Yizha, Eli, Marek, Yuzek, Lonek and our master of disguise, Tatek."

Everyone nodded to Moishe and he returned the gesture. "Are you an actor?" Moishe asked Tatek. The boys laughed.

"I wore girl's clothes and had long hair. I walked like a girl with small steps and moved my hips from side to side. I even carried a doll. My parents gave me false identity papers as a girl so the Germans would not look to see if I was circumcised. You do know that girls aren't circumcised, don't you?"

Everyone laughed again.

"This is my gang," Yonik said "We're all over thirteen. We don't mix with the others, only eat with them. They get more food up here than they give the adults downstairs. They give us soap, toothbrushes and shirts and we sell them on the streets for money."

"What do you use the money for?"

The boys laughed again.

"Ice cream, schmuck! Ice cream and movies," Yonik replied. "Do you want to join us?"

"Yes!" was Moishe's enthusiastic reply. The boys shook his hand and pounded him on the back. Moishe was part of a gang and for the first time in many years, he had friends. For the next three weeks, Moishe and his friends roamed the streets of Krakow, stealing food from vendors at the market or playing card games in the side streets by inducing people to play a few hands of what was a crooked game. From their profit, they would treat themselves to movies and go on ice cream binges.

Sara left the hospital and was taken to another building run by the Jewish Committee where she regained her strength and health. Moishe visited her, but he had found a new life with his friends who were always busy accomplishing nothing except getting themselves in and out of trouble. It was for Moishe a time of marvellous memories of camaraderie that he had never experienced before. The many years of loneliness had embedded in him a need for friends in the same way that he needed food, but this was a different kind of hunger. It was a period in his young life he would cherish for all his remaining years. The life and needs of anyone other than his friends at Dluga Street 38 were not his business, nor his concern – that is until Lena Kuchler entered the big room on the third floor carrying a child with three others holding her coat.

MRS. BELLA WAS SERVING SOUP IN A CORNER NEAR THE WINDOW, ladling from a large cauldron. She was an angry, boisterous, mean-mouthed woman who caved in from the pressure of the children's demands by responding in an uncaring and defiant method. Many of the children were crowded around her, holding out little dishes in their outstretched arms, shouting, "Give me too! I want more!"

The older boys resented her indifference to the younger children and the fact that, in their opinion, she took more than her share of the soup, ignoring the children's pleas.

"Excuse me," Lena inquired, "are you in charge of the children's home?"

Mrs. Bella's response was, as usual, abrupt and sarcastic. "Home?" she exclaimed angrily, "do you call this a home? Do you see what's going on? This is hell, not a home! They're all criminals!"

"Please," Lena interrupted, "I have four Jewish children who were brought from a cloister and abandoned. They are hungry and in need of care. This little one can't walk," indicating the one she was carrying.

Mrs. Bella looked at Lena as if she were speaking to an idiot. "So what if they're Jewish? What should I give them, tap water or a piece of my flesh? When I go to the kitchen to bring them soup, they all attack me. They want to beat me up as if I were stealing it for myself."

When Moishe and the older boys heard Mrs. Bella make this remark, they nodded their heads and made obscene gestures. Their dislike for her was apparent.

"And they curse me too. I'm fed up with this whole business. There's no food, no clothes and no mattresses. The children sleep on the floors and on the stairs. There is so little here, they go out and either beg or steal. The little ones are always wetting and soiling themselves. They cry all night long and I have no rest, day or night. It's worst than the labour camps, and here you come with more children, more demands they should be cared for. It's so easy to say you're sorry for the children. If you're such a saint, look after them yourself! I've had it!" Mrs. Bella threw the soup ladle on the floor, picked up her bowl and left the room slamming the door hard behind her.

The older boys cheered.

After Mrs. Bella left, the children rushed to Lena, the only adult in the room and cried, "I'm hungry, I'm hungry! I want soup!" They tugged at her arm and pulled at her dress trying to get her attention. One boy pushed her and plunged his hand into her coat pocket searching for something to eat. Lena's face turned to shock, being pushed and pummelled by the hungry children. Clutching the child she had entered with, she seemed affixed to the floor unable to move while the screams of, "soup, soup, soup", rang throughout the room.

She watched two boys climb the table where the empty soup kettle sat and drag it off and lick the inside. One of them crawled right inside the pot, but the other one pulled him back by his leg. Everyone was dressed in rags, most were barefoot, constantly scratching themselves and screaming from hunger.

Moishe and the older boys moved to a corner and watched, amused by what was happening. Lena Kuchler was not a tall woman. Her face had the lines of tension, but there were signs of determination in her posture by the way she held herself together. It was apparent she had withstood previous pain and suffering, defeating it by determination and stubbornness. Her soft eyes were filled with compassion as she looked at the scene that surrounded her. The children's screams and pulling should have been enough to frighten any normal person not accustomed to witnessing such a display and the boys expected her to run out of the room behind Mrs. Bella. Instead she gently pushed the children aside and made her way through them to the pile of blankets in the corner where she placed the child.

She turned to the children, some clinging to her coat. "Come with me," she said. "Let's make a circle and we'll play a game." But the children did not understand and not one extended their hand to make a circle.

"Come let's all sit on the blanket and I'll tell you a story. Once upon a time, there was a mighty king . . ."

But the children were not listening.

"Food! Food!" they cried loudly. "Give us food. We want food!"

She stood in the midst of the screaming children, her facial expression revealing the pain of the children's plight, realizing she could not reach them unless they had food. They were hungry and understood only one thing, to feed that hunger. Her attempts at settling down the younger children proved futile and finally she ran out of the room while everyone cried out their hunger to each other. In time the room returned to its original state of personal terror and a few of the children began to play with each other. Others sat on the floor, arms wrapped around their waist and cried. Yonik made an uncomplimentary remark about women being soft and the older boys laughed and agreed. They had no respect for differences in gender. Only the use of power had any significance to them.

A few hours later the door burst open with a loud bang, startling the children. They looked to see Lena standing in the centre of the doorway between two large suitcases. She lived in a house with her brother Sani who was in the Polish army. After leaving the room, she purchased several loaves of bread on the black market and took them home. Using everything she could find in the house, she made sandwiches from jam, butter and fat and put them into the two suitcases with boxes of biscuits, candies and cookies. She also took all the towels and soap she could find. Again she was confronted with the same confusion and deafening noise she had experienced earlier. She dragged the two heavy suitcases to the table as everyone surrounded her.

"Children!" she announced in a loud voice. "I've brought you food."

At first the children didn't believe her. A few of the braver ones touched the bags she was removing from the suitcases. She opened one and showed them what was inside and they all crowded around, pushing and shoving to get at the bags.

"Stop!" she shouted. "Whoever sits nicely on the blanket will get served first." Everyone rushed to the blankets; the older boys among them. "Quiet! I want quiet." She pointed to two of the older girls and asked them to help. Lena and the two girls gave everyone a sandwich. Several children hid some of their food under their shirts and then complained they didn't get any.

"There is enough food for everyone to get seconds," she announced. "Eat slowly. You will all get more. And after you finish, there is dessert. Why don't you look at what you're eating? Not everyone has the same." The children examined their sandwich fillings and bargained with each other for tastes of the different sandwiches.

"No!" Lena shouted over the noise. "Each of you must eat your own. You must not touch anyone else's. Whoever is good can pick his next sandwich with whatever filling he likes." The children cooperated. When all the food was gone, she distributed the candies. The children were now calmer, sucking their candies slowly and happily, trying to make them last as long as possible.

While they were enjoying dessert, she moved a bench to where the sink and faucet were and removed the soap and towels. "Who knows how to wash a small child?" she asked.

"I do," volunteered a small, clean girl.

"But you're so small – you won't be able to do it alone. How old are you?"

"I'm eight years old," she replied, "and I know how. I helped Mrs. Bella."

"I can help too," said an older girl shyly. Lena glanced at her hands, which were red and swollen, and was about to object, but the girl anticipated the objection and continued, "I used to do a lot of laundry for my mistress and wash the floors. My hands became frozen and that's why they are red. But it's nothing – it doesn't hurt anymore."

And so began the next stage in Lena Kuchler's efforts to win the confidence of the children. The older boys did not take part in what was happening, but watched and laughed at the scene that unfolded in front of them. The three undressed the children. They washed them under the running water, drying them quickly, after which Lena combed their tangled hair with the only comb she had. Many were unbelievably skinny, nothing but skin and protruding bones with hardly any flesh on them. Their stomachs were bloated like balls and covered with black and blue bruises from beatings and fist fights. The hands and feet of most of them had been frozen from the cold, their skin dry and cracked and covered with running sores. Their heads full of abscesses, lice and ringworm. Some had twisted and crippled bodies, broken limbs that had been improperly reset caused from jumping from the trains taking them to their deaths. Many had deep head wounds. Afterwards, the children wore the same filthy rags, since there were no others. When Lena finally left, it was in a state of total exhaustion. The jungle she had entered earlier had developed cracks and the children for the first time were fed, clean and looked more human than they had in the last few years.

The older boys still viewed her with suspicion. No one does what she did without a reason. She obviously intended to profit from her actions, but they couldn't figure out what that might be.

Lena became a permanent fixture at Dluga Street 38. She took over the third floor and through her brother's contacts was able to obtain food and clothes. She tried to persuade the Polish Director of the Supply Mission in Krakow to give her food for the children, but was unsuccessful. However, he was so taken by her convictions and passionate pleas, that he gave her two thousand kilos of sugar, without official authorization, which she sold on the black market. With this money, she was able to feed and clothe the children until other funds could be obtained. The older boys still used the house as a base, but now they knew they could get food at the house easier than stealing it on the streets.

After the surrender of Germany, Jewish children showed up by the dozens, hidden by Poles and Polish institutions during the war. The gentiles waited for the children's parents to return for them. When it appeared that was not to be, they were dropped off at the gate and abandoned, in some cases without wearing any clothes. Occasionally, parents came to Dluga Street 38 and found their lost children and claimed their off-springs, but the children that remained, and continued to grow beyond the capacity of the building.

Moishe, Yanek, Sevek, Yuzek and Tatek

Money was found from different sources but never enough. The sick and the healthy slept next to each other in the crowded house. Word reached them of a suitable house for rent in Zakopane, a resort in the hills, known for caring for tuberculosis patients. The landlady was willing to rent to Jews, but she wanted one year's rent in advance as a precaution in the event that if something happened to them before the lease expired, she would have her money. Her condition was based on the known fact that the area was notoriously anti-Semitic. In spite of this, every effort was made to find the money to rent the house in Zakopane.

Another serious problem arose as a result of the arrival of many Jewish girls hidden in convents or the homes of

Polish gentiles. Several girls found it difficult to admit they were Jewish and continued to wear the Christian cross on chains around their necks or to pray in a manner that was not Jewish. The older boys called the girls *Musselmen* and treated them with contempt.

Yonik and his gang would enter the girls' room and taunt them, pull their hair and try to rip the crosses from around their necks. The girls took to locking their door and remaining in their room except to eat, afraid of the boys. After a few such incidents, Lena went to the boys' room to explain what they were doing was wrong.

Naiten sprang angrily to his feet. "Please Mrs. Lena, those girls don't belong to us. Why do you keep them here? Why do you feed them? When they hear the word Jew, they spit! Let them go back to their priests and Sisters. If I ever see one of them spit again, I'll kill them, I swear I will!"

Shocked by Naiten's outburst, Lena explained, "Don't you ever, ever lay a hand on those girls. I know it bothers you to see the girls wearing their crosses and reciting their Catholic prayers but we must all understand the reasons. These girls were raised in convents. It will take them time to realize they are not Catholics and little by little, they will give up the prayers and the other things. You can't force them! You must never force them to do anything, do you understand?" She looked at her angry charges, hoping they did understand.

Naiten was not convinced. "You mean we have to listen to them praying and making fun of the Jews – here, in this building?"

"Yes, that exactly what I mean." Her voice showed no anger, her eyes gazed at her charges, willing them to understand that pain comes in various dimensions and that patience, with a lot of understanding, was a healer. Somewhat more calmly, she continued, "they think the word Jew is an ugly word and it will take lots of time for them to get over it. Help them."

When she left, the boys argued amongst themselves. Most refused to accept her comments but they agreed not to pull the crosses from the girls' necks.

The crowding in the building made it impossible for the children to play inside, which meant for them to play outside, it was necessary they go to a park, but that was impossible. There was the fear that gentiles would throw rocks at them. The older boys heard about the adults being reluctant to take the smaller children to the park. "Let me see somebody even reach for a rock," Yonik assured Lena. "I'll take care of him." Stefan, Marek, Moishe and others also volunteered to guard the expedition of the children to any Krakow park they wanted to visit.

"Don't worry," Stefan assured Lena. "Nobody would dare throw a rock at the kids, not while we're around."

But the consensus was that the children should stay at the building until arrangements could be completed to move them. Money was raised and the resort in Zakopane was rented for a year. Workmen were converting it into a building that would give the children an environment needed to become healthy, normal boys and girls. Everyone anxiously awaited the day they could leave Krakow.

The house on Dluga Street was as depressing as ever. The older boys were still hostile to the girls. The little children spent most of their time lying on their mattresses, looking at the sun through a window. Occasionally their room was filled with children's laughter, but most of the time the silence of inactivity prevailed.

The committee's finances improved and another house in Rabka was rented for seventy children and the regular staff. Dluga Street now had about one hundred and seventy children. It fell on Lena's shoulders to find adults willing to go to Zakopane, to a place ridden with anti-Semites, unprotected against any provocation and at risk for their lives. Lena gathered a staff of women survivors from Auschwitz for this task. For the most part the women were completely alone, having lost their families. For them the children were a new chance at being mothers and in time, they became as devoted to their charges as a natural parent.

One Sunday morning, when most Krakow residents were returning from church services, there arose screams of "pogrom, pogrom!" Pandemonium broke out. Everything happened very quickly. The Jews barricaded themselves in the building, terror on their faces. Someone ran into the office screaming. A mob of several hundred people had formed outside the gate shouting, "Kill the Jews! They've taken a Catholic girl to kill for their matzos! Kill them – Kill the Jews!" Many were pushing against the locked gate, trying to break it down.

The adults were petrified. The younger children cried. People in the street screamed for Jewish blood. Suddenly the ranting of the mob ceased, its attention attracted to a window on the second floor. Standing on the windowsill, a bottle in his hand was Stefan. He shouted, "Get away from here. Get away fast or I'll throw this bomb! We have bombs and grenades. You have two minutes to get out of here!"

"Bombs! The Jews have bombs!" the would-be pogromists shouted in panic, and within a few seconds they dispersed. The near-riot was over. Still clutching the bottle containing strawberry preserves, Stefan reentered the building to the acclaim of everyone.

When the day of departure finally arrived, two large trucks came at five in the morning. The drivers agreed to take the children to Zakopane only on condition the tarpaulin be closed, concealing the children so the Polish people did not see their cargo. What the children were not aware of was that they were leaving one fire for another. The Germans had poisoned the people in Zakopane with their fascist lies. The valley had a reputation for being anti-Semitic, but after the Germans left, they were worse.

Lena was reminded by the committee, "If there is trouble, there will be no one to help you, no men to protect you and a hundred children to worry about." The war had been over in Poland for many months. "How many Poles have come to you and said they wished to help you? Do you have friends at all? The Poles love us like the Germans loved us! Reconsider," they pleaded.

Her answer was, "The children in this building are very sick and Zakopane is the only cure for them. If we wait, we'll lose some of them and that is something we can't afford."

They continued to argue, but to no avail. Lena refused to be deterred from her goal. The committee reluctantly supported her decision, but made her promise that if trouble developed, she would leave Zakopane and return to Krakow with the children.

Once outside the city, the trucks picked up speed, the drivers anxious to reach their destination without being discovered. Crowded against each other, most of the children fell asleep. The trucks entered the snow covered mountains of the Tatras and began its ascent along the mountain route to Zakopane. Over narrow bridges and through a tunnel that entered the valley, the trucks wound their way to its ultimate destination. A little after noon they arrived and the children looked with awe and amazement at the impressive, inviting resort building, surrounded by trees and grass. Far off on the horizon as though painted for a scenic stage background was the tall giant of the Tatra Mountains, the proud and sure Giewont.

IMMEDIATELY UPON THEIR ARRIVAL, LENA ORDERED THE CHILDREN to throw off their dirty clothes and to take a bath. The children scrubbed themselves clean using soft towels and sweet water and when they were finished, they were given clean clothes, shoes and undergarments. Their rags were thrown away, their hair was cut and they were treated for sores and lesions from head to toes. Their beds had real sheets and pillows with covers and all the children were amazed at what they saw before them.

Moishe threw himself on his bed, basking in the sensations and aroma of luxury. This was heaven – a place of dreams. The boys yelled their excitement, releasing their tension. They were in the country where everything smelled and looked clean and they had sheets, soap and even clean clothes. Overcome by their surroundings, the exhilaration of this moment was intoxicating as they marvelled at their good fortune and their new home.

Bronia, their cook, prepared a feast for lunch that was from a fairy tale. The table was covered with clean cloths, the room filled with sunshine as the waitresses placed course after course in front of each person. Never had Moishe seen so much food at one time. The soup was thick and delicious, the long fresh bread was torn apart with the enthusiasm of the hungry and devoured with relish. This was heaven to them, the likes of which they had never seen and they loved it.

Every day brought new surprises. Programs were implemented, toothbrushes introduced and the older children shown how to make their own beds. Most were afflicted with a wide variety of sores, rashes and pimples; several were infested with lice. Minor surgery was provided, a delousing program introduced and everyone took hot baths, hot shampoo treatments and frequent applications of DDT powder. After three days, they were all given a clean bill of health as the sound of laughter rang throughout Zakopane.

As the months passed more children arrived from Warsaw and Lodz. Bitter clashes broke out every now and again between the veterans of Krakow and the newcomers. Gradually both factions blended into one and the fights ceased.

A new doctor took Naiten to Krakow for three days. When he returned, Naiten no longer wore his eye patch. He had been fitted with an artificial eye and this changed his outlook on life. Some of the children left, reunited with relatives. Yonik had been found by his uncle and Stefan went with him.

Moishe had earned a reputation as a tough kid in Krakow and though he was overwhelmed by Zakopane, his attitude did not change. He was rude and aggressive. To him girls were tolerated with a minimum of patience, respect was earned by power. A survivor from the concentration camp noticed the way Moishe treated the girls and befriended him. Edith became his teacher and confidant. Gradually Moishe's toughness dissolved as she taught him how to love his friends, to treat others as he would like to be treated. His resentment towards the girls finally diminished and he began to understand the meaning of respect instead of power.

An attempt was made to enroll the older children in the government school system in Zakopane but was met with resistance and hostile anti-Semitic rhetoric. Government requirements allowed any child who could pass the entrance examination the right of enrolment and sixty-two children submitted applications for the examination. All passed.

When the children began attending the school they were met with insults and curses of Zyd! Zyd! – Jew! Jew! Rocks were thrown at them and there was shoving and pushing. It was decided to keep the younger children at the resort, while the older ones continued to attend the government school. There were a few fist fights, but when the Jewish students fought back, the fights stopped. The name calling continued, but the older children ignored the taunts.

In November it became worse. At recess, the school teachers miraculously disappeared and fifty Polish children surrounded the twelve Jewish children. The gentile students formed a circle, threw rocks at them, struck them with their fists and sticks until the snow was covered in blood and all the Jewish children were bruised, bloodied and cut. Subsequently, the children stopped attending the schools in Zakopane.

Reports of violent anti-Semitism throughout Poland reached the resort. Funds were dwindling and the Jewish Committee was having difficulty affording the two children's shelters. The food supply became dangerously low and they had only a few days of coal. Travel for Jews in postwar Poland was dangerous as Jewish passengers were attacked and thrown bodily from moving trains. Lena Kuchler needed to go to Krakow and argue for financial help in person. Her telephone calls had been met with arguments of lack of money and the difficulties of protecting the children in such an isolated location. When she arrived at Dluga Street, she was told the treasury was empty. Realizing she could accomplish nothing further in Krakow, she took the train to Warsaw to see the Warsaw Central Committee Chairman, but was met with the same answer. Empty handed, she returned to Zakopane.

A few weeks later, Lena was attacked and robbed. Richard, one of the younger boys was almost thrown into the freezing river by Polish boys, but was saved by a peasant. Yizha, Yanush and Melik had to use knives to keep from being attacked in a theatre. The home in Rabka was attacked and Lena expected the rabble would also attack Zakopane.

Lena took a train to the office of the Ministry of Public Security in Krakow. Unable to obtain soldiers to protect the children, Lena accepted guns and ammunition – she would arm the children. In her purse she carried a letter to the commander of the army post in Zakopane authorizing him to give to Lena one heavy machine gun, six regular guns, six rifles, six pistols, two dozen grenades and three boxes of ammunition. Lena would have her own army.

When Lena returned to Zakopane, and gave the commander the letter, he was more than cooperative, installing a powerful searchlight on the roof of the main building and a siren. He posted two men in three eight-hour shifts to help defend the resort if attacked. He also supplied her with a flare gun to be used to bring him and more men to her assistance and he added more automatic rifles to her arsenal.

Zakopane became a miniature fortress. The heavy machine gun was placed on one of the balconies and covered with a tarpaulin. Winter dragged on and the children were not allowed to leave the building for despite constant patrolling, stones crashed through the windows, at first at night and then during the day. Stories of murders and beatings were heard. In Zakopane a botanist who had hidden his Jewish background was uncovered and murdered. By mid-January of 1946, the children had been taught how to use the guns, rifles and machine guns. All the windows of the basement were sealed and supplies brought down to the basement level as everyone waited for the inevitable.

When the attack came, it was sudden and on an overcast night. One of the soldiers sensed something was amiss. Immediately the younger children were ushered into the basement and all the lights in the building were extinguished. Another soldier uncovered the machine gun and fitted it with the ammunition belt. Lena fired the flare gun and started the siren. She went to the telephone to call for help, but the line was dead.

The first shot rang out.

Flashes of gun fire appeared from the trees. From the roof, the machine gun began clattering, the siren screeched as the searchlight roamed back and forth over the grounds. Yizha and Naiten fired their rifles from their posts, while another child tossed a grenade. Moishe had an automatic machine gun with a seventy-two-bullet canister and raked the grounds in short bursts from behind the sand bags. For fifteen minutes the boys screamed at the top of their lungs while shooting, with neither side appearing to be affected in any telling way. Shots from the intruders ricochet off the walls, glass shattered as the bullets sped through to impact against the furniture inside. Never had Moishe felt such adrenaline surge as he ran behind the bags in a crouched position firing into the darkness.

Suddenly the attackers' fire grew weak. Militia trucks appeared and the soldiers joined in the battle, dispersing the attackers. The older boys raised their weapons, screaming abuses at the fleeing intruders, laughing hysterically at being the victors. By some miracle, none of the children were injured, but all were scared, regardless of their boastful claims.

Lena knew it was time to leave Zanopake – but to go where? Several of the older boys and girls approached Lena looking very serious and adult. One boy said, "We want you to help us get to Palestine. We don't want to stay here." The others nodded.

Lena didn't know how to reply. "Children, do you know how many borders you have to cross before you can reach Palestine? How will you get across the Polish border, the most difficult of all?" The children pleaded. The discussion lasted late into the afternoon without Lena being able to persuade them from their goal.

The children from Rabka arrived, stretching the capacity of the resort home to its limit. Moishe received news from Krakow that Gershon had turned up and was very sick. He was told his mother had given so much blood to him that she became ill, but Gershon still was not responding to the treatment.

Devastated by the news, Moishe asked to return to Krakow. Reluctantly, he said farewell to his friends. The parting was difficult and painful as Moishe was one of those who wanted to go to Palestine. The boys shook hands and hugged him. Moishe climbed into the truck and watched the building and friends he had come to love disappear from view.

Not long afterwards, six boys and six girls left Zakopane for Bytom to go over a guarded mountain pass into Czechoslovakia, their first step to Palestine. *(They never* succeeded in their attempt, but eventually some made it to Rosenheim, Germany.)

When Moishe arrived in Krakow, he was taken to a house for Jewish adults. His mother was ill. She had lost weight, her complexion was pasty white, fatigue was in her eyes and tired of body. He learned when Gershon arrived, the doctors said he was in need of a blood transfusion, but no one would donate any. Sara gave blood three times until the doctors refused to take any more because she was jeopardizing her own health. Her efforts were in vain for Gershon died from the neglect of the stomach wound.

They decided to go to Palestine to find Sara's relatives, but to do that, they had to be part of a group with roots in Palestine. Throughout Krakow, there were different groups that trained immigrants in kibbutz living in Palestine. These organizations found ways to smuggle people out of Poland and into the promised land. Sara wanted Moishe to join one that would allow him to say kaddish for his brother and take them to Palestine. They joined a kibbutz organized by Mizrachi.

Moishe had a lot of clothes from Zakopane and with the little that Sara had they presented themselves to the people who ran the kibbutz. The officials took away their suitcases, with all their clothes, informing Moishe they now belonged to a collective community – what they had was no longer theirs – it belonged to everyone.

Moishe was not pleased, nor did he appreciate the way they interpreted every aspect of living. When in need of clean clothes, he went to the official to ask for a replacement for what he had been wearing.

"I came with clothes, why can't I have back what was mine. I can't wear the same things over and over again."

"Others have them. They no longer are yours."

"I know. I see them wearing my clothes, but I have nothing."

"We have nothing left to give you."

"Just give me back what was mine. Even you are wearing my clothes."

"It's not yours any more – it's mine. Find your own clothes."

Before they left Krakow for Berlin, Moishe was told he and his mother were to be separated. He was angry. There was no way he and his mother would be parted. He threatened they would not leave if they continued with their plans. The officials relented. One night, about forty people left Krakow to make their way to Gorlitz, a border city that was partly in Poland and partly in Germany. With false documents, they crossed the dividing line separating the two countries and went to the railway station, to get to Berlin.

A man approached with smiles and greetings and spoke to them in Yiddish, befriending some of the people. Before the train for Berlin arrived, the German police came and arrested them. The man who had befriended them was an informer and had notified the police they were illegal immigrants.

Everyone was placed in jail cells. Moishe and his mother shared a small cubicle, with two cots and an exposed toilet. For ten days they remained in prison, without any contact from the outside world. The food was bad and the guards were anti-Semitic, showering them with verbal abuse. Only once a day were they allowed out of their cells to exercise. Ten days passed before they were taken back across the dividing line into Poland.

It was enough for Moishe. This wasn't getting them to Palestine and his respect for the organizers had reached a point of disrespect and uncooperation. They left the group and journeyed north to the Baltic port of Szczecin which was under the authority of the British government. The British presence was to stop any Jews from leaving the country specifically for Palestine. For the next several days, they tried to find a ship that was leaving Poland, but were unable to smuggle themselves aboard. They heard of a ship returning over five thousand Germans to Germany. When the ship was about to depart, they mixed with the Germans and boarded with them.

They set sail for Lubeck where everyone was placed in a camp until the authorities could figure what to do with them. A member of an Israeli brigade discovered Moishe and his mother and arrangements were made to get them to Munich. At night they left the camp and boarded a train.

When they arrived in Munich, Moishe and his mother were separated against Moishe's wishes. Each was taken to a different kibbutz, his mother outside of the city, while Moishe was sent to one inside. Before long, Moishe became fed up with kibbutz living, tired of the spartan existence and the rules that didn't allow freedom of choice. He walked out of the kibbutz to find his mother. When he arrived at the railway station to take the train to his mother's kibbutz, he was pleasantly surprised to meet her climbing the steps from the platform as he was descending to the train. She too had become depressed with being separated and left to find him. Together they returned to his mother's kibbutz where they remained for the next two years.

Moishe was taught a trade in the tool and die industry, but it was not what he wanted. He went to school, while his mother worked. In the area of the kibbutz were different Displaced Person camps and whenever he was near a Jewish agency, he would check the bulletin boards to see the lists of refugees in the camps. On one such occasion, he discovered the names of some of his friends from Zakopane in a DP camp at Rosenheim.

Again some of the boys from Zakopane were together, but only for a very short time. The year was 1947 and the boys were on their way to Palestine. They had left Zakopane on their own when Lena Kuchler had vacated the resort house. She didn't have enough funds to buy everyone a passport and she had to tell the older boys they had to find their own way to Palestine. The boys joined a kibbutz and were able to get themselves into Germany, but no further. They were waiting for the next stage of their trip when Moishe discovered them. Moishe didn't want to lose them again. He ran home to tell his mother when he heard they would be leaving. He wanted to be with them. By the time he reached Rosenheim, they were all gone. Saddened by his loss, Moishe returned to his mother and told her the disappointing news.

THEY EMIGRATED TO CANADA IN 1948 AND MOVED TO TORONTO. Life was better, but Moishe could not find himself. He became an automobile mechanic, but it wasn't what he wanted. His uncle had a bakery and he asked to be taught the bakery business. Fifteen hours a day Moishe apprenticed at Perlmutter's Bakery in Toronto until he became a full-fledged baker. In 1950, he purchased Quality Bakery in Hamilton on Barton Street and later sold it to his employees, opening another near Cannon Street, which he later sold in 1957.

What he wanted was to find his friends. He flew to Germany and took the train to Munich, where he rented a car. He drove throughout Europe searching for information that would lead him to his friends. On November 1957, he arrived in Israel with a few leads. With the help of an uncle, he found Sevik. From Sevik he found Marek who was in the army and then Yusik who lived in Haifa. He learned that Yonik and Tatek were living in Paris, France. One by one, from city to kibbutz, Moishe tracked down his friends from Zakopane. His was a quest of joy. His need was to journey back to a time of pain and grief mixed with joy and happiness. His purpose was to bond himself with friends who had absorbed the pain of the war, shared the experience of survival and whose lives paralleled his own. By doing this, he found he could accept what had happened to him and to live with the memory. He had left the dark and needed to come out into the light. By the time Moishe left Israel to return to Canada, he had found most of his friends and more importantly – he found himself. He found he could go on with his life and he discovered Malka, a wife to share that life.

* * *

"In 1947, the older boys and girls did not wait for the new Jewish state to be created. They left us earlier, once again as 'illegal' migrants and joined in the battles that preceded the creation of Israel.

A few months after the proclamation of the State of Israel, all my children arrived with me to our Homeland. Our long journey from night to the bright new day had ended. We are now free men in a free land. The crowds on the dock were shouting and waving. Shalom! Shalom! Bruchim l'medinat Yisrael! (Welcome to the Land of Israel!) For the first time in my life I had the feeling of being reborn. Two of my boys are gone forever. Lonek and Yizha were killed in the fighting in 1948. Small envelopes containing their medals and their papers repose in my desk. That is all that remained of them.

In the Book it is written, 'There is a time to build up.' This is the time. We are building up. And we are being rebuilt."

LENA KUCHLER-SILBERMAN
Born: January 28, 1910
Died: August 6, 1987

*The italics on this page are from the book, *My Hundred Children* by Lena Kuchler-Silberman.

Moishe

The Boys from Zakopane

Leon

Marek

Yizha

Yuzek

Naiten

Tatek

Moishe   *Sara*

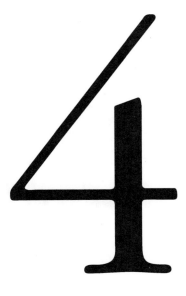

I HAVE A MISSION

"It is no challenge to die like a Jew; the true challenge is to live like a Jew."

— THE CHOFETZ CHAIM

Israel

Shaar-HaGolan: *A kibbutz near the Golan Heights where Dubi Arie lived and married. From here, his life would branch out to fulfill his mission.*

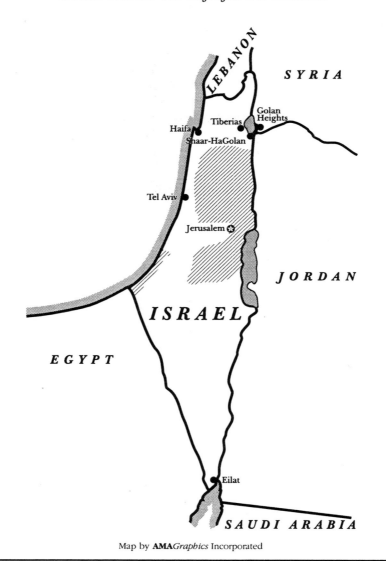

Map by **AMA**Graphics Incorporated

I HAVE A MISSION

The Story of
DUBI ARIE

Colonel Gur's 55th Parachute Brigade was assigned to General Narkiss's Command and he was instructed to break through the built-up area, north of the Old City of Jerusalem. The city was defended by a very heavy concentration of Jordanian forces. An hour before midnight of June 5, 1967, the historic battle for Jerusalem began. Dubi and his brigade were wearing the wrong type of uniforms for street fighting, heavily loaded with their packs, they were used to clear the mountains surrounding the city of Jordanian troops. The battle was fierce, with many men on both sides being killed, but those still fighting were too involved to stop or shed a tear. Smoke from exploding grenades mushroomed in the air, cannon fire swallowed the land creating large craters, machine gun bullets tore into the night amid the screams of pain from the wounded and the dying on both sides. The noise was deafening and the fighting continuous, with each side giving little and paying in lives for what they gained or lost.

After a fierce night battle, resulting in heavy casualties, the Israeli's entered St. Stephen's Gate by 8:30 in the morning and by 10:00 a.m. reached the Western Wall. It was during the final bursts of gunfire of the bloody Six Day War, that Dubi discovered the purpose of his survival. In the midst of the fighting, his face black from the dirt and smoke, he heard the shrill, piercing sound of the shofar preceded by the long awaited words over a transistor radio held by one of the paratroopers that the Western Wall was once again back in Israeli hands. Dubi was overcome with emotions and cried.

When the Israeli soldiers heard the news from the radios carried by the paratroopers, they could not contain their joy; the same men who were unable to cry for their fallen comrades, shed tears for what had been lost for two thousand years and was now theirs again. A paratrooper near Dubi opened the collar of his uniform and removed his tallit (prayer shawl) and kissed it. The announcer's voice was filled with emotion, his voice broke as he could no longer contain his own feelings. Music poured from the radio as the song, "Jerusalem of Gold", filled the air like a national anthem and for an instant, time stopped inside every Jew as his soul soared to the heavens with the knowledge of their victory.

Jordanian gunfire was intense, the battle never wavered for an instant, with both sides wanting to succeed. The excited voice of the announcer rose over the sound of the shooting as the Israeli soldiers, realizing that two thousand years of exile had come to an end pushed ahead until they stood before the Western Wall.

Jerusalem was Jewish.
Jerusalem was united.
Jerusalem was Israeli.
When Dubi heard the shofar, he felt the first spark of an idea that would lead him to the creation of the mission in his life.

BORN ON AUGUST 4, 1939 IN WARSAW, DUBI WAS ONLY THREE weeks old when the Germans marched into Poland. He never knew the city as his parents did, never saw the many parks and public gardens, nor the numerous theatres famous for drama and ballet. He had no memory of the city of his birth because his mother, Sarah, sensing the Germans would not settle for any peaceful means to their demands, anticipated the impending invasion of her beloved country. With her young son Isahar and newborn Dubi, she left Warsaw before the Germans made leaving impossible.

Her husband joined the Soviet army, receiving a commission as an officer and had gone to Russia. There was no one to protect her children except herself. What few members of her family still lived in Warsaw were preoccupied with their own problems as the black clouds of war hovered on the horizon. She packed what she could carry and joined the thousands of refugees escaping the brutality of the expected German invaders. She left without money or food, only with the premonition that to stay was more dangerous than the unknown she and her children were about to face. By the time the Germans entered Warsaw on September 8, 1939, Sarah, Isahar and young Dubi were on their way to the Siberian wilderness.

By her sheer wits and cunning, Sarah wandered across a continent ahead of the refugees that followed, surviving in a jungle of disease, starvation and death. Holding the hand of Isahar and cradling Dubi to her bosom, she trekked for endless hours, receiving food for Isahar from the farmers she passed, while she breast fed young Dubi. Racked with pain from her ordeal, hungry from the lack of food, she endured because behind them was the advancing Germans and ahead, although unknown, was freedom from what she fled.

Unknown to Sarah, Hitler's crazed ambition to dominate the world was closely bound up with his concept of the Jew being his implacable enemy. The war he waged against his imaginary foe was an integral part of his overall military and political campaign and would dominate many of his decisions. Millions of Jews were living in Eastern Europe, the very region sought as Lebensraum for the German people and hence their annihilation was one of the war's primary objectives.

Hitler's mechanized forces swept into Poland with the strategy of a new concept in war called *blitzkrieg* (lightning war). They converged from the Baltic Sea in the north to the Slovakian border in the south, crushing the Polish army in a massive pincer movement. Constantly on the move, never stopping longer than was necessary, Sarah and her two children survived each crisis, always one step ahead of the advancing Germans, but at great personal sacrifice and hardship.

"I don't know how we got away or how we managed to survive, but my mother was a very brave woman. How my mother withstood the dangers of wandering with a young boy and a newborn child, when all of Europe was aflame and Jewish blood was being spilled, amazes me. How was mother able to foresee and foretell the unseen and the unimaginable? How did she comprehend what the millions who were to be slaughtered failed to understand? We spent five years in Russia. She worked very hard, cutting trees, doing all sorts of manual labour. I have no doubt, that a divine hand led my fate and that fate strengthened my mother's wings to protect and save myself and my brother from certain death. Who told mother to escape? Where did a young woman of twenty-five muster the strength and courage to leave home and family?"

Like the ebb and flow of the sea, the battle surged forward until a year later the German forces were fighting defensively on the banks of the Volga at Stalingrad and in the foothills of the Caucasus. Everything did not go according to Hitler's plans. In occupied Russia, hundreds of thousands of Germans, together with their accomplices and their appointed officials were shot or taken prisoners by the partisans. The war was turning against the German army and their ultimate defeat appeared on the horizon.

Separated by thousands of miles, Sarah learned her husband, Israel, had been killed in an airplane crash in some isolated place. Confronted with the knowledge that the life she had before the war could never be the same, she exhibited the determination for survival that had kept them alive by closing the book on her past and concentrating on her future. Her life was now totally in her hands. Without any hesitation, she continued to slave at her work, waiting for the day when she could return to Warsaw with the memories of a life that was now dead.

By November 1943, the Soviet army was on the offensive in Northern Kiev and the German army was being pushed back towards Poland. Once more Sarah and her children were on the move, always struggling, eating from hand to mouth, existing on crumbs and substandard food, suffering the pangs of hunger and near starvation, but with the hope that tomorrow would bring a new day for them as they moved westward behind the advancing Soviets. The instinct to survive, always present, became the inspiration for life. The protection of her children and the need to know that a normal life could be reclaimed, strengthened Sarah's desire to survive and she found the strength to continue while her body was punished by hard work. Victory seemed only months away when Soviet troops liberated Riga. The Germans were backed into Germany and the Allied troops were winning the war in Greece, Norway and Italy. Dubi had become four years old.

By January 17, 1945, the Soviet forces reached Warsaw, and as each successive month passed, the infamous concentration camps were liberated one by one and the gory, inhuman details of Buchenwald, Auschwitz, Sorbibor, Treblinka, Chelmno and Theresienstadt were revealed. The story of the six million Jews who died in the Holocaust became the horror of the war and the world reeled from the magnitude of what had taken place.

On May 8, 1945, the war against Germany ended and the Third Reich that was to last a thousand years came to a fitting end in less than twelve. The Soviet government approved the return of all immigrants to their country of origin, and Sarah and her two children journeyed back to Warsaw to put the pieces of their lives together – but there were no pieces left. Warsaw was a mere skeleton of what once had been a major centre of Jewish civilization. When they returned to Warsaw, it was to find the smouldering ashes of a once vibrant and colourful Jewish community, the largest in Europe, obliterated. There was no one – no friends – no family and no community. Only the ruins and ashes of a life that once existed. The Jewish section of the city was destroyed to the very foundation of the buildings as every landmark had been erased by the hate and evil of those who thrived on delivering death to the innocent. When the Jews returned to what had once been the Warsaw ghetto, they saw and felt the meaning of the Holocaust.

The Poles had already begun the slow and painful process of rebuilding their shattered city and re-establishing their interrupted lives and careers, but the Jews could not do so. There were far too few survivors *(no more than 200 Jews had survived in Warsaw, the remnant of more than half a million)* to build a viable community and all the Jewish buildings had been levelled. Polish Warsaw was able to return to life as the capital of modern Poland, but Jewish Warsaw was destroyed forever and with it the Jewish Nation in Poland.

NUMB WITH THE REALIZATION THAT SHE AND HER TWO CHILDREN were the only survivors of their family, Sarah sought the help of a Jewish agency. They were shuffled to a refugee camp. *"When we couldn't find our relatives, a Jewish organization took us to a refugee camp in Austria. They took away our rags and gave us clean clothes and food. It had been a concentration camp during the war and I remember entering the gate and seeing the piles of human hair and bars of human soap."*

Life in a *Displaced Person Camp* (place for homeless refugees) was not a life, but an existence. The days merged with each other without substance or purpose as the monotony and routine ate away at every fibre of a person's body and soul. Sarah waited and hoped for the day they could build themselves a new life. When the camp became over-saturated with refugees, the Arie's were relocated to another camp near Salzburg.

The family suffered three more years of confinement in the camp. *"I remember seeing a poster of a child eating a piece of bread with butter. I was so jealous. Then I saw a child with his father. That too, made me jealous. Though one day, I would be able to have the first, I would never realize the second."* The impressions of a shattered world had made their mark on Dubi, and whenever he was able to obtain paper and a pencil, he would sketch. He was six years old and within him burned a new hunger – to be an artist.

After three years in the camp, nine year old Dubi and his older brother grabbed their mother's hand once again. In 1948, the family had a choice, either to emigrate to the United States or to the new State of Israel. Sarah chose the latter. *"My mother really had no burning desire to go to Israel. It was a matter of people being together. People she had met in the camp chose Israel and she wanted to protect us. To her a country of Jews offered that protection, but I always wondered whether there was some power from above leading us to those decisions."*

Young Dubi had lived a struggle that most don't suffer in a lifetime. Forced to grow up fast, under extraordinary circumstances, even the return to the promised land would not change the fate that awaited him. Three years would pass, when the cruelty of time would challenge Dubi to question that higher power, when it moved in a cruel fashion. The unbelievable hardships placed on Sarah took its toll and on June 21, 1951, at the age of 36, she died.

Too young to live alone, but ever the survivor, Dubi found a new home and life on a *kibbutz*, a collective settlement in which society flourished and individuals excelled. His experiences during the war were constant images that invoked the feeling of pride that he was a Jew, and his desire to put those images onto paper haunted him. He could not shake the feeling that maybe it was this reason that he had survived.

Nestled in the Jordan Valley, the agricultural kibbutz Shaar-HaGolan thrived. Here Dubi learned to farm by day and draw by night, to develop his natural artistic talents, spending his free time painting and sculpting. Kibbutz officials enrolled him in art classes in Tel Aviv. *"All my life I did art, even as a child in Russia. I always loved the pencil. All I ever wanted to be was an artist."*

The boy became a man . . . the man became an artist and then he became a soldier. In 1957, at the age of eighteen, Dubi began his military career, volunteering for the paratroopers' division. The boy was taught to be a professional fighter, disciplined to perform under the most stressful conditions, made aware of life outside the security of his kibbutz. He found himself with new goals and different specifications for living, and a sense of pride in being a soldier defending his adopted country. Ultimately, he completed his mandatory three years and returned to farming and his art.

It was on the kibbutz, that he met and married his beloved Raya on December 15, 1961. Together they planned their lives, Dubi to become an artist and she to raise a family. But there would be endless interruptions in Dubi's life before he was to realize his dream.

On May 22, 1967, President of Egypt, Gamal Abdal Nasser declared the Straits of Tiran closed to Israeli shipping. Before long, Israel was surrounded by 250,000 troops, over 2,000 tanks and 700 front line fighter and bomber aircraft. Without the strait open, Israel had lost an important shipping port and could not allow this action to go unchallenged.

Dubi was recalled to duty and was part of an elite paratrooper brigade that volunteered for a very dangerous assignment. They were made to understand the mission was fraught with many risks; estimated casualties to be high on the drop alone. They would be required to parachute behind the enemy lines, deep into the Sinai at an altitude of 400 feet with their heavy gear, making it impossible for any adjustments to their chutes. Once on the ground they were to proceed to where suspected missile launchers were located and blow them up. The mission was a number one priority, for Israel to maintain air superiority, it was mandatory that all rockets and artillery be eliminated before the Israeli air force flew by on their way to destroy the Egyptian tanks.

On the night of the raid, the men were loaded down with ammunition, explosives, food and water. Each man had to carry what they needed when they made the drop adding an additional risk to the jump. When they hit the ground, it would be impossible to find anything in the darkness of the desert, and it became imperative that each man be his own supply depot. They waited for takeoff, not knowing when they jumped, that they would survive not only the jump, but the logistics of getting back into Israeli-held territory. Just before takeoff, the plans were changed, they were ordered to the East Line to fight the Jordanians.

The Israel's did not want to open another battle front, and made overtures to the Jordanian government promising they would not attack its territory if they would agree not to

The Six Day War: June 5-7, 1967.

Israel *completely encircled the old City on June 6, despite fierce opposition by the crack Jordanian Legion. Early next morning, Israeli commandos fought their way into the walled city itself.*
In late June, Israel annexed Old Jerusalem.

Map by **AMA**Graphics Incorporated

enter the engagement. On June 5, 1967, the Jordanian Army launched a barrage of artillery fire from its positions along the armistice line against Jerusalem. The Jordanians were convinced the Egyptians were winning their fight against the Israeli's, they chose to support what they believed was a winning cause. It was evident what was developing was not an isolated skirmish, but an outright effort of the Arab community to reclaim the whole State of Israel. With Jerusalem under bombardment from the guns of the Arab Legion, General Narkiss moved over to the offensive to stop the barrage from damaging property sacred to the Jews. The idea of recapturing East Jerusalem and the Old City was not the initial intention of the Israeli army until the Jordanians started bombing West Jerusalem. Plans to mass their armies against Egypt were altered, and portions of their limited forces were redirected to take the Old City of Jerusalem from the Jordanians. The opportunity to recapture Jerusalem could not be ignored.

Jordanian gunfire was intense, the battle never wavered for an instant, but the excited voice of the announcer rose over the sound of the shooting as the Israeli soldiers advanced, knowing that two thousand years of exile had come to an end.

Jerusalem was Jewish.

Jerusalem was united once again.

Jerusalem was Israeli.

When Dubi heard the shofar, he felt the first spark of an idea that would lead him to the creation of the mission in his life. He vowed that if he survived, he would create a monumental piece of art that would instill in every Jew the sense of awe and pride that he was feeling at that moment. He promised to devote his life to fulfill his dream. His was a personal awakening, capping a life-long search for an understanding of the struggle of the Jewish people to survive, and finally crystallizing in what he saw as the true purpose of his whole life.

"Something happened to me at that moment. It became the centre point of what I call the urge for a profound creation. I wasn't certain what it would be, but I knew that whatever I did would be a monumental expression of the answers for which I have been searching."

The nation trembled with joy that Old Jerusalem was in Jewish hands again. Battle weary soldiers, heavy with the burden of witnessing their comrades killed, hardened to the horrors of pain, lowered their weapons and rejoiced. Some sang, others wept and many prayed.

My City Jerusalem
No more blood to stain your stone
Your walls, your gates
Forever will be open
With our blood we have vowed, the paratroopers.

The Israeli's estimated that Egyptian casualties totalled 15,000. The Egyptians lost 800 tanks and several hundred field guns as well as 10,000 vehicles. The Israeli's suffered casualties of 300 men. The Jordanian casualties were 6,000 with Israel losing 550 men. Syrian losses were not recorded.

Dubi entered the Old City and gazed at the wondrous sight before him. He touched the stones and an overpowering feeling deepened within him. *"No one asked you then if you wanted to be a Jew. You were a Jew and they killed you or you survived."* All of these thoughts came rushing back to Dubi Arie during those moments. Jews again were forced to fight for their survival.

"When I draw an imaginary line connecting milestones in my life, I find it difficult to identify which events, conscious or subconscious, affected my way in life, but I believe that the divine led me in my way . . . my fate and my mission, and that these were etched in my soul before my birth."

Out of these experiences came a remarkable series of drawings and poems, many of them reflecting the terrible violence of war. Meanwhile, under the guidance of Israel's most distinguished artists, he became a master of many techniques. Death was the environment of war, but Dubi endured and the young paratrooper again wondered if this was the reason his life was spared during the Holocaust. Again and again, his life would be interrupted by the savagery of war.

In the autumn of 1969, Dubi was again on active service in the Sinai, fighting the never-ending Wars of Attrition. He was part of a special unit sent behind the Bar-Lev Lines to create a pincer movement against the Egyptians. In mid-April 1970, Egyptian commando units crossed the Suez Canal regularly and attacked Israeli fortified positions. This led to a counter-bombardment by Israeli forces and reprisal raids along the Egyptian line by Israeli parachute and commando units. The fighting escalated with Israeli forces attacking targets in the Gulf and inside Egypt. The initiative passed to Israel and the War of Attrition became a war of counter-attrition. The final phase of the war occurred in late April 1970, when the Israeli's attacked along the Suez Canal, pushing the Egyptian army back into Egypt. The war reached a ferocious pace, with the Israeli army advancing towards Cairo. Then the unexpected occurred – on September 28, 1970, President Gamal Adbal Nasser died.

Again the young paratrooper for the elite Red Berets thought he was being kept alive to fulfill a mission and it was not luck that was doing it. All along, his creation percolated in his mind. His past and present became entwined in a pattern that gave him glimpses of an idea that captured his imagination. He returned to his kibbutz after fulfilling his duty, to work on his idea.

"Nothing happens to me. My kibbutz had 600 civilians and soldiers and was near the Syrian border. There was bombings every night and we hid in the tunnels that were underneath the buildings." By this time, he was an accomplished artist. Dubi knew he wanted to set down on canvas everything he was feeling, with the Jewish struggle as

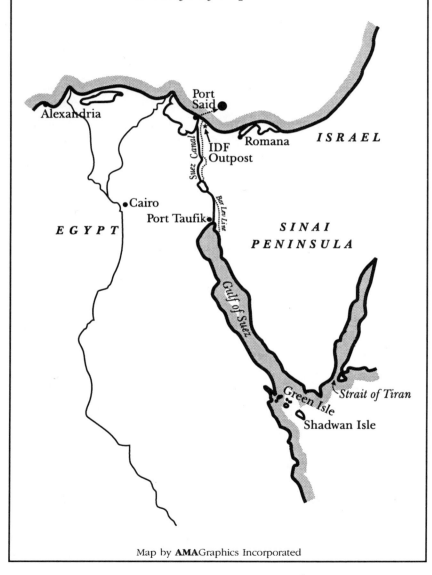

a centrepiece. *"I began to feel I had a mission to fulfill, not with a rifle – with a brush. For reasons that I cannot explain, inspiration overcame me."*

Once again Dubi tried to put his life into perspective. His vision had become more tangible in his mind, but the scope of his idea frightened him. He sketched many pictures that gave life to his goal as the images burst from his imagination onto paper giving substance to the vision that only he saw.

At 2:00 p.m. on October 6, 1973, the Yom Kippur War began with the Egyptian and Syrian armies striking out together. 800,000 troops, 2,200 tanks, 2,300 artillery pieces, 150 anti-aircraft missile batteries and 550 aircraft were thrown into the battle. Unprepared for the attack, the Israeli's took heavy casualties at the beginning. By midday on Wednesday, October 10, almost four days after the attack, 1,100 Syrian tanks were destroyed. The pride of the Syrian army lay smoking and burnt out along the countryside they had travelled. For nine days, the Israeli army met the enemy countless times in life and death struggles. On October 15, 1973, the Israeli's crossed the Suez Canal and fought their way to the main Cairo road. All resistance had crumbled. On October 22, the Syrians accepted a cease fire. The Israeli's had fought the Egyptians, the Syrians, the Iraqis and the Jordanians and had become victorious, but the number of lives lost was too large a price for victory.

> *Stand up David, Goliath is upon you*
> *Israel, your walls have shattered*
> *Your holy day stained*
> *A day of prayer for Israel*
>
> *From the four corners of earth*
> *A mighty and cruel enemy besieges you*
> *To capitulate a stubborn nation*
> *To sow death and destruction*

We have vowed again this time
To defend our nation
Until the last drop of blood
Our country we shall not forsake

By the time the 1973 Yom Kippur War came, he said, *"I have to start. I can't wait anymore. I remained on the front line for six months after the war end before I was discharged. I made a decision to leave Israel after the war and chose Toronto, Canada as the location where I could create my vision. I left the kibbutz to fulfill the true purpose which fate destined for me. I do not relate to the mission as the work of my life. This work sums up an important period in my life; a hatch to open, to ascend to other important milestones in the future . . . challenges in which I see a natural mission."* Despite physically leaving his homeland, there was no change in his spirit.

In 1974, Dubi, his wife Raya and their two children, Gilad, who as a soldier took part in the Lebanon campaign and Doron moved to Toronto. To make ends meet, Raya worked in a day-care centre, all the while devoting herself to raising the two children. Later Yonat *(named for slain Entebbe hero Yonatan Natanyahu)* was born in Canada. Raya was Dubi's biggest supporter, a devoted companion and a constant source of inspiration, enabling him to fulfill his dream. *"I started to research the Holocaust. I talked to survivors. After two years, I discovered a lot had led up to the Holocaust and that many things happened at the same time."* He threw himself into studying Jewish history, the Torah and other religious and philosophical books with an almost maniacal passion.

He discovered a rich spiritual sphere difficult to grasp in depth and his desire to learn only intensified. The work created as a result of this period inspired him. His ideas received new dimension. Many of the spiritual questions that had plagued him for years were answered. *"One of the deepest questions was about spiritual and physical struggling – to die for God or the nation. On the kibbutz, we believed that it was important to struggle physically for the nation."* But the more Dubi read, the more he questioned his own philosophy.

After his intense study, his feelings began to change. *"I found that the spiritual struggle was equally important. It took so much strength to keep the faith in all those terrible times throughout history. That is why we were able to survive. I believe we have a mission in this life even though we pay for it."* For six years, Dubi absorbed everything before putting his brush to canvas. Thirteen years had passed since he felt the first inclination of his purpose in life. Before he began, he was to be inspired by an event that took place in Canada.

"Terry Fox, the young marathon runner who died from cancer, gave me a lot of strength and made me believe anything was possible. To watch with awe and amazement the young man ignore his handicap and attempt a feat unparalleled in history gave me determination and a very deep belief in my mission. I found his motto inspired me, 'If I can dream it, I can do it,' and I began to draw."

At first there were only rough sketches. The research added vision, and the vision became the composition. Finally, a definitive sketch . . . the blueprints for the composition began to unravel. From the first to final brush stroke, the painting would take seven years, but there was more to it than the composition.

Like the life of the artist, the art did not unfold in a sequential line. Sections literally took weeks to dry and the composition developed in a seeming splatter of logic, as the artist moved from position to position on the canvas. But art, like life, does not stand still. As the creator changed over the years, so did the creation. After seven long years, the canvas was finally finished, but the struggle had only begun.

***

UNDER THE WINGS OF GOD AND THE SHADOW OF AMALEK consists of seven panels beginning with the Birth of the Nation: The biblical dictum, *"The deeds of the forefathers will serve as a signpost for their descendants"*, sets the stage for the first panel of "The Mission."

THE FIRST PANEL. This section depicts key events in the lives of our patriarch that foreshadows both the struggles and triumphs of the Jewish nation throughout its history. The unfolding of the painting begins with Abraham, father of the Jewish nation, the first person to embrace the concept of monotheism. God reveals himself to Abraham through three heavenly messengers who come to the tent of the elderly patriarch and his wife, Sarah, to announce the incredulous news that the childless couple will be blessed with a son. *"And I will make of thee a great nation and I will bless thee and make thy name great and thou shalt be a blessing."*

The origins of the Jewish people through the birth of Isaac is truly miraculous. It is this quality of "higher than nature" that has enabled the Jews to overcome awesome challenges and to continue to exist until the present.

In the sacrifice of Isaac (upper centre of panel), Abraham's consummate trial comes when God commands him to sacrifice his beloved son on the alter, *"Please take your son, your only one, whom you love, Isaac . . . bring him up there as an offering."* (Genesis 22:2). As Abraham reaches for the knife, he is stopped by an angel who entreats him not to harm the boy, instead he catches a ram caught in the thicket to offer in Isaac's place.

The patriarch's unique ability to subjugate his own desires to fulfill the will of God is a legacy that has been endowed on his descendants for all time. Consequently, every Jew possesses the innate power to surmount whatever difficulties he faces in his daily life and to ultimately triumph over them.

In conclusion, Abraham is told that overcoming his supreme test will lead to an ascent to ultimate good. *"I shall surely bless you and greatly increase your seed like the stars of the heavens and like the sand on the seashore . . . And all the nations of the earth shall bless themselves by your offspring"* (Genesis 22:17-17).

Two generations later, the patriarch Jacob is forced to leave his home and flee from the wrath of his jealous brother, Esau. Stopping to sleep for the night, he dreams of a ladder that stretches upwards from the earth to the heavens on which angels are ascending and descending (middle right of panel). According to Biblical commentary, this ladder symbolizes the connection between the physical and spiritual worlds, a link forged through prayer and righteous deeds.

Many years later, Jacob wrestles until the break of dawn with a "man" regarded as the guardian angel of his brother Esau; at the apex of their struggle, Jacob emerges victorious and is blessed by the angel. *"No longer will it be said that your name is Jacob, but Israel, for you have striven with the Divine and with man and have overcome"* (Genesis 32:29). This incident represents the eternal battle between good and evil that will manifest in Israel's continuing struggle, both spiritually and physically, with powerful adversaries.

The pyramid, an enduring artistic structure (triangle), is symbolic of the Jewish exile in Egypt, which begins when the twelve tribes (the sons of Jacob) migrate there as a result of a severe famine in their own country. Superimposed on the pyramid is an image of the Angel of death, the last of the ten plagues inflicted on the Egyptians; the Hebrew letters written in green spell out the names of the other nine plagues.

Originally welcomed as an honoured guests of Pharaoh, the status of the Israelites deteriorates to affliction and bondage with the passage of time. *"A new king rose over Egypt, who did not know of Joseph"* (Exodus 1:8), and who had no appreciation for his many contributions to the country. Significantly, the Egyptian exile is a prototype for the rampant anti-Semitism that Jews are to later experience in the many countries where they sojourn throughout the centuries, in which the ruling powers retain and harness the talents of their Jewish subjects through enslavement.

THE SECOND PANEL. Depicts the Exodus from Egypt, the event that transforms the Jewish people into a nation and sets the stage for receiving the Torah. Moses, the greatest prophet of all time, is shown with an outstretched arm and staff, the 'faithful shepherd', leading his flock to redemption.

Acknowledging the covenant that He established with the patriarchs to give them the Land, God commands Moses to inform the Jewish people that He is about to redeem them. *"Therefore, I say to the Children of Israel: 'I am God, and I shall take you out from under the burdens of Egypt; I shall rescue you from their service; I shall redeem you with an outstretched arm and with great judgements. I shall take you to Me for a people and I shall be a God to you'"* (Exodus 6:6-7). Each of these four expressions represents a progressive stage in the process of redemption.

The Jewish people are led out of their bitter exile under the protective wings of the Creator. *"And God took us out of Egypt not through an angel, not through a seraph and not through a messenger; but the Holy One, Blessed be He, in his glory and essence, took us out Himself"* (Passover Hagaddah).

Throughout their wanderings in the desert, God accompanies the Israelites, going *"before them by day in a pillar of cloud to lead them on the way, and by night in a pillar of fire to give them light, so that they could travel day and night"* (Exodus 13:21). God tells Moses to relate the following to them: *"You have seen what I did to Egypt, and that I have borne you on the wings of eagles and brought you to me. And now, if you harken well to Me and observe My covenant, you shall be to Me the most beloved treasure of all peoples"* (Exodus 19:4-5).

Israel's first encounter with its archenemy, Amalek, occurs soon after leaving Egypt, when the latter launches an unprovoked attack on them in the desert. The grandson of Esau, Amalek represents the leading force of evil in the world; the eternal struggle based on the legacy of Easau's implacable hatred for Jacob, clothed in the garb of many hostile enemies over the course of history.

However, in the Book of Deuteronomy, the commandment to erase the memory of Amalek is articulated in strong terms. *"Remember what Amalek did to you, on the way when you were leaving Egypt, that he . . . struck those of you who were . . . weaklings at your rear, when you were faint and exhausted, and he did not fear God . . . You shall wipe out the memory of Amalek from under the heaven – you shall not forget!"* (Deuteronomy 25:17-19).

After forty-nine days, the Jewish people arrive at Mt. Sinai, where they encamp *"like one people with one heart"* and prepare themselves for receiving the Torah, the most monumental event in their history. The Torah provided the Jews with an eternal blueprint of God's commandments, enabling them to lead spiritual lives within the confines of the material world. The Torah established a foundation for the development of the Judo-Christian ethic, the framework of western civilization.

Shortly after receiving the Torah and the Ten Commandments, the people force Aaron the High Priest into fashioning a golden calf for them to worship, thus violating the commandment against idolatry. This episode exhibits a fundamental lack of faith in God, who had recently liberated them from Egyptian bondage with wonders and miracles, and sustained them in their wanderings in the desert.

After descending from Mt. Sinai with the two Tablets of the Law, Moses is crowned in glory as the leader of the Jews and pillars of light radiate from his head (right middle). The revelations of divinity that emanate from the receiving of the Torah allow heaven and earth to meet and embrace;

spirituality to permeate all aspects of the physical realm. Henceforth, the entirety of Creation will be forever altered.

The configuration (in red) above the head of Moses is a seven-branch menorah. An eternal construct of the unity of the Jewish nation, the menorah represents the cycle of creation, comprised of the six days of the week crowned by the seventh day, Shabbat. Ultimately, the menorah symbolizes the spreading of Israel's light throughout the world.

Forty years after leaving Egypt, the Jewish people, now transformed into a mighty nation, stand prepared to enter the promised land to their forefathers. This is accomplished with the conquest of Jericho (bottom left of panel) under the leadership of the prophet Joshua, successor to Moses: *"And it came to pass, when the people heard the sound of the horn, that the people shouted with a great shout, and the wall fell down flat, so that the people went up into the city, every man straight before him, and they took the city"* (Joshua 6:20).

THE THIRD PANEL. Chronicles the Biblical period of the Prophets and Kings, when Jerusalem gains ascendancy as the religious and administrative centre of Israel. An incomparable epoch in the history of the Jewish people, it is marked by the establishment of monarchy through the ruling dynasty of King David, the judicial system (the *Sanhedrin*, or High court), and the existence of the Holy Temple *(Beit Hamikdosh)*.

Following the reign of King Saul, the prophet Samuel crowns David as the new King of Israel (lower right corner). The Holy Temple built by David's son, Solomon, is destroyed by the Babylonians, and the people are led into captivity (upper right corner). The destruction of the Second Temple by Roman legions culminates in the 2,000 year dispersion of the Jewish nation into an exile that endures to the present day. Hovering over these tragic events is the mighty eagle, an ominous symbol of both the Imperial Roman Empire and the Nazi Regime.

Several significant characters in Jewish history emerge in this panel. Collapsing the pagan temple of the Philistines, the might warrior Samson (right middle of panel) employs a strategy of 'no other choice' that parallels the heroic resistance against the Romans at Massada, and of later Jewish resistance movements. The fight between David and Goliath (just left of Samson, right middle of panel) symbolizes the proverbial struggle of the State of Israel – a small nation facing the many and mighty.

At the bottom of the panel is a depiction of the period of the Maccabees, showing the rededication of the Holy Temple and renewal of sacrifices after the desecration of that edifice by the Hellenists (Greeks). These events are connected with the miracle of Chanukah, where a small band of zealots (Maccabees), were able to defeat a mighty foreign power (the Greeks), through intense determination and piety. This victory of 'the few against the many' is a theme that will be re-enacted many times throughout Jewish history.

At the far left is a striking image of a rabbi in a *tallit* (prayer shawl) holding a Torah, perceived as 'the pillar of fire.' He is one of two main figures that play a major thematic role in the painting. Manifesting steadfast faith in God and adherence to His precepts, the rabbi personifies the spiritual strength through which the Jewish people have endured throughout the ages.

At the far left of the panel (and continuing into the next) is a panoply of flags of the various countries and mighty empires that sought to obliterate the Jews. Although most have long since disappeared or fallen into obscurity, the Jewish nation still exists.

THE FOURTH PANEL. Details the horrific events of the Holocaust, in which one-third of the Jewish people was annihilated on the continent of Europe. The six tombstones that comprise this segment are images central to the entire painting, signifying both the lowest ebb in the history of the nation, and also its greatest hopes for triumph and ascendancy.

Ostensibly, the stones are a memorial to the six million martyrs of Nazi brutality; however they are envisioned by the artist as life-stones, monuments to the continued survival of the Jewish nation in spite of near extinction. In fact, it is from the ashes of the Holocaust, the most profound manifestation of darkness, that the modern State of Israel will eventually be reborn.

Each of the six stones is a silent witness, bearing testimony to milestones of Jewish history; one by one, they recall centuries of cultural, political and spiritual aspirations, calling forth forgotten remnants of significant meaning. Dates are engraved in Hebrew and arranged in chronological progression related to a specific dimension of Jewish experience. Collectively, the stones are monuments to; (1) the Diaspora; (2) the Holocaust; (3) Uprising; (4) Heralds of Zion; (5) Sovereignty; and (6) Battles of Israel.

The large circle above the stone portrays the vibrant lifestyle that flourished in the Eastern European communities that existed prior to this period. It provides a glimpse into the traditional observances of Jewish holidays and rituals amidst times of joy (weddings) and sorrow (pogroms and expulsions).

Rising from the unspeakable images of death at the bottom of this panel is the prophet Ezekiel, proclaiming the Biblical prophecy of the dead coming back to life in the Valley of the Dry Bones. *"The hand of the Lord God was upon me . . . and set me down in the midst of the valley which was full of bones . . . and, behold, there were very many in the open valley; and lo, they were very dry. Thus says the Lord God to these bones: 'Behold, I will cause breath to enter into you, and you shall live' . . . And the breath came into them, and they lived, and stood up on their feet, an exceedingly great army. Then He said to me, 'Son of man, these bones are the whole house of Israel. Prophesy and say to them, Thus says the Lord God; Behold, O my people, I will open your graves, and cause you to come out of your graves, and bring you into the land of Israel . . . And you shall live, and I shall place you in your own land'"* (Ezekiel 37:1-14).

Following the desolation of the Valley of the Dry Bones, there is a perceptible transition from darkness to light that introduces the next panel, the birth of the State of Israel. At the top left corner is Theodor Herzl, founder of the modern Zionist movement, the first to envision a Jewish homeland. The term "Zionism" is derived from "Zion," one of the names used in the Scriptures for the Land of Israel. The development of political Zionism becomes the impetus for the return of the Jewish people to their historic homeland.

At the First Zionist Congress, held in Basel, Switzerland in 1897, Jewish delegates from all over the world assemble and decide that the purpose of their movement will be to establish a national home for the Jewish people in the Land of Israel. According to Herzl's beliefs, Jewish suffering will cease only when this goal is realized.

An invisible line runs from Herzl to a group of young people (between first and second monuments) who represent the earliest origins of Zionism. Responding to centuries of pogroms and massacres, this new generation is willing to rise up and fight to protect Jews. Swirling above them are the words (in Hebrew): "Jewish blood will not be cheap".

A unit of partisans, Jewish underground fighters of World War II, is pictured just above the stream of red that stretches from the Monument of the Holocaust; ideological heirs of the early pioneers of resistance described above, their movement culminates in the Israeli soldier (depicted in the fifth panel), as protectors of the Jewish people in their own land.

The appearance of a rainbow can be interpreted on a number of levels. To the artist, it is an ominous symbol – a

"UNDER TH

Panel 7

Panel 6

"I feel personal responsibility as a Jew, a human being and as an artist to strengthen the belief of the eternity of Israel. I believe that every Jew who will see, contemplate and understand the symbolism in my creation will feel proud to be part of this great nation."

DUBI ARIE

DUBI ARIE takes great pride in presenting the *"Scroll of the Mission"* based on his monumental work, *"The Mission: Under the Wings of God and the Shadow of Amalek."* Twenty years from inception to completion, this creation illuminates 4,000 years of Jewish history, beginning with the patriarch Abraham and culminating with the Redemption of the Jewish nation. The panoramic creation, which takes the form of a seven-panelle oil on canvas measuring 38.5 feet by 7 feet, radiates with brilliant colour and imagery; never before has the story of the Jewish people been depicted in sucl a vibrant manner.

To view *"The Mission"* is a

WINGS OF GOD AND THE

Panel 5   *Panel 4*

profound intellectual and emotional experience, evoked by its visually stunning synthesis of artistic symbolism and historical content. Indeed, the viewer is drawn into the rich texture woven from an interplay of elements and archetypes that are icons of the Jewish odyssey throughout the ages. The canvases comes to life as a tapestry of events – past, present and future – which transcend linear time. Instead, they reveal an internal awareness shaped by the collective experience of the people of Israel in their transformation from an ancient tribe into a modern nation.

    The dream, perceived by the artist as a "national mission," was conceived on June 7, 1967, the day that East Jerusalem was liberated during the Six Day War by Israeli paratroopers, who regained control of the Western Wall, the focus of the fervent Jewish hopes for redemption over the centuries. It was in this emotionally-charged atmosphere that the inspiration to create "The Mission" first burst forth in his heart and mind.

I believe, with a
destiny was guided
guided by the power
biggest and most imp
my life – the imp
creation. When I
mission I will kn
purpose for my life.
tests which I
preparation for thi

SHADOW OF AMALEK"

Panel 3   Panel 2

l my heart, that my
nd continues to be
above, towards the
rtant challenge in
lementation of this
ucceed in this holy
w that there was a
will know that the
ave faced were the
esteemed purpose.

DUBI ARIE

RT as a universal vehicle of communication, transcends reason in its ability to speak to the heart and soul of another. As such, art is truly a unique resource for educating mankind to work together in mutual cooperation and harmony.

We are in the midst of a flourishing of interest in Jewish spirituality, manifested as a desire to unlock the treasures of our past. This resurgence of identity finds expression in a diversity of artistic forms which reveal the many dimensions of the Jewish experience.

The ultimate purpose of the *"Scroll of the Mission"* is to inform Jews of their shared purpose and common destiny – enabling them to perceive the connection of the Jewish people over time and space, and to forge bonds of unity amidst diversity. In addition, this resource will build bridges of understanding and tolerance between the Jewish nation and the other peoples of the world.

Panel 1

"*I* shall surely bless you and greatly increase your seed like the stars of the heaven and like the sand on the seashore ... And all the nations of the earth shall bless themselves by your offspring"

(Genesis 22: 17-18)

portent of universal destruction and despair – warning of a future atomic holocaust that would not distinguish between nation, creed, or nationality. The lessons of history are clear, and it is man's responsibility to learn from them.

The Torah describes the rainbow as a sign of God's covenant with Noah and his descendants until the end of time, a reminder of His promise to never again destroy the earth and its living creatures. As such, it is a harbinger of hope and goodwill, reassuring us that no matter how bleak the future may seem, God will lead mankind to its ultimate goal.

THE FIFTH PANEL. With the realization of the Zionist dream, the birth of the State of Israel, in 1948. The young soldier holding the Israeli flag presents a bold visual image that is significant to the entire painting. Counterpoint to the figure holding the Torah (mentioned in panel 3), the soldier is an archetype for the many heroic warriors who have defended the Jewish nation over the centuries.

Together, the rabbi and the soldier comprise the duality that has preserved the people of Israel unto the present day: a nation whose spiritual strength is based on belief in God and Torah, protected by soldiers girded with the faith of their people.

At the bottom right of the panel is the ship Exodus, which attempts to penetrate the British blockade of Palestine to bring to the beleaguered remnants of European Jewry to a safe haven; unfortunately, the boat is not allowed to dock, and its 4,500 survivors are returned to Europe. The Exodus becomes a symbol for the many heroic vessels that try to run the blockade.

The conflict with the British authorities intensifies with the rising tide of "illegal" immigration, and thousands of refugees, newly freed from the Displaced Persons' camps in Europe, are sent to new internment camps in Cyprus. Representing the Sephardic aliyah is the Egoz, a vessel on which 43 Moroccan Jews perish when their ship sinks in the

Straits of Gibraltar; this tragic event captures the fervour of Sephardic Jewry to reach the Holy Land.

Jews who return to their homeland are known as "Olim," from the Hebrew word "aliyah," to go up or ascend. The process of emigrating to the Land of Israel is therefore an elevation; the heartfelt desire of Jews the world over during the interminable centuries of their dispersion and becomes a reality with the establishment of the State of Israel.

The fortunate survivors and immigrants who have managed to gain entry are welcomed by the outstretched arms of the resistance fighters, while an angel hovering above rejoices at the fulfilment of the two-thousand-year-old promise of return: *"And your children will return to their borders"* (Jeremiah 31:17). Again, physical and spiritual join as biblical prophecy is fused with modern Zionism. However, the establishment of the state does not mark the end of the struggle; for the inhabitants of the young country, especially those who populate the kibbutzim and other collective settlements of the border areas, there will be a need for continued vigilance. The barbed wire fences and observation towers at the bottom left of the panel tell of the measures required to ensure security and safety.

Massada (lower left), a high rocky fortress built in Judean times under siege from the Roman conquest, is a hallmark of Jewish resistance. Its inhabitants demonstrate a fierce resolve not to submit to their captors, preferring death in battle over servitude and enslavement to Rome.

Finally, the image in the upper left of the panel is Jacob once again locked in struggle with the angel of his brother Esau, progenitor of the enemies of the Jewish nation. It informs us of the threat that our adversaries continue to pose to us.

THE SIXTH AND SEVENTH PANELS. Together these two panels comprise a thematic unity that departs from the chronicles of Jewish history, beckoning us into a future era: the ultimate

Redemption of the Jewish people and the events that are to occur in the messianic period.

According to tradition, when the Messiah comes he will stand on the roof of the Holy Temple and proclaim, *"Humble ones: the time for your redemption has arrived!"* The souls of all the previous generations will be brought back to life (Resurrection of the Dead) and reunited in Jerusalem. And the Holy Ark that once held the tablets *"etched with the finger of God"* will find their final resting place there.

We observe that the Gate of Mercy (lower left corner of sixth panel) is blocked, in anticipation of the spiritual redemption that is to occur. The structure depicted on top of the Gate of Mercy is King Solomon's Temple (First Beit Hamikdosh), an edifice of great magnificence that marks a golden age for the Jews. Its destruction by the Babylonian king Nebuchadnezzar leads to the conquest of the people of Israel and their subsequent exile in Babylon. (The Second Beit Hamikdosh, set aflame by the Romans, is depicted elsewhere, in Panel Three.)

The primary focus of the Era of Redemption will be re-establishment of the Holy Temple, an activity highly correlated with the termination of the exile: *"Rebuild your House as in former times, and establish Your sanctuary on its site; let us behold its rebuilding and make us rejoice in its completion."*

According to Maimonides (one of the greatest scholars and philosophers of all times), the climax of the Redemption will be the 'ingathering' of the Jewish people to their historic homeland: *"Gather our dispersed from among the nations, and assemble our scattered from the ends of the earth."*

During this time the pilgrimages to the Holy Temple for the festivals will be instituted once again: *"We will go up and appear and bow before You on the occasion of our three pilgrim festivals . . . on the Festival of Matzot (Passover), on the Festival of Shavuot, and on the Festival of Sukkot."*

Additionally, these panels depict the return of the Ark of the Covenant and Menorah to the Temple; these holy artifacts are borne with great rejoicing by the figures below, as the temple musicians sound trumpets to herald their restoration: *"Restore the Kohanim (priests) to their service, and the Levi'im (musicians) to their chanting and song."* (The events that will take place in the Era of Redemption, as described in the four preceding paragraphs, are widely documented in both written Torah (Scriptures) and Oral Torah (Talmud); the material quoted above is from the traditional Siddur (prayer book), Mussaf service for the Three Festivals.)

The Lion's Gate (lower right of the seventh panel) symbolizes the physical redemption of the Jewish people, since it was an entry point for the Israeli forces in the 1967 War (for this reason, it is known as the Gate of the Paratroopers) and enabled the recapturing of sites holy to them. The structures pictured on top of the Lion's Gate correspond to spheres of government and administration: on the left is the Citadel of David (which still exists today), dominion of royalty during the rule of King David; adjacent to it is the Israeli Knesset, the current seat of government administration.

In these panels we see the re-emergence of key figures encountered earlier in the painting. Pictured in the upper right of the sixth panel are the matriarchs: Sarah, Rebecca, Rachel and Leah: mothers of the nation, they embody the strength and greatness of Jewish women throughout the ages. In fact, it was in the merit of the righteous women of that generation that the Jewish people were redeemed from Egypt (Gemorrah Sotah 11:b); according to commentary, women will once again be in the forefront of the future redemption of our people.

Just below the matriarchs are the three patriarchs: Abraham, Isaac and Jacob, corresponding to the trials of *Chesed* (kindness), *Gevurah* (severity) and *Rachamim* (mercy). Collectively, the patriarchs represent a fusion of divine energies that achieve consummate perfection in Jacob, blending opposites into the harmonious balance referred to a Beauty.

To the left of the fathers is Moses, once again the redeemer of the Jewish people, forming a triad with Joshua the warrior and Aaron the High Priest. Similarly, the pyramids are an illusion to the three foundations upon which the world stands: [the study of] service [of God], and deeds of kindness (Mishna Pirkei Avot, Ethics of the Fathers 1:1).

The image of King David with his harp represents the restoration of royalty through the David dynasty, hinting to the coming of the Messiah, who will be descended from that lineage. The prophet Elijah descends in a fiery chariot to herald that the time has come; he is accompanied by seven angelic hosts playing trumpets and harp.

An interplay of spiritual forces converges, (top of the panels), resulting in unification that enable the Creation to achieve its ultimate perfection. In the centre of this dynamic visual configuration we see the Ten Commandments, the foundation of the Torah. The next level is the mystical sephirot, manifestation of divine attributes in the world, described in the esoteric writings of Kaballah. Finally, the names of the twelve tribes of Israel, and the blessings that Jacob endowed to each upon his passing, are interwoven with the Hebrew months; each constellation (mazal) corresponds to one of the tribes and reflects its specific essence. Also appearing in the circle are the seven fruits for which the Land of Israel is praised: wheat, barley, grapes, fig, pomegranate, olives and dates.

The circle encompassing this matrix is not yet closed, signifying that the arrival of the Messiah is necessary to complete the preparations. The reappearance of Jacob's ladder (centre of the last panel) portends that the long-awaited event is close at hand – the link between the spiritual and physical realms has been wrought to perfection. For artist Dubi Arie, the six points of the Star of David express the elements of faith, land, people, justice, hope and power – which together will lead to the closure of the circle.

The Era of Redemption will be ushered in for the people of Israel, and indeed for all the nations of the world, and we will witness the fulfilment of prophetic visions: *"No more will violence be heard within your boundaries and you will certainly call your own walls salvation and your gates praise"* (Isaiah 60:18) . . . *"And they will beat their swords into plowshares . . . nation will not lift up sword against nation, neither will they learn war anymore,"* (Isaiah 2:4).

MANY OF DUBI'S QUESTIONS HAD NOW BEEN ANSWERED. THE struggle for the Jews has certainly been a physical one, but it has also been spiritual. *"The spiritual struggle of the Jews is important. For the Jews to maintain their belief in God throughout the centuries of persecution, this is a miracle and we survived. We had a mission."*

He finds it difficult to accept the premise that money is the healer of old wounds. On the kibbutz, he was offered money from Germany for being a survivor – he refused. Money cannot buy back the lives and the grief. He sold a series of etchings to a gallery on condition that none of his paintings be sold to German distributors. When his client reneged on his promise, he discontinued the series. When offered a huge amount of money to create thirty-two stained windows, it was on condition the glass not come from Germany, even though he recognized they manufactured the best glass. They agreed. When he found the money to pay for the windows was coming from Germany, he refused the commission, even after they increased his fee. Dubi Arie has received very large offers for his painting, He has turned them down. The painting will be donated. *"I could go to the telephone right now and become a millionaire, but I don't want any benefit from this. I was led to this. It's not mine. The time was given to me for a specific reason. A mission means you don't have to be paid."*

Some day he hopes to return to Israel. *"I left physically, but I never really left."* If he can help young Jews to better understand their history, *"I know there will be some meaning to my life."* Despite the gloom and murky content of horrific events, his intention is to stress the positive; that out of unspeakable horrors came Israel, that out of death, life can sometimes spring. There is a small sign in his work room displaying a quote from Theodor Herzl which states, "If you will it, it is no legend."

> *"It is my belief that education is the hope of the world, and art is its inspiration. I feel a personal responsibility as a Jew, a human and as an artist to strengthen the belief of the eternity of Israel. I believe that every Jew who will see, contemplate and understand the symbolism in my creation will feel proud to be a part of this great nation."*
>
> – Dubi Arie

I would like to thank Nacha Sara Leaf, Associate Director of Art Judaica Educational Foundation (Detroit, Michigan) for permission to reprint her description of The Mission.

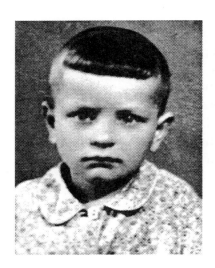 

The Years of Growth

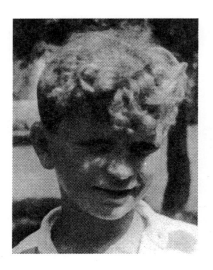 

Sarah Arie

Dubi Arie

5

I KNEW MY ENEMY

"The selection was a constant threat, like a drawn sword over our heads."

— ABRAHAM KSZEPICKI
Treblinka

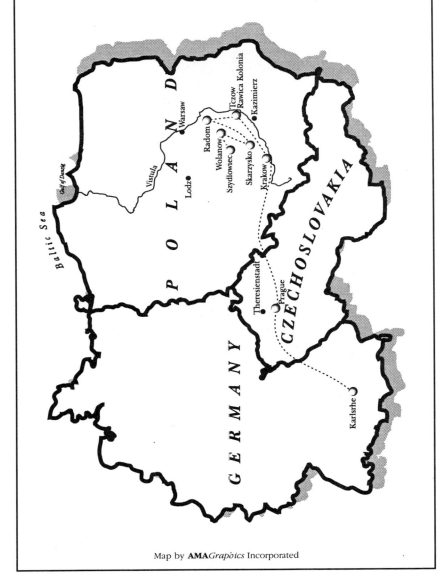

I KNEW MY ENEMY

The Story of
MARJAN ROSENBERG

"Why won't you marry me, Marjan?" For months she had been wanting him to marry her. "Marry me, Marjan," she asked again.

Marjan groaned.

What was he to do? It would have been perfect to accept her proposal, for who would suspect him, if he were married to a Roman Catholic farm girl? But that was out of the question; he definitely could not marry her. He had deliberately avoided becoming involved with girls because of *a secret he could not reveal. This girl was persistent, she wanted to get married and she had made no secret of her intentions – she wanted him. If he succumbed to her persistence, his secret would be uncovered, so he could not accept her offer. He knew, if he exposed himself and revealed his penis, she would know that he was not what he claimed.*

"*Come on, Marjan. Poppa likes you. He thinks you're the smartest boy he's ever met.*"

Marjan tried to think of an excuse, but he didn't know what to do. If she became angry, there was no telling what she might do or say to others. That was all he needed, someone investigating him.

"*All right! I'll marry you,*" *he finally blurted out, regretting his words even before they left his mouth.*

"*You will? You will never be sorry. I'm going to tell my family.*" *She ran out of the barn.*

As Marjan watched her leave, he began to tremble.
My God, he thought. What have I done?
I can't marry her.
She'll discover I'm circumcised.
She'll realize I am Jewish and tell the Germans.

BEFORE 1939, OVER SEVENTY PERCENT OF POLAND WAS dependent on agriculture, with farming being the dominate source of revenue. Many of the buildings gathered into small communities could be seen as outcrops, dotting the flat, rolling fields, meadows and woods. Szydlowiec was ideally located between the industrial city of Krakow on the south and its capital, Warsaw to the north. Just outside the city, a main highway, lined with a variety of stores, served both the local residents and the travellers. Szydlowiec's sprawling community lacked tall buildings, consisting of small clusters of homes spread over a wide area, with few modern amenities and fewer conveniences. The main streets were made from cobblestones and the residential roads covered with hard-packed stones and gravel from the nearby quarry.

The City Hall was the hub of this sprawling city, surrounded by a community of non-Jews and outside this inner circle, the streets stretched in all directions like spokes in a wheel into the Jewish district. Szydlowiec's population numbered about sixteen thousand, of which more than half were Jewish. They were governed by a strong core of gentile politicians with only a handful of Jewish representatives amongst those administering its day-to-day operations.

On the outskirts, a major industry employed many of the area residents, for Szydlowiec was famous for its leathercraft with fourteen tanneries surrounded by many small family shops. They also operated shoe manufacturing businesses as a secondary industry offering an economic stability in which all the residents prospered. As well, there were quilt-making and tailor shops, while nearby, builders obtained many of their raw materials from a stone quarry.

Szydlowiec's toilet facilities were outhouses built next to each home or a few yards from a main building and periodically, the residents would hire someone to drain the contents to prevent excessive seepage. They did not have any running water, purchasing their needs from a water carrier, who drew his precious liquid from a large pure well located near the centre of the city.

Szydlowiec's pace of living was much slower than the bigger cities with very little occurring to cause undue excitement. The routine of each day offered little stress from within and even less pressure from outside the city to disturb the status quo as most Jews led pious, traditional lives concentrated around the synagogue, the study house and the *shtibl* (house of worship). Szydlowiec was populated by two major religions reluctantly suffering each other's presence. Roman Catholic and Jew lived in close contact with each other, in reasonable harmony, albeit with a thin veil of cruelty hiding the distrust and dislike between them. It was this way for years and so it was expected to continue, for many more years to come.

I WAS BORN ON APRIL 5, 1926. THERE WERE FOUR IN MY FAMILY; my father Pinchas, Hela, my mother, Abraham my older brother and myself. Between my father and mother, they had a total of ten brothers and ten sisters of which my father was considered the most liberal by the Jewish standards of those days. Although he ran a very disciplined house, he tended to look upon business as a game in which he interpreted the rules loosely. He owned a newspaper kiosk two miles from the City Hall, just inside the Jewish district. His kiosk was a meeting place where many Jewish residents spent their time *shmoozing* (gossiping) over the news and events of the day. Many were not Jewish, coming from the surrounding area to purchase their reading needs from his kiosk. My father proudly boasted he had the distribution rights to sell any of the newspapers or magazines in any language printed in Poland and his was the only such kiosk in Szydlowiec. He also sold manufactured tobacco products. It was this, more than any other item that got him into trouble more than once.

My father was not active in politics, but when a regulation was passed financially assessing petty traders who sold their wares from stands to pay a daily 2-zloty tax to the city, my father called a meeting together of all the vendors and politicians and appealed to them to have the law rescinded. After long negotiations, the law was revoked.

To suggest my father followed the guidelines governing business people would misrepresent his character. He had a tendency to bend them just enough to make them work in his favour. His favourite *shtick* (mannerism) was selling newspapers to his cronies, then buying them back for less money. This scheme could only succeed because of the attitude of the times and the cooperation of his customers. When his supply of newspapers had all been purchased, which was always the case because he never ordered enough, the original customer would sell his newspaper to someone else for half price. That person would then sell it

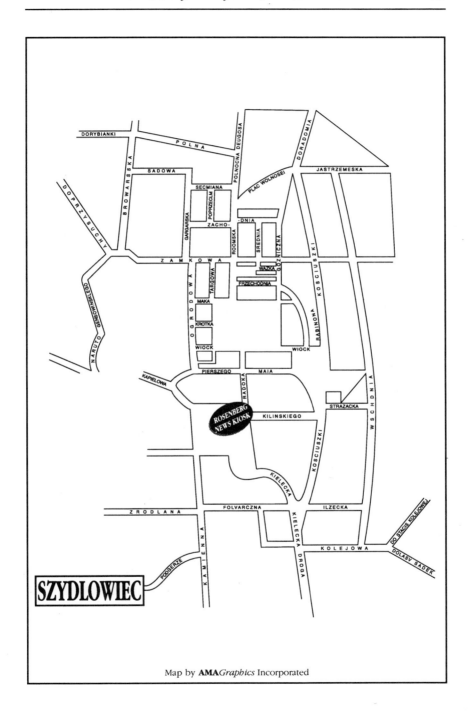
Map by **AMA**Graphics Incorporated

to someone else for a quarter the price, and that person would sell it back to my father below his initial cost. Those reading the newspapers were careful not to tear or mutilate the title page, which my father returned to the distributor as unsold. The distributor would then credit my father's account and everyone was ahead except the confused distributor, who could never understand how my father made a living selling so few newspapers.

Another of my father's business escapades was to take tobacco sold in a can, and roll it into home-made cigarettes and sell them individually for much less than the manufactured cigarettes. It was against the law for a retailer to do this; it was also illegal to sell less than a full package of cigarettes. The unprofessional appearance did not concern any of my father's clients, since they didn't have to buy a full pack and were being charged a bargain price. He was caught, when one of his customer's purchased three cigarettes in front of an inspector investigating business improprieties. My father was arrested and taken to Radom where he pleaded not guilty. His nephew defended him unsuccessfully, but my father was only sentenced to sit in jail in Szydlowiec during the day. For seven days he sat in a chair in an empty room and did nothing. At the end of the day he went home to sleep. My mother would pack him a lunch and a drink because his jail sentence did not include meals. To think that being in jail was a deterrent for future infractions would be a misconception of my father and his roguish manner.

My father rarely showed any emotions or feelings of affection towards my brother and me, nor was there any doubt he considered himself the head of the family and its final authority. At dinner, he always took his place on the short end of the table, signifying this was where the head of the family sat. We had to address him in the third person. "Would father please pass the potatoes," not, "Can I have the potatoes?" Tradition and respect required when the head of the house was not seated at the table for his meals or had died, his seat remained vacant, not to be used by other members of the family again. The seat of authority had great significance to my father, but there were times when he would find himself in conflict with my mother because she had a mind of her own.

The marriage of my parents was arranged by relatives. Love played no part in their union. A cousin of my mother told my father that he knew a nice Jewish girl who would make him a lovely wife. They were introduced and not long afterwards they were married. My mother was a dutiful wife, but was intellectually superior to my father. She loved to read, and was able to argue most subjects with intelligence and foresight. She was extroverted in nature and not afraid of responsibility being the founder and the first president of the local *WIZO Chapter* (Women's International Zionist Organization), and an equal partner in running the kiosk, functioning without guidance and with complete confidence. She kept our home according to Jewish tradition, and catered to the needs of my father, as was the role of a Jewish wife. When my mother needed the freedom to be herself, she would visit with her parents in Krakow or with her family in Warsaw. This was done to help regain her perspective as an individual, and to prepare herself for her role in the family and what was expected of her.

My brother was an apprentice electrician. We were good friends as well as brothers and we shared many experiences in our preteen years. Abraham was shy and very reserved. He had difficulty making friends, often joining me and my friends when we did something that interested him or when he wanted company. Life for young boys in Szydlowiec was hardly exciting, except on Wednesday – market day, when farmers for miles around would come to the city with their produce and set up their stalls. It was a day of fun as we played between the stalls, sometimes getting into mischief.

Our home was a two-storey circular complex with each apartment having access to the inner courtyard. Everyone had to pass our door to get to the street, since ours was the first apartment. Like many of the homes, ours lacked running water and inside toilet facilities. My family occupied a main floor apartment and one of my father's sisters had the apartment on the second floor. Two of my father's five brothers also lived in the same apartment complex. They were strict disciples of the Talmud, referring to Abraham and me as Pinchas' *goyim* (gentiles). They did not look upon us as Jews, for in their eyes we did not live by the rules of the Talmud. Whenever my uncles or my cousins passed our apartment, they would look away from our door to show us in their eyes we did not exist.

Szydlowiec boasted two synagogues and several shtibls. My father was more liberal in his interpretation of the Torah, belonging to a shtibl in which a different member from the congregation led the services every Sabbath. Our shtibl was pro-Zionist, which was another reason my uncles disapproved of us. They frowned on anyone who believed that Palestine should be the land of the Jews before the Messiah returned.

My cousins went to a yeshiva, while Abraham and I went to a public school run by the government. We became very fluent in Polish, to the extent, we were often mistaken for Poles until we revealed our names. At home we spoke Yiddish and Polish. This was a necessity, for my father and mother needed to talk to their customers in both languages if they wanted to make a sale.

There are many memories of Szydlowiec that I cherish, but there is a memory of one person that always cheers me when I reflect on those precious early days of my youth. His name was Itzchak – Itzchak the water carrier. I don't remember what his last name was or if I ever knew it, but Itzchak resembled someone out of a book by Sholom Aleichem. He brought two pails of water to our housing complex every day, pouring it into a large container for each tenant to draw from. He was a short man with large shoulders and walked with his head down from the weight of having to carry the water. His hands were large, his knuckles were like burnt leather from being outside every day for hours. A long pole across his shoulders held two large pails filled with water. Whenever one of his pails was heavier than the other, the pole would tilt, and Itzchak would try to balance that which would not balance. To equalize the pail meant pouring out some water, and water meant money to Itzchak and he could not pour money onto the ground.

Every day, in all types of weather, he would arrive at our building with his two pails of water. In the winter months, with ice and snow on the ground, he would balance his load with precision as he wobbled on his small legs, picking his way around what he perceived was a patch of disaster. During a snowfall, he would trudge into our apartment with his long pole wet from the snow, a mound on his hat, and icicles forming on the pail. His eyebrows would be sprinkled white with snow powder with little splinters of melting ice dripping off his face and his hat. He would stand at the door unable to do anything but appear comical. Without Itzchak, we could not wash, do laundry or quench our thirst. He was essential to our existence and the brunt of everyone's sharp tongue.

"Nu, Itzchak," my mother would say. "Where have you been? The morning's almost gone and I have work to do. Gossiping with Mrs. Shapiro, I bet, you no-goodnick?"

The poor man was everyone's friend as well as everyone's whipping dog. Every day he would be back with his load of water and every day he would hear the complaints and smile. It was a different world to that of today's and our priorities were much simpler and easier to understand. People like Itzchak were an important facet of our lives that has been lost forever.

My ambition was to be a lawyer. When Abraham and I finished public school, I continued my education at a high school in Radom, while Abraham went to work. Szydlowiec was too small a community to support a state high school, which meant for me to continue with my education, I had to enroll in a private school for higher learning in a larger city and pay tuition. To be eligible to attend a state high school, which was sometimes difficult for Jews, it was necessary to move to a larger city.

In 1937, I moved to my grandmother's home in Krakow (my grandfather had died in 1935) to attend a private high school. The Kirshenbaum family were different from the Rosenbergs. Whereas my father's family was reserved, my mother's was warm. Their friendliness made the transition to a bigger city much easier because of the genial hospitality and affection my grandmother, aunts and uncles showed me. They helped pay my tuition and took care of me during the school term. For summer vacations, I went home to Szydlowiec.

By 1939, I was thirteen, a graduate of public school, two years of high school, with good marks and the ambition to make something of myself. Rumours of a German invasion were being ignored by the Jewish population, who appeared filled with their own self-confidence and arrogance about their own personal importance. When the Germans invaded Poland on Friday, September 1, 1939, and overran Krakow in six days, our way of life came to an abrupt end. Within two months, Poland's army was defeated and Poland surrendered. My schooling ended in November 1939 when the Germans closed all the Jewish schools and most newspapers were forced to stop publishing. I feared for my family in Szydlowiec and told my grandmother I wanted to return home to be with my parents. I packed what little I had, and hitched a ride by truck back to Szydlowiec to a life that would never be the same again. All my dreams and all my plans had come to an end.

AT THE BEGINNING OF THE GERMAN OCCUPATION, LIFE IN Szydlowiec appeared normal, but all that changed within a few weeks. More noticeable was the element of verbal abuse that surfaced against the Jews, surprisingly from the gentiles. There was very little physical contact; the Jewish population kept to themselves, but with the arrival of the Germans that changed – and changed for the worse. German soldiers roamed the streets of the Jewish district intent on creating constant fear by intimidating and threatening those whose appearance was too obviously Jewish. The refinements for their cruelty were reserved especially for pious Jews, whose traditional garb – hat and long black coat, beard and sidelocks identified them easily. Fear of being accosted made staying indoors more acceptable and my orthodox uncles and cousins remained in their apartments, depending on their wives to venture outside to obtain their food and to their other needs.

Even attending a synagogue was too dangerous for the orthodox. Polish gentiles would position themselves by the synagogue steps and swear and curse at those who entered. Pushing and shoving followed next, rotten vegetables would be pelted at them and someone was eventually hurt. When it became evident the Germans were provoking incidents against them, the orthodox men remained at home. In other places, the Germans selected observant Jews forcing them to desecrate and destroy the sacred articles of Judaism, even to making them set fire to their own synagogues. They piled the Torah scrolls in the marketplace compelling the Jews to set fire to the pile, making them dance around it, singing "We rejoice that the shit is burning." Feeding pork to pious Jews or plucking beards, hair by hair was another of their sports, as well as setting beards aflame, while the pious Jew ran about trying to extinguish the fire with his hands.

Those belonging to neighbourhood shtibls continued to attend, because the Germans had not discovered what a shtibl represented until much later. When winter came, the

Germans created labour details and conscripted Jewish men and boys to clear the main roads of snow. The old and the young, without concern for health, wealth or position in the community used straw brooms and shovels, as they were escorted from one street to another and forced to do backbreaking menial work in every kind of weather. A few times, someone was shot for disciplinary reasons or just to inflict fear.

By early 1940, the Jews were moved into a ghetto. Fortunately, our apartment was already located in the section designated and we were not forced to vacate our home. As other families moved into our section of the city, we accepted families to share our apartment.

By mid-1940, the Germans created a Judenrat, a committee of Jews, fully responsible for the directives issued by the German Commandant in charge of a much larger district of which Szydlowiec was a part. The Jewish Council were men of influence and wealthy residents whose participation was not always voluntary. Upon penalty of reprisal, they had to assure the Germans that the Jews in Szydlowiec would cooperate and comply with all directives being issued. One of the first orders had to do with housing the Jews from outside the city who were continually being brought to Szydlowiec's ghetto. Jewish communities with less than 500 residents were sent to Szydlowiec and the vacated community was liquidated. The herding of Jews into ghettos did not meet with any serious opposition from the Judenrat, fearing more that the local population might be motivated by outbursts instigated by the Nazis than the confinement. To be confined was deemed preferable to being killed. If there was an advantage to being in a ghetto, it was that it preserved the family, an advantage missing in the labour camps.

The Judenrat recorded the Jewish population by gender and occupation between the ages of twelve to sixty to be exploited for labour, and all labour was not of the same nature, being divided into menial work, skilled, technical and clerical work. Movement was restricted and the rationing of food became a major priority. Anyone found outside the established boundaries were dealt with severely.

It was also decreed that Jewish businesses essential to the war movement must continue to operate under German supervision. Periodically they made demands for silver, copper, gold and jewellery, and if the stipulated amount was not collected by a deadline, hostages were hung or shot. This was the fearful climate we lived in. An environment that led to many deaths. We had become pawns in a bigger game and we were unable to control our own movements. My father took Abraham and me aside one day to counsel us on what to expect and to prepare us for any unforeseen developments. The German presence had changed him into a very solemn and quiet man.

"Listen to my words. No one can help us except ourselves if we are to survive. There is a rumour we will be sent to a labour camp and if this happens, we will need money to buy food and bribes. The Germans think they took everything of value, but I have hidden a few gold coins that each of us must hide for the time it is needed."

Abraham asked, "Where can we hide something that will not be found when they search us?"

"In our shoes," my father answered. "In the heels of your shoes. My friend the shoemaker will fix our shoes so we can put a gold coin into each heel without anyone being aware the heel has been tampered."

"When do we use the gold coin?" I asked.

"When you must . . . only when you must," was my father's reply.

The next day, we went to my father's friend the shoemaker and he altered our shoes, creating a hollow heel. From then on, under our feet were two French Napoleonic gold coins that could mean life or death for each of us. Life, if we needed to use it to buy food and death if found on us by the Germans.

The Judenrat submitted names of men to be part of a labour detail away from Szydlowiec. Abraham's name was on the list, but when he was told, he was afraid to go and asked me to take his place. I agreed. The next morning, trucks drove into the courtyard, and when Abraham's name was read out, I stepped forward. We were driven to Rejow, near a munition factory. When the guards ordered us out of the trucks, those too slow to respond were shoved or clubbed. They pushed us into a single line. An SS officer made his appearance. He walked in front of the line screaming insults, showing his contempt for those in the line.

I was fourteen-years-old, fair-haired with blue eyes. If I wasn't Jewish, I could have been considered the poster person for the young German Aryan role model. The officer approached me shouting, "You blonde Judas," and punched me in the mouth, knocking me to the ground. Dazed by the unexpected blow, I lay on the ground confused and in pain. His blow had loosened my teeth. I spit out the loose teeth and tried to muffle the pain. He did not stop, but continued down the line, hurling his verbal abuse at everyone he passed.

I slowly got up and returned to my place in the line, holding my hand over my mouth. When the SS officer returned, he stood before me, an exaggerated smile on his face, finding my appearance amusing. I had a look of pain, blood trickled from the side of my mouth, and my face was distorted by my expression of trying not to make a sound, and to him it was funny.

He laughed.

He pointed his finger at me and said, "You will work in the kitchen." The SS officer ordered a guard to remove me from the line and I was led away from the work detail and into a building. I remained in the kitchen until the camp closed, and because of where I worked, I was never hungry or ever physically hurt again. The rest of the work detail was sent to Skarzysko to build foundations for barracks to house the workers for the munition factory. For as long as I remained at this labour camp, the SS officer never tried to hurt me again, although he was relentless with everyone else and I never knew why I was spared.

They closed the camp in the early part of 1941 and we returned to Szydlowiec. I learned that my mother and father had been taken away after I left and sent to Skarzysko to work in the munition factory, living in the same barracks my work detail had built. Abraham had arranged to smuggle food to them every day by bribing Polish workers living in Szydlowiec who worked in the munition factory.

I asked Abraham. "Where are you getting the food to give to our parents?"

"The black market," he said. "I have been selling our possessions to barter for food. Last week, I sold Momma's Shabbas candlesticks. I know how much she prized them, but they were made from silver, and for their weight I got enough food for a week."

"How do you know you can trust the Pole to give our parents the food? He could keep it for himself."

Abraham smiled. "He does it for a profit. Others use him. Sometimes, I hear from another Pole, who lets me know she is doing fine. Momma sends me messages through friends, saying the food I send her is a blessing from heaven. She is always hungry, but if not for what she received from me, she would be in greater difficulty."

"What do you hear of Poppa?"

Abraham shook his head slowly, his eyes pained with his sorrow. "He's not well. They have him working with gunpowder, without any protection from the fumes. He coughs a lot, inhaling the fumes into his lungs."

I asked more questions and each answer Abraham gave told the situation had worsened in Szydlowiec since I left the city. Everyone wore a yellow Jewish star on their outer garment. Food could only be purchased at fixed hours and at designated shops, Jewish doctors no longer could treat non-Jews, all radios were confiscated, gentile doctors were no longer permitted inside the ghetto, and all Jewish educational and religious places were closed.

". . . And my friends?"

The look on his face said it all. "I'm not sure. The Germans make raids every day into the ghetto and take people away. Some must be in labour camps, and others I think are dead."

Soon afterwards, we learned our father had died of malnutrition and gunpowder poisoning, but my mother was coping better because of the extra food she received.

The Judenrat posted new names to go to another labour camp and this time my name was on the list. Once again, I was put into a truck, but this time I was taken to Wolanow, a different type of camp surrounded by high barbed wire. Our guards were Ukrainians but the Camp Commandant was an SS officer. Every day we were trucked to a factory manufacturing uniforms and returned to the camp at the end of our shift. Being the youngest in the detail, the Director of the factory, also a German, made me a gooseherder.

The Factory Director had in his possession more than 200 geese which he was fattening for resale. My responsibility was to feed and care for his geese in a small compound he had built in the courtyard within the factory. Each morning, I was taken to where the geese were housed and left to attend to them. The work was not hard. In fact it bordered on boredom and it was difficult to motivate myself to keep active. A few times, I fell asleep and once when discovered by the Director, was beaten for being lazy. He was obsessed with his geese, taking great pains to make sure they were well fed. He sold them to his German employees and shipped them to their families in Germany.

A crisis developed one day with the geese. I was uneasy about the health of some of them, and went to the

Director's office to inform him that several of his flock did not appear well. I never had a reason to enter the office before, and when I did, I could not believe what I saw. Fortunately, the Director was not in when I entered, for my look of surprise was too hard to hide. Behind a desk was a woman working on the accounting books; she was my mother's sister. I stared at her with my mouth open wide. She looked up, saw me and quickly looked around to see if we were alone, placing a finger in front of her mouth, suggesting I was to be silent.

I tried to rationalize what she was doing in the Director's office. Aware of my confused look, panic in her eyes, she shook her head frantically, waving her hands before her face, but said nothing. Realizing my aunt's presence was not what it appeared, I made I did not know her.

"Who are you?" Her eyes roamed over the room anticipating someone's entrance. She held a sheet tightly in her hand, afraid releasing it might make a noise.

"Marjan Rosenberg. I take care of the Director's geese," I responded.

"What is it you want?" She asked. There was a weak smile on her face as we play-acted the scene.

"I came to see the Factory Director. There's something wrong with some of his geese. They're acting sick."

"The Director is not here today," she answered, while indicating with her head for me to leave. "I will tell him and have him see you when he returns."

If overheard, our conversation was innocent. The look on her face made me understand she would contact me later. I nodded my head to let her know I understood and returned to my section of the compound. Later, I learned why her presence was not to be revealed and I was sworn to secrecy.

My uncle was an electrical engineer. He had purchased forged documents claiming he and his wife were German nationals working in Poland when the war broke out. They spoke German and Polish flawlessly and the authorities never questioned their background. Both applied for jobs at the uniform factory and were accepted; my aunt to the office, and my uncle to design electrical plans for buildings under construction on the grounds. They had been able to get away with their impersonation for almost a year. I was the first person who recognized them, and they made me promise not to come into the building except for business, otherwise I would jeopardize their safety. I, of course, agreed.

In time, as I came to know the Factory Director, I found him to be a likeable person. He helped reunite Jewish worker's families by bringing them into his work detail when he learned they were undergoing hardship. We were fed regularly, and although the hours were long, the work was not hard. I got a message to Abraham, in hopes of convincing him to come to the factory. He refused, afraid that if he were not in Szydlowiec, he would not be able to continue smuggling food to our mother, and without the little he was able to get to her, she might die.

I informed the Director about my mother and asked his help. He agreed. A message was smuggled to her, instructing her to walk out the gate on a predetermined day when the Polish workers left at the end of their shift. The Director would be waiting outside in his car. We received word that she agreed. Security was lax at the munition factory because the Germans were confident that if anyone tried to escape, they couldn't go very far and would be picked up almost immediately. To be caught while escaping meant death.

On the day of her escape, the Director and I sat in the car across from the entrance. The workers began leaving the compound and the street was congested with everyone moving in all directions. We kept our eyes on the front gate, waiting to see if my mother would make it through the security and out into the street. When she appeared, I pointed her out to the Director and he opened the car door, signalling my mother to come to him. When she saw me, she immediately entered the car. We hugged and kissed each other as the Director drove away. We returned to his factory and my mother mixed with the workers as if she was part of the original crew.

The next step was to bring Abraham to the camp. Before we could make arrangements, the Germans instituted other plans. The following morning, we assembled for roll call, forming ourselves into rows inside the barbed enclosure. The first indication that something was amiss was when the Commandant entered the enclosure. We should have become wary but no one gave his appearance any thought. He stood facing us, clutching a riding whip in one hand, beating a silent tattoo against his thigh, while Ukrainian soldiers surrounded the camp. He ordered all the men and women to separate into two groups. Everyone regrouped. Using his whip as a pointer, he strolled between the rows of 900 workers, repeating only two words, 'left' or 'right' as he passed his unsuspecting victims. Later, I recognized this routine as the selection process. When he reached my mother, he said 'right' and when he passed me, he said 'right'. After he was finished, the compound had been divided into two groups of about 450 people with the Commandant standing in the middle. He waved at the two trucks parked outside the enclosure. They entered, with the rear of the trucks facing those on the 'left'.

We watched.

From the rear of the two trucks, the guards removed machine guns and set them on the ground facing the group on the left. The Ukrainian's continued to point their rifles at everyone, to discourage any movement.

The group on the left became restless.

We realized what was going to happen, but before anyone could formalize any resistance, the Commandant ordered the soldiers to shoot and the machine guns began to chatter.

Bullets flew across the short distance striking the men, women and children. Only a few minutes passed before the guns became silent. Four hundred and fifty survivors screamed hysterically until the Ukrainian's clicked the bolts from their rifles and took aim at the living prisoners, their intentions obvious. Silence was restored, and the Commandant ordered the men to drag the dead bodies to a ditch not far from the camp. Lime was poured over the corpses and buried.

It was the early part of 1942.

It was Hitler's Final Solution for the Jews

It was total annihilation.

IT WAS POSSIBLE THAT ABRAHAM'S LIFE HAD BEEN SAVED BY HIS refusal to come to the labour camp. His devotion to our mother had conceivably, at least for the time being, been his salvation. Had he come to our camp, he might not have been selected, but as it turned out, I never heard from or saw Abraham again, nor have I discovered what happened to him. The phrase "what if" has haunted me ever since.

That week the labour camp was closed, and most of the survivors including my mother and myself were shipped to another labour camp called Blizyn. Blizyn was another barbed wire compound where uniforms were manufactured and labourers transferred gravel brought from the local stone quarries by trucks, onto the trains. My mother was sent to the uniform factory; I unloaded the gravel trucks at the railroad. My work detail consisted of Poles, who were paid for their labour and Jews, who were slave labourers. To distinguish a Jew from a Pole, the Jews had a yellow star with the word 'Jude' sewn onto their outer garment.

For ten hours a day, seven days a week, I was assigned to shovel gravel from off the trucks into rail cars. The guards were very lax and indifferent. Any attempt at trying to run away, either by going up or down the tracks meant instant discovery, because the area was flat, open countryside, without any places to hide – to attempt an escape was suicidal. The guards would keep watch over the prisoners for a little while, then enter the railroad shack for coffee or schnapps. Occasionally they would look out the window to see what we were doing, but the effort was more token than interest. When we stopped to eat, which usually consisted of weak turnip soup and stale bread, they would come out from the shack and watch us until we returned to our labour.

For the next four months, I shovelled gravel into the rail cars. I became aware of a passenger train that came through on the way to Radom. Each afternoon, it slowed as it approached the station and then increased its speed after it passed. It seemed possible, that I could probably grab hold of the caboose handrail before the guards became aware. Each time it passed, I studied the speed and calculated the effort needed to take hold of the rail. I watched the shack to see what the guards were doing as the train approached, and I gained confidence in my plan when I realized that they never looked out of the window when the train came alongside the building. If I was to make my escape, it had to be before the train schedule changed or my shift was altered. The night before I intended to escape, I went to my mother to inform her of my plans.

She voiced her fear for my safety.

"It's dangerous Marjan," she told me. "If you are caught, they'll hang you as an example to prevent others from trying. Are you sure this is wise?"

My plan for escaping the work detail had its risks, but I was prepared for what might happen. The killings at Wolanow had convinced me that the Germans held Jewish life too cheaply and any day could be my last.

"No, I'm not sure," I answered, "but I must try now before they send me to another labour camp where the opportunity to escape might never occur. It is you that I am worried about. They might hold you responsible because you are my mother, and your life could be in danger. There is also the chance since we see each other so rarely, they might not bother you."

"But the longer you stay, the less chance you have to survive. I don't think you have a choice, but to try."

"Before I go, take the gold coins. You may need them to bribe someone to get you food. I have a plan that if it works, I will not need the money."

"What is your plan?"

"Better that you shouldn't know."

"You're right. Better also I should have a story ready in case they come to me with questions. I will make one up to protect me in case they are looking for reprisals."

Using a small piece of metal, I loosened both heels and removed the gold coins, giving them to my mother. We cried and hugged each other. I left quickly, praying she would be safe until the horrors of the war were over.

The following day, I was shovelling the gravel as usual, but this time, I positioned myself on the side of the railway car facing the adjoining tracks. As I threw the gravel into the car's interior, I kept my eyes on the shack and the horizon from where the train would appear. The passenger train whistled in the distance and I could see the black plume of smoke on the horizon. As the train slowly came alongside of me, I gave a quick glance at the shack to see what the German guards were doing, saw no movement, reached out, grabbed the bar that supported the rear platform and let the momentum swing me onto the steps. I crouched in front of the caboose door, trying to make myself as small as possible, as the train picked up speed and continued out of sight of the building.

Unknown to Marjan, after he escaped, a story was fabricated by his mother and relatives with the cooperation of the Jewish police (an authorized unarmed force whose responsibility was keeping the Jewish population under control) to allay suspicion against her. The Gestapo were told that Hela was not Marjan's biological mother, but his stepmother; Marjan was an illegitimate child whose mother had died many years ago. This story was confirmed by his aunt and his father's sister, and the Gestapo accepted Hela's story and did not take any action against her.

I had made good my escape.

My only fear was for my mother.

As soon as I felt confident that I was free, I removed the Jewish star from my outer garment. By the time the train approached Wolanow, I was hungry and tired and having second thoughts about my escape plan. When I first conceived the idea of escaping, it appeared ingenious, but as I thought over what I was about to do, I wasn't too confident my idea was practical. I was returning to where I tended the geese. It seemed logical if I hid with my relatives from the uniform factory, no one would think of looking for me in the house of a German national. My purpose was to hide in their home until something else could be arranged and move on to a safer place. They told me they never locked their front door. Once inside, I only needed to wait for them to return. The train was approaching Wolanow. I jumped off and ran into the woods. It didn't take me long to reach their empty house. Once inside, I hid underneath the bed, thinking it to be a safe place to be concealed in case they came home with other people.

I fell asleep and was awakened by voices. When I crawled from under the bed, my relatives were shocked that I had returned. Recovering from their surprise, they agreed to hide me until they found a way to get me to a safer place. When they left for work, they locked the front door to prevent anyone from accidentally entering and discovering me. After two weeks, they were feeling the tension of my presence. The risk of detection was becoming too great and they suggested I seek refuge in the Radom ghetto and I agreed.

They gave me money and food and I left their house for Radom. *(My aunt and uncle were eventually betrayed by a Polish employee, and taken to Bergen Belsen, where both perished two weeks before liberation.)*

I WAS NOW SIXTEEN YEARS OLD. IF I WANTED TO SURVIVE TO MY next birthday, I would have to live by my wits. When I entered Radom, I discovered there were two ghettos, with the smaller one having less security. Radom was 30 kilometres from Szydlowiec, and I recalled my father had friends living in that part of the city. The problem was how to smuggle myself into a ghetto. While walking along a street, I saw a Jewish labour detail returning to the ghetto, and when the guard wasn't paying attention, I joined them before they entered the gate. The German guard did not notice that I was the only one without the word 'Jude' on my coat. After all – who would want to break into a ghetto, but a fool?

I walked the ghetto streets asking people if they knew where I could find the friend of my father's, and finally someone knew who I was looking for and where he lived. When I found him, he let me spend the night in his room, but in the morning, he told me where I could find a room for myself. It did not take long to become familiar with the routine of the ghetto and I started to establish myself as part of the Jewish population.

One day, while on the street, I was stopped by German soldiers. They were rounding up men to work in a munition factory in Pionki-Zagorzdon where they manufactured guns and rifles. I was ordered into a truck already filled with Jews and taken out of Radom to a barbed wired compound. My initial fears were that I would meet the same fate as my father, and forced to carry the gunpowder, but fortunately for me, I became a bricklayer's helper in the construction division of the plant, supervised by a German civilian. He taught me the skills I would need, and by an extraordinary bit of luck, I discovered he had previously worked in Wolanow when I was the gooseherder. The food portions at the camp were paltry, but he was very helpful in getting me additional food and cubes of sugar. While working, he told me about his family and his son, who was my age. The news he received about his son from time to time was not promising for his return from fighting at the Russian front. He showed a fondness for me, looking upon me as another son. In time, I felt confident he would not betray me, and I asked his help to escape. He said he would see what he could do.

In the early months of 1943, the German bricklayer heard the camp was being closed and the Jews were to be shipped to a concentration camp. He warned me I had to escape and soon. Desperate to find a way out of the camp, I allied myself to twenty Jews who planned to dig a tunnel out of the compound to beyond the barbed wire. The tunnel would be about one kilometre long to exit inside the pine tree forest surrounding the camp. We dug every night, using loose timber scrounged from within the camp to shore up the walls. For one week we dug until we recognized what we were doing was impossible. We couldn't get rid of the earth we brought up and we were unable to find wood to keep shoring the tunnel walls. We realized our plan was faulty and impractical, so we abandoned the escape.

The Russian army had advanced to the Vistula River. We heard the guns and saw the flashes in the sky from the shelling and knew the Germans would withdraw. Everyone assumed the Russians would soon cross and liberate the area. Unfortunately their time table would not be soon enough for us. News of our relocation became common knowledge and time was running out for us. A Polish labourer offered to help me escape providing I gave him something for his risk. I convinced him with the Russian army crossing the river shortly, he could be richer for his cooperation. I told him I came from a wealthy family from Szydlowiec and if he got me out of the compound, my father would give him one of our houses after the war for his help. The greed of owning a city house, and the pending Russian invasion convinced him he had everything to gain and nothing to lose by cooperating and he agreed.

Being the bricklayer was a German national, his movement was not monitored. He could enter and leave the compound at his leisure, sometimes taking Jews with him to work somewhere and then returning later with them. The next day, he and I walked out of the camp together. Instead of going to the factory, he took me to where the Polish farmer waited and the farmer hid me on his farm. A few days later all the Jews were shipped to Auschwitz.

For two months I remained hidden in the farmer's barn, waiting for the Russians to cross the Vistula River – but they never did. To escape detection from the Poles, I had to convince them I was a Catholic. I asked the farmer if he would teach me some of the more common prayers that might be asked of me if I were questioned. The next day, he brought me a book of prayers, and I memorized every one as well as several hymns he said were popular to most Catholics. He taught me how to pray, to cross myself properly and how to conduct myself in a church. I read about Catholicism, and practised what I learned in anticipation of what might be the difference between living and dying.

The Russian's remained on the wrong side of the river. The farmer became anxious about my presence in his barn. He no longer cared about the house, only fearing he would be executed for what he had done. Finally, he insisted I leave. At nightfall, I began my trek into the unknown, hiding by day and moving by night until I came upon Tczow Rawica Kolonia; a small village with a Roman Catholic church, surrounded by small farms. Cold and hungry, I trudged from farm to farm looking for work and food. Everyone turned me away, until I came to a farmer, who offered me lodging and food in exchange for work. I accepted his offer.

When I planned my escape from the labour camp, I anticipated many problems that I might encounter. Not wanting to be caught meant I had to prepare myself with many stories that would be difficult to verify. The farmer asked, "what is your name?"

"Marjan Rozanski," I answered.

"Where are your papers? I need your papers."

"I don't have any. My father has them."

"Where is your father?"

"We lived in Kazimierz on the other side of the Vistula River. My father was an anti-communist and had voiced strong opinions against them. When the Russians came, my family fled across the Vistula River at night. There was a lot of shooting and I got separated from him in the confusion. He was carrying all our documents. My mother's family name was Helena Badowska, and our family has lived in Kazimierz for many years."

"You cannot work without documents. How can I verify what you say? I can't go to Kazimierz, the Russians are there. Tomorrow, you must go into the village and get new documents. Tonight, you can stay here. I will give you supper, and you can sleep in the helper's room, but tomorrow you have to see the German police in charge of this village and tell him your story."

The German police officer had an office in the church rectory. Could I convince a German official as I had the farmer? If he became suspicious, and ordered the removal of my trousers, they would discover I was Jewish and the chances of my leaving the village alive was slim. I spent a restless night worrying about all the negative possibilities, envisioning a number of plans that were all impractical. Finally, I knew I had no choice but to do what the farmer asked. My hope was the German would believe my story and wouldn't think to check my penis. I could not sleep that night worrying.

The next morning, after breakfast, I proceeded to the back of the church. The German police officer was behind a large desk. He glared at me when I told him the same story I had told the farmer and I waited for him to respond.

"The Russians occupy the town of Kazimierz. How am I to prove your story?" He said.

I said nothing.

He stared at me hard. "Wait here. I will call the priest." He got up from his chair and left the house. Panic set in as my gaze swept the room. The smallness of the office was suffocating, and as I was preparing myself to run, he and the priest returned.

"Ask him," the officer said to the priest.

The priest offered me a friendly smile and asked that I recite a particular prayer.

I did.

He asked me to recite another prayer.

I did.

He asked me to cross myself.

I did.

The priest told the German police officer he was satisfied I was a Catholic. The officer appeared undecided at my performance and continued to glare at me, hesitant in giving his decision. Finally he accepted the priest's judgement, and filled out the documents in the name of 'Marjan Rozanski'. When I left the house, I was sweating and shaking from the experience, but I now had a new identity. All that remained for me was to live my lie until the Russians crossed the river – whenever that might be.

But they did not cross for fourteen months.

WITH MY NEW IDENTITY AND A RESPONSIBLE PLACE IN THE community, it appeared my troubles were over. It seemed only a matter of time before the Russians would cross the Vistula River and I would be free, but time became my enemy because the Russians decided not to move. Instead they appeared to be content to stay where they were and stay they did for the next fourteen months. During that time, I became Marjan Rozanski, farmer's helper and a devout Roman Catholic. I was to learn that having identity papers was the least of my problems and that my biggest obstacle would be my penis.

It became a delicate balancing act in trying to figure when to expose it and when to hide it. Where I worked, the bathroom was an out-house, which offered some degree of privacy, but when in the field, the bathroom was where you worked. When a man needed to urinate, he turned his back on the others and did what he had to do. Sometimes there were workers all around and it was impossible not to expose that which I needed to hide. If there was a need to move your bowels, the worker put some distance between themselves but still exposure was critical. I had to learn to control my bladder and bowel movements if I wanted to survive. To be caught would result in my being shot. My fellow workers did not show me they were sympathetic to the Jewish problem. If anything, they were eager to find a Jew for the reward the Germans were offering. That meant, that the simplest act of going to the bathroom became a major undertaking, which required no error or misjudgment on my part.

During the first two weeks, I became familiar with the farmer and his family. Although not a bad man by the standards I had seen, he and his friends always talked about catching a Jew and beating him. After beating him, they would turn him over to the Germans for the litre of vodka, which was the reward for catching a Jew. "Its good riddance to the Jewish trash," I heard more than a few times. I stood a few feet from them, and listened as they fantasized what they would do if they ever caught a Jew. I knew my life would depend on my ability to outwit them, not on their compassion to help me.

In rural Poland, it is customary for the farmers to go to confession often. The farmer reminded me, I had not gone since my arrival and urged me to go that week. Again I was confronted with a serious dilemma. I did not know what to do. I had no clue what was expected of me or what the protocol was when confessing. The same logic prevailed as when I applied for my identification papers. If I left unexpectedly, the farmer would become suspicious about why I did not return. If I went to church, I had to hope circumstances would favour me with good luck by not revealing my lack of knowledge and expose me as a Jew. To leave the farm and not go to church could also be dangerous because when the farmer went to confession, and he asked the priest, "was Marjan Rozanski here?" The priest would say, "who?"

I entered the church and looked around trying to assess my surroundings. I had never been inside a Christian place of worship, but from what I overheard, I had a general idea what to expect. The inside was dim with the rays from the sun casting beams of light from the small windows into the sanctuary. There were rows of pews with the altar on a dais farthest from the front entrance. I knelt at the top of the aisle and crossed myself before proceeding down the outside aisle towards a cubicle. Inside, I could barely make out the silhouette of a man. I entered the empty side, closed the curtain, sat on a stool and waited. A few nervous minutes passed, while I became accustomed to the dark interior.

From the other side of the partition, a voice spoke. "Bless you my son."

I waited, unsure what to say. The priest remained quiet, and the silence became heavy. Confused and frightened, I blurted out, "Father. I don't know what to do – I am a Jew."

Again there was silence. The confessional window separating the two cubicles opened, and the priest looked at me, saying, "Do not be afraid my son, I will not betray you." We looked at each other for a few minutes, and finally he asked me if I knew any prayers.

I nodded.

He began to pray, "God bless Poland . . . please help the oppressed . . ." and I repeated the words after him. When he finished, we talked, and as I was leaving he said, "when the hyena leaves Poland, and if you do not find any of your family, I will sponsor you for baptism, if it is your wish."

For as long as I lived on the farm, the priest kept my secret. "Come to me whenever your heart is heavy and we will talk," he told me. Over the next fourteen months, we had many conversation on numerous subjects. At no time did he make any attempt to convert me to a Catholic, nor did he make any offer to help me to escape.

The weeks became a year and still the Russian's did not advance. My assimilation into the community was complete and my presence became a matter of acceptance. After I turned eighteen, the problem concerning my penis arose, causing me a great deal of trouble. Being eighteen and never to have kissed a girl was something I had become accustomed to, but eighteen, and never having slept with one was a battle between urge and common sense, especially since there were invitations. The accidental bump, and touch of an innocent hand in a place where my problem lay concealed created sensations that were biologically pleasurable and mentally frustrating. The sexual feelings awakening in me became too awkward to conceal from the naked eye, although buried beneath many layers of clothes. It was impossible for me to engage in any form of sex, no matter how much I wanted to do so. Once naked, instead of an orgasm, it could be the climax to my life.

Tczow Rawica Kolonia, being a small community, I mixed with the same girls socially. It was imperative I avoid any sexual involvement with them, which meant my not seeing any one girl too often. I was successful – except for one young lady who was much more persistent than the others. Finally, unable to offer any more excuses without endangering my secret, I agreed to marry her, for no other reason than to give me time to figure how to escape before I was forced to commit to my promise. Her father and mother were overjoyed. My prior education, and the ability to converse on a variety of topics impressed them. They were proud their daughter was going to marry a clever boy, and had the 'bans' published.

I knew I could not go through with the marriage because I was unable to sense whether she would keep my secret or reveal to the authorities my true identity. I agonized over what to do. The risks were astronomical, and it wasn't smart on my part to have let myself be compromised as I had, but the die had been cast and my options became fewer and fewer. Three weeks passed, and I had yet to develop a strategy to remove myself from my predicament. In the meantime, there were suggestions of having sex now that we were betrothed. My many excuses were not being met with any undue understanding from her and my position was becoming untenable. Running away seemed the only solution and I began making plans to save myself. On January 1, 1945, the Russians finally crossed the Vistula River and overran our village on January sixth.

I was no longer a prisoner.

Using our new found freedom as an excuse, I told my future father-in-law I was returning to Kazimierz to find my parents. Once I found them, I could bring back all the missing documents to confirm my identity and speed-up the marriage process. He thought that was a very good idea. I informed my employer, I would be leaving to find my father. Before I left, my future father-in-law gave me two bottles of homemade vodka, which he had brewed. He was a bootlegger, and had access to large inventories of illegal made spirits, that he sold to supplement his income.

He told me to hurry back.

I shook his hand.

I left.

I never returned.

I REMAINED IN RUSSIAN-HELD TERRITORY UNTIL THE WAR ENDED and then returned to Szydlowiec. It was a sad place as there were only three Jews left in the whole city, an uncle of mine, his son and my former public school teacher. They had been hidden by a Polish farmer until liberated by the Russians.

I did not want to remain in Szydlowiec with memories that haunted me of my lost family. There were no records of what had happened to my brother and the camp where my mother had been, no longer existed. I journeyed to Radom in hopes of finding some of my relatives. At this point I did not know if my aunt and uncle had survived or for that matter any other relatives from my father or mother's side. While there, I registered with the Jewish committee in charge, and posted signs on the different bulletin boards, stating I had survived, and if anyone knew the whereabouts of anyone from my family to contact me.

Applications were being accepted for the police force and I submitted myself as a proposed candidate for no other reason than to earn an income while in Radom. In the unlikely case my mother or brother were alive and came looking for me, I had a permanent base where I could be located. The only documents in my possession were those of Marjan Rozanski and under that name I completed my training and was assigned to be the desk sergeant at one of the police stations.

I took it upon myself to help Jewish refugees gain access to their former homes. Jews would come to the station, and ask for the Jewish sergeant and they were directed to me. The refugee whose premises were now occupied by gentiles would reveal to me where he had hidden jewellery or valuables in his house or apartment before being forcibly removed. They needed to gain access to their premises. Could I help them?

We would go to the apartment or house, knock on the door, and explain we needed to get something from inside belonging to the previous owners. Wearing my police uniform, the residents found it difficult to object and would reluctantly let us enter. The Jew would point out where he had hidden his valuables, and I would break a hole in the wall, tear up the floor or open a couch and remove the valuables, to the amazement of the people occupying the premises. We would leave quickly, but the gentiles would complain we had removed items that were now theirs and follow us, venting their anger. Sometimes official protests were lodged against me, but to no avail, because the valuables, and the owner had disappeared and it was now impossible for the complainer to get financial satisfaction. For my part, their complaints were ignored, and since I had very little money, there was no way the gentiles could get from me any compensation.

One day, my past life finally caught up with me. The father of the girl I was to marry was arrested for bootlegging. As luck would have it, the arresting officers brought him to my precinct to be held for trial. Two policemen entered with the farmer between them and brought him directly to my desk. He looked up at me, recognized me and exclaimed, "Marjan Rozanski! So here is where you went? We have been looking for you. You broke my daughter's heart by not coming back. How could you do this to her?"

He was the last person in the world I had ever expected to see, I was struck dumb when I recognized him. Composing myself, I leaned forward, so our faces were close to each other. I said, "I could never have married your daughter. I am a Jew."

Straightening himself quickly, he stared back at me with a look of amazement and then anger on his face. He shouted, "I knew it! I knew it! You were just too smart to be a Pole, you fuckin' Jew." He was locked in a cell. The next day, I arranged for his release and had his vodka returned to him. He left the building and it was the last time I ever saw him.

In the meantime, I posted more notices throughout Krakow stating I had survived the war and if someone was aware if anyone from my family survived, to contact me in Radom.

My mother called.

She had been in Theresienstadt Concentration Camp when she was liberated. She arrived in Radom, and stayed with someone she knew while I continued with my desk job and helped Jewish refugees get their valuables. One day, someone tried to kill me for being a troublemaker and it seemed prudent that I relocate to another city. I had myself transferred to Lower Silesia, where I joined the police force with the rank of lieutenant. By the fall of 1946, I had become disenchanted with what I was doing and the direction in which my life was going. One night, I left the police station, and crossed the border into Czechoslovakia. It would be fifty years before I would return to Poland again.

I went to Prague, Czechoslovakia where I remained for one month. It was a difficult time for me, trying to decide what I wanted to do with my life and where to take myself. I registered with J.I.A.S. *(Jewish Immigrant Aid Services)* who were able to get me into Germany, to an uncle and aunt in Karlsruhe. He was the managing director of a large textile mill and he gave me a job. He later found another aunt and uncle who survived as Oskar Schindler's employees and brought them to Karlsruhe. By this time, my mother had joined us.

The question arises: How many survived? From my original family, only my mother and I survived. From my father and mother's family, from ten brothers and ten sisters, only two of my mother's sisters and one of my father's sisters survived the Holocaust.

In 1947, my uncle located two Polish friends with their niece Lily Ingber and a nephew who had been in Hungary and brought them to Karlsruhe as well. My mother remarried. She remembered a member of the Kirshenbaum family had emigrated to Canada in 1920 and had become a rabbi. With the help of the Jewish agency, she traced him to London, Ontario and he agreed to sponsor the family.

In 1948, before we left Germany, I proposed marriage to Lily Ingber and she accepted. My mother and I left for Canada and Lily joined us a few months later. On February 5, 1949, we were married.

I HAVE BEEN BLESSED WITH A WONDERFUL MARRIAGE, CHILDREN and grandchildren. My life has been structured to help others overcome the trauma of the Holocaust and to improve the quality of life for the aged and the needy. My experiences have made it impossible for me to ignore the suffering and pain of others less fortunate. At first I became motivated by my guilt because I survived and later by a genuine need to do something positive with my life. I have been told my presence has made a difference to many, and for that I am grateful for it would be a shame to have survived the Holocaust, and wasted my life.

I was able to put the past behind me. After a lot of mental adjustment, I placed what had happened to me into an acceptable perspective that eased the pain of remembering, and calmed the anger of hate for what had befallen not only myself but the millions that died and the few that survived. That is, until I was interviewed by The Toronto Star on Thursday, December 3, 1992. My portion was a small part in a supplement that gave a general overview about the way Holocaust Jews lived in Toronto. Subsequently, I received a letter on July 1993 that reawakened the memories and events I had experienced between 1939-1945, forcing me to analyse portions of those events with more care because of what the letter requested.

The letter was from a Polish Committee in Toronto. The writer informed me he had read the supplement and had contacted the parish of the priest who kept my secret, and the farmer's family where I was employed. They would be contacting me personally. Forty-eight years after the fact, my past had caught up with me.

When I received the first letter, it was from another priest of the parish. He stated, he was glad I was doing well, and informed me the priest whom I had known during the war had since died. He asked if I would like to sponsor a holy mass for the priest for keeping my secret, and offer a testimony on his behalf to Yad Vashem for saving my life.

The request was sincere, yet in trying to respond, I was forced to ask myself many questions I had never had to consider. For fourteen months the priest was the only one with whom I could talk to without pretending to be someone else. Our relationship was never as friends, but as two people who despised a common enemy, and in some way recognized we had a common God. Until 1953, I wrote letters, and sent parcels to him, grateful for his Christian charity, and in recognition of what he had done for me. One day, my last letter was returned marked address unknown.

After much soul searching, I replied. My answer was difficult but I believe it was correct. I included with my letter, a money order for $100.00, and requested it be used towards a holy mass in the priest's honour. I informed the writer I could not in all good conscious give testimony for him as a righteous gentile to Yad Vashem. My confession that I was Jewish occurred in a confessional box. As a Catholic priest, he was sworn to keep secret that which was told to him within that sanctuary. I have no hesitation in recognizing he was a man who believed in his responsibilities over any personal views he had or felt. The priest exercised his beliefs with integrity, and kept my secret because that was what he was sworn to do and for that I will always be eternally grateful.

During the fourteen months I lived in his parish, he never made any overtures to help me to escape. At no time did he propose, initiate or volunteer any plan that would remove me from the sphere of the German's or to lessen the risk of capture. I know he risked his life to keep my secret. If it ever came out he always knew who I was, his life would have been forfeited, but that could only have happened if I told or if he told.

He was not my enemy nor was he my friend.

In April 1994, I received a letter from the widow of one of the farmer's son. She wrote that her husband's father had passed away, and they were glad I had survived and was doing well. They asked if I would like to visit with them? The tone of the letter implied that they always knew I was a Jew, even during the war years.

I wrote, reminding them, they never knew I was Jewish when I worked for their father. Had they known, based on conversation I had often overheard between them and their neighbours, they would have denounced me for the litre of vodka that was being offered by the Germans. I enclosed a money order for $100.00, and I requested the money be used to purchase gifts for the farmer's grandchildren, and they be made aware the gifts were from a Jew.

I never heard from the parish priest or the farmer's family again. In retrospect, I am convinced if my real identity was uncovered, the farmer would have turned me over to the Germans without hesitation and ultimately my life would have been taken. With the priest, I was safe. Revealing who I was to anyone in that community would have been tantamount to committing suicide on my part. It was not a safe haven in which to hide.

I have asked myself many times, why did I survive and not my brother? Why did I survive and not any of my religious uncles or cousins? I have never been able to find an answer that satisfied me. Was my life spared so the work I am doing in the community could be done? Was I lucky or was it preordained? So many questions – so few answers. Circumstances obviously worked in my favour or maybe it was God's will? For every answer, there appears to be two more questions.

Who do I blame?

Maybe a passage from a diary of a young girl might be the answer to a question that has many answers:

> "Who has inflicted this upon us? Who has made us Jews different to all other people? Who has allowed us to suffer so terribly up till now? It is God that has made us as we are, but it will be God too who will raise us up again. If we bear all this suffering, and if there are still Jews left, when it is over, then Jews instead of being doomed will be held as an example. Who knows, it might even be our religion from which the world, and all peoples learn good, and for that reason, and that reason only do we have to suffer now. We can never become just Netherlanders or just English or representatives of any country for that matter . . . we will always remain Jews but we want to, too."
>
> – Anne Frank

Monument to the Jews of Szydlowiec

MICHAEL ROSENBERG

Michael Rosenberg was the recipient of the Commemorative Medal for the 125th Anniversary of Canadian Confederation from his Excellency The Right Honourable Ramon Hnatyshyn. "The award is being given to those persons who, like you, have made a significant contribution to Canada, to their community or to their fellow Canadians. The decoration is a reminder of the values of service, individual respect and community effort on which Canada was built and which its quality of life will always depend."

DON'T WORRY: IT WILL BE GOOD

"The good die but live on in the example they provided."
— ADAPTED FROM TALMUD

Batia Schmidt remembers: Helmut Rauca stepped onto an earthen mound at the end of the square and ordered all Jews to pass by him. By late afternoon, all 26,000 Jews passed him on his review stand. On his right, Rauca had 2,007 men, 2,920 women and 4,272 children, a total of 9,200 Jews. It was these who would be marched to their deaths.

Map by **AMA**Graphics Incorporated

To the Teitelbaums, קוראים
Thank you for listening to my story from Darkness to Light. With Love,
Faigie Schmidt Libman
Feb. 23, 2015 ♡

Batia   Feiga

DON'T WORRY: IT WILL BE GOOD

The Story of BATIA and FEIGA SCHMIDT Libman

The sheet of paper in her hand was small and the words on it barely occupied half the space that could be used, but their meaning was worth more to her than any gift. Over the years she had received hundreds of these messages, written in scrawls of imperfection with spelling mistakes and crooked lines, each one cherished for the treasure they represented. Somehow the pain she suffered, the hurt she experienced, softened when her heart was touched by the magic words.

A half century has passed. Where have all the years gone? The dead have long been buried, but the memories of those who are no more are fresh and alive because not enough time has passed to erase what happened. For the moment this and all similar papers in her possession were her only cure. She placed it lovingly on her desk and raised another. Tears formed, but she smiled with enjoyment at what she read.

"They should never feel the pain we suffered during the war," she said, "but must grow up and understand who they are and what they are, and realize that we survivors are an integral part of their future. We are pages in a book. Each one a story. Some read like fiction, because it is too unbelievable to accept what was experienced. Others are dramas that make the reader grip the pages with hope and expectation. Some have happy endings. Most do not. Each person has a beginning, a middle and an end. Yet, in that end, even though the main character survives, are they still alive?"

She lay the papers on top of the desk and fanned them across its surface. The colours were alive, most messages were in pencil, some in different coloured ink. "The children will someday become books of their own," she said quietly, "but now they are unfinished manuscripts on the threshold of understanding. They are innocent as I was until 1941 when the Germans invaded my homeland. At the age of seven, I learned a new way to live . . . a way that continues to haunt me fifty years after the war has ended. If only I could be seven again . . . ."

She closed her eyes and pointed her finger to the fan of sheets and touched one. Her eyes opened and she read the letter and smiled, then laughed. "They call me Morah (Teacher) Faigie. It sounds like a rank in the army, but a different kind of army, an army of knowledge. I remember during those terrible years, hearing the adults refer to a soldier as untersturmfuher (lieutenant), to the kapo *(prisoner in charge of a detail), to the lagerkommandant (commandant of the camp) or the kommandofuhrer (supervisor of work detail). They held a rank – a rank that sent fear through every part of my body.*

"Many people strive to attain a position of merit. It is usually the culmination of a life's ambition. Over the years, I have acquired four, each as important as the other, but some giving me more pleasure at different times. Rank that does not inflict fear – but love. When Benny asked me to be his wife, it was a moment that took away some of the ugliness in my life. Two survivors united to plan a better future. When my children call me 'ema' (mother) it is like silk caressing my skin. My grandchildren call me 'bubby' (grandmother) and I see the future that Benny and I have made and I know the past is behind me, but I cannot let it be forgotten. Maybe that is why these letters are important. They call me Morah Faigie and I know in their hands goes our future, our memories and our hope. They have told me they owe me more than they can repay for the knowledge I have imparted, but that's not true for it is I who owe them, as I owe my mother for saving my life. If it were not for my mother, I would not be here. I would never have known Benny, had children and grandchildren and feel what I do now when I read these precious words of love. They say they owe me and I reply they have repaid me a million times over, but how do I repay my mother. Some debts last a lifetime."

ALONG THE BALTIC SEA, SURROUNDED BY LATVIA, RUSSIA AND Poland is the small predominantly Roman Catholic country of Lithuania. It is a flat land covered with many farms and lakes with heavy emphasis on animal raising. Only 25,200 square miles in area and a population before World War II of about two million people of which 150,000 were Jews. Over the years Lithuania was occupied by Poland, Russia, Austria and Prussia but after World War I, it gained its independence. In 1940 it was again occupied by Russia.

Lithuania was not a tolerant country and the Jews were repeatedly subjected to pograms. Although subjected to increasing hostility, their economic, cultural and public achievements were unparalleled among Jews. In many ways, the Jews of Lithuania were different from Jews of other European countries, in that they spoke a special Yiddish dialect that differed from the Yiddish spoken anywhere else. They were known as Litvaks well-educated, sharp-witted, a flair for humour as well as being aggressive. Their influence on Jewish culture around the world was historic. Their way of life was based on the Written and Oral Law, resulting in Torah learning flourishing throughout the country. They lived in Vilna, Minsk, Kaunas and Pinsk and were in the majority in many of the smaller rural towns.

Kaunas was the capital city of prewar Lithuania with a population of about 128,000 people of which 35,000 were Jewish. It was a cultural city with elementary schools, commercial high schools, technical schools and universities. For the Jews who could afford higher learning, there were Hebrew high schools and Talmud Torahs as well as five daily Jewish newspapers, a Jewish hospital and an orphanage. Kaunas was considered a modern city with wide boulevards and many shops and theatres. A city of beauty that became ugly with the changes that befell it.

Faiva and Batia Schmidt had one daughter, Feiga, who in 1940 was six years old. They had a second floor apartment in a beautiful large stone and brick three-storey building in a middle-class district in Kaunas. Their apartment consisted of two bedrooms, sewing room, kitchen and dining room. Faiva's parents lived nearby on the same street. Faiva was a tall, good-looking, gentle, soft-spoken man and a successful businessman who owned an international bookstore on the main street of the city. Theirs was a more affluent lifestyle, one of the few families in possession of a telephone and an apartment that had guest facilities with a bath tub.

Favia had four well-educated sisters, three of whom left Lithuania before the war for France, Israel and Argentina. Chava, the youngest, was attending a local university in 1941. Favia had a deep appreciation for learning, possessing the ability to speak five languages; traditional Yiddish in the home and Lithuanian outside as well as German, Russian and Hebrew. To him, life was a continuous education and he was always eager to expand his knowledge, whether it be through books, art or theatre.

Faiva and Batia were exact opposites in many ways. Batia, although not a tall woman, had a tendency to dominate a discussion or situation by her physical energy and take charge attitude. Born in the small community of Krakinova, she aspired to be a nurse, a vocation her father thought unsuitable for a Jewish girl. Strong minded, refusing to abide by protocol, she convinced her father to let her go to College in Kaunas. Reluctantly he agreed and Batia over the next three years spent many hours learning not only to be a nurse, but to be the best nurse possible. Upon graduation, she was immediately hired by the Jewish Hospital and quickly became the head nurse of the surgery department, spending long hours beyond her allotted time making sure that everything functioned according to her requirements. She ruled with authority and an iron fist, unwilling to tolerate sloppiness or indifference when it came to attending the sick. The demand for obedience was carried over to her home and into her married life.

Batia's dedication to her work made her an absent parent, replaced by a governess-cook who cared for Feiga during the day. They also had a maid. Batia's absence from the early years of Feiga's life resulted in Feiga becoming more attached to her father, and as a young girl, she had a inner fear of her mother because of the way she controlled their lives. Faiva accepted his role, content to allow Batia to govern, allowing him the opportunity to concentrate on his never-ending search for knowledge.

THE GERMAN INVASION OF POLAND ON FRIDAY, SEPTEMBER 1, 1939 was followed by the Soviets occupying Polish territories east of the Vistula River. On June 15, 1940, the Soviet army invaded Lithuania, ousted the government, followed by widespread arrests and killings. Public life in Lithuania underwent very little change once the Soviets were in control. The Soviets encouraged the population to involve themselves in the many cultural events sponsored by the government.

Favia encouraged Feiga to participate in several of the sponsored events, wanting her to expand her educational horizons, transferring his passion for knowledge to her. She was also being taught to play the piano to make her aware of the beauty of music. As the only child, her parents doted on her with many material items, buying Feiga expensive clothes for her extensive wardrobe. Batia enjoyed showing off Feiga when not confined to the hospital, but these excursions were too few to change Feiga's opinion of her mother. A constant visitor to Feiga's maternal grandparents in Krakinova, as well as being spoiled by her paternal grandparents who lived down the street, Feiga enjoyed all the comforts of a child who had everything.

The Soviets tried to prevent news of the German atrocities in Poland from reaching the Jewish population, not wanting to upset them into responding with measures that would be counterproductive. However, they were unable to stop the flow of refugees escaping into Lithuania with first-hand news. When the Schmidt's and their friends discussed what they had heard, Batia voiced her opinion that what the Germans were doing in Poland could be repeated in Lithuania if they ever chose to break the Pact with Russia. Her friends could not conceive that Germany would want to fight Russia and they felt their lives were not in jeopardy. Batia felt they were wrong.

Her fears were realized on June 22, 1941, when Germany invaded Russia and subsequently entered Lithuania two days later. The lives of the Jews in Kaunas changed forever. In one day, Germany overran the Baltic countries and the Schmidt family entered the European conflict. German bombers flew over Kaunas at dawn on June 22, 1941 and with deadly accuracy bombed the industrial section of the city, meeting no resistance from the Soviets. Fearing what the Germans might do, many Jews tried to leave the city, but only one train left Kaunas. Many tried to leave on foot, intent on trying to reach Leningrad. At the border, the Russian army would not let them enter and the majority returned to their homes and their eventual deaths. Later, history would record of Lithuania, its near total annihilation of the Jewish population from a single country.

With the help of Batia Schmidt's writings, Feiga's memory and facts from history, the massacre of Kaunas becomes a living memory of the inhumanity of the Holocaust. Kaunas was the hotbed of Lithuanian nationalistic aspirations, with many eagerly awaiting the arrival of the Germans, vowing to eradicate their Jewish enemy. The Germans became the excuse for the anti-Semites to raise their heads from the filth of their prejudice and to make barbarism into an art of butchery.

Batia wrote about the first three days of war when German bombers dropped their cargo of death. *"It was one of those lazy days in June in 1941. The sky was clear, there was no stir of leaves on the trees and the sun had wrapped everything with her rays. But something strange and ominous were in the air. Then night came. The Jews of Kaunas went to sleep with the hope to meet another day. It was now Sunday the 22nd of June 1941. Suddenly at four o'clock in the morning, a deafening series of crashes broke the stillness of the night. As if by signal, everybody was in the streets. The airfield and the outskirts of Kaunas had been bombed by the Germans.*

"The Russians who had occupied Lithuania for nearly a year abandoned our city and Kaunas was left without any administration. The Lithuanian anti-Semites now had a free

hand to plunder and rob the Jewish stores. With robbery alone, they were not satisfied, they ransacked Jewish homes, attacked and murdered innocent people.

"All the doctors and nurses of the Jewish Hospital were immediately mobilized by the director of the hospital. Being the head nurse of the surgical department, I went on duty at once, as hundreds of casualties were being brought in. Not knowing what the next few hours would bring, I took my husband and child along to the hospital. We worked all night to give first aid to the wounded.

"The condition of the wounded brought to our hospital was indescribable. The hospital looked at that time like a morgue. Still vivid in my mind is one of the wounded, a little eight year old girl. Her arm was shot through and had to be amputated. 'They killed my parents,' she told me. 'I am all alone now . . . why did they have to shoot me?'

"It is impossible to describe the suffering and the conditions. Under normal conditions the capacity of the hospital was about 500 beds, but as the wounded were brought in, every available place was jammed. Nevertheless the great suffering of the Jewish community in Kaunas at that time was nothing to compare with the degradation and punishment we had to endure in the later years of oppression.

"Three days after the bombings, the Germans entered the city. They came in motorcycles and in automobiles. With their greyish uniforms and gray faces, they all looked alike. The sky looked gray too, and so looked the sun.

"The streets were soon deserted by the Jewish populace. All was quiet in Kaunas and in our homes the living-dead crouched. The first one's to feel the German power were the Jews. We were ordered to leave the city and to move into a special suburb. We had to crowd three and four families into each small house. That was the beginning of the Kaunas 'ghetto'.

"At the same time our hospital was transferred to a building near the ghetto. We worked day and night to *organize the hospital, to make the patients somehow comfortable and to give them emotional and physical help. For about five weeks we all worked together as one team. We took turns during the day to return to our families.*

"Late one afternoon, when most of the staff was away to see their families, the hospital was mined and blown up. All the patients, a doctor, a few nurses and the rest of the help who were on duty at that time perished. I was one of those who had left for the afternoon."

FEIGA REMEMBERS: "THERE ARE MEMORIES SO VIVID, THEY ARE AS if they took place only a few days ago. On the other hand, I seem to feel that certain things happened, but I find it difficult to know why I feel that these thoughts must have happened. I was only six years old and my world was my father. My mother, although only five feet in height, was a dominate force in our home and my thoughts of her were more of fearing her than devotion. I loved my father and I had trust in anything that he said or did. When it came to my mother, however, I knew if you followed her instructions, everything would be turn out good for us. But you followed them not because it was what must be done, but because she insisted it had to be done.

"My father allowed her to control the events in our home. His passion for learning occupied much of his time and for him to be allowed the freedom to do what he enjoyed even if it meant relinquishing his authority, he didn't mind. The irony of my mother's energy was that she seemed to have a negative perspective on people and events, always seeing the worst rather than the best. In this way, she focused her actions on resolving what she was experiencing to her satisfaction, instead of adapting to it. It was this perspective that was the edge for survival that we needed.

"I remember my mother complaining about some situation that she was critical of, or about a person who didn't exert what she felt was the maximum effort and whose results were unsatisfactory. After she finished speaking, I would say, "don't worry . . . it will be good," and although my comment often fell on deaf ears, it seemed an expression that was often spoken.

"The German's bombed Kaunas. My mother woke me and I dressed quickly. I was frightened by the noise and explosions in the distance. Our telephone rang and my mother rushed to it, made a few remarks, but listened more than talked. When she got off, she ordered, and that is how I recall, *ordered,* that we were going to the hospital with her. She had been instructed to go alone, but she would not let us stay behind. My mother made her own rules and my father offered no objection. While my mother put a few essentials into a bag, my father helped me to get ready. Holding my hand, we rushed from the apartment and ran to the hospital. There was black smoke over the buildings and tremendous noise. Lots of noise. People were crazed with fear, running in many directions at once, neither knowing which direction was safer than the other. My mother pushed ahead, determined to reach the hospital regardless of the chaos that engulfed the city.

"We entered the hospital to a scene of bedlam and utter chaos. People arrived on their own, some bleeding profusely from wounds that were gaping holes in their bodies, arms broken, some using planks of wood as crutches, their heads and bodies swathed in home-made bandages. Ambulances arrived and departed, cars with injured civilians and trucks carrying the maimed and dying drove to the emergency door, one behind the other creating an impossible jam. My mother was given instructions on where to concentrate her skills and we were told to go to a room where the family of the staff were staying. We were told to keep out of the way while the injured were being attended. When we entered the room, it was to find men, women and children subdued and frightened, some crying, some hysterical and many numb with fear.

"Later, I went to the doorway and looked down the corridor. Laying on portable cots, tables and stretchers were small children, and I went to them and talked to those able to talk. I spent the rest of the day in this manner until my mother showed up, tired and exhausted to take my father and me to a room where we had something to eat. That night and for the next two nights we slept in the hospital ward, laying on the floor beside the wounded and the sick. My mother worked around the clock, controlling her area with an iron fist and the discipline of a general. The reference 'general' became associated with my mother and her authoritative manner, but never to her face. On June 25, 1941, we were ordered to return to our homes and await the next crisis."

BETWEEN JUNE 25 AND 26, MORE THAN 3,500 JEWS WERE murdered by Lithuanian students and released convicts who roamed the streets of Slobodka carrying iron bars searching for Jews – intent on only one purpose: the deaths of any they found. Within hours of the Germans' arrival, hundreds of Jews were seized from their homes and forcibly taken to the Ninth Fort, *(one of the fortifications that surround the city)* where they were murdered. They organized pogroms, rounding up non-Jews to show them how to mock, abuse, injure and murder Jews without fear of reprisal or prosecution from the law. The Germans re-enacted Kristallnacht in every town and city they occupied. They took hundreds of Jews to the cemetery and shot them, seized others in the streets and dragged them to a garage, where hoses were placed into their mouths until their stomachs burst. Unable to hide and no place to flee, the Jews were found, taken from their homes, tortured and beaten. Using revolvers, axes, rifles and knives, the students and convicts spent two nights in an orgy of death and violence, killing, decapitating and robbing without fear of reprisal and with the blessings of the German authorities.

After the massacre ended, the Germans took charge of the remaining Jewish population. First came the reign of terror, followed by a more sophisticated terror – the systematic elimination of an entire city population in stages.

From the moment the Germans entered Kaunas on June 26, 1941, the Schmidt family never knew whether the next moment would be their last. It was Batia's ability to make the right move at the right time as each successive purge of the Jewish population took place that made them survivors. In the ensuing confusion, it would have been easy to integrate with the non-Jewish population because their surname was Schmidt, but the Lithuanians pointed them out to the Germans as Jews and they were caught in the web of destiny that was to take them from the heights of social standings to the subterranean level of living in the bowels of hell. Anti-Semetic rules governing the lives of the Jews were implemented. They were ordered to wear the symbol of Zion on the outer portion of their clothes, front and back. They could not hire any non-Jewish help, doctors were forbidden to treat non-Jewish patients and food could only be purchased at designated shops during specific hours and all radios had to be turned over to the Gestapo.

On July 15, 1941, the Kaunas ghetto was established in Slobodka, a suburb of Vilijampole; surrounded by high barbed wire and patrolled by dogs and soldiers. Living conditions lacked sanitation facilities and had very few amenities. It was an old section, next to the Vilija River, neglected by the city government, lacking sewers, running water and with only a few paved roads. Before the ghetto was formed, the district housed about 7,500 people of which 3,000 were Christians. Christian residents were forced out of Slobodka to make room for the 35,000 Jews of Kaunas and told to take whatever Jewish homes were vacated. A Judenrat Council of five prominent Jews were appointed by the Germans, to govern the ghetto and to represent the German authority.

They gave the Jews only three days to leave their homes and forbid any wheeled vehicle, whether it be an automobile, a cart or a child's wagon to be used to transport their belongings. Everyone was forced to carry whatever they could on their backs or in their arms. The Schmidt family packed their suitcases with valuables and extra clothes to be used for barter – especially Feiga's exquisite clothes. Wearing multi-layers of wearing apparel, Batia prepared herself for the time when these items may someday be needed to secure food.

In Slobodka, they were assigned to a room with many people. As many as eight people in one room, which meant in most cases, more than one family shared the room. That month between 6,000 and 7,000 Jews were taken away for a work detail outside the city. By the end of the month, some survivors staggered back physically maimed and psychologically scarred, reporting the mass execution of everyone.

By mid-August, ghetto living had become a way of life, with the promise that although hard, it was at least liveable.

Batia continued to write in her diary:

"Regardless of the great loss, we built in the ghetto a new hospital. On account of unsanitary conditions, the number of patients increased, but we worked with great zeal to help them all. Surrounding the ghetto was barbed wire and everywhere inside that barbed wire was hunger, suffering, spiritual and physical pain. The Germans and Lithuanians were guarding us day and night, but we went on."

Batia made the rounds of the ghetto with a doctor, seeking the sick, even though they had very little medicine. She changed bandages, made them comfortable, encouraged them with her promises of a better tomorrow, instilling in them the strength to survive another day.

Then a day that Batia dreaded occurred. Feiga came down with scarlet fever. To be sick was in itself a death sentence, but to have scarlet fever, a communicable disease, was death for anyone that contracted it and that made Feiga an undesireable liability. Batia placed Feiga in their makeshift hospital and used her skills to prevent the illness from spreading. When the German doctor came to determine who would be transported to a concentration camp, Batia moved Feiga from room to room with the help of the other nurses, until the doctor left. This procedure was repeated until Feiga's fever broke and Feiga returned to their room well enough to be cared for away from the hospital.

The Lithuanians and Germans randomly entered the ghetto and invaded homes, using any excuse to instill fear when no excuse was needed. If it was dirty, everyone was removed and shot. Batia would encourage people to keep their rooms clean, not to give those who enjoyed inflicting pain an excuse. But they needed very little excuse.

Feiga remembers . . . living in a room with a lot of people. "We were always hungry. My mother was never one to allow circumstances to control her life, so one day she covered her Jewish star with some matching cloth, took some of my expensive clothes and smuggled herself out of the ghetto. Later she returned with food. I don't know where she got it, only that whenever circumstances warranted, she would disappear with my clothes and return with food. Years later, I learned that my mother would brazenly walk the streets and knock on doors of people she knew from the hospital; non-Jews she had helped. She would barter my expensive clothes for food and arrange for future purchases by being told what other of my clothes these people were interested. To be caught outside the ghetto meant death. To live without food meant death. To my mother it was not a matter of bravery but of necessity, and when hunger could no longer be ignored, my mother did what had to be done. Her initiative repeatedly was the deciding factor between living and dying. To my mother, dying was not an option to be considered but one to be overcome. I lost track of how many times she saved my life."

ON AUGUST 18, 1941, SS HAUPTSCHARFUHRER HELMUT RAUCA entered their lives and each day became the last for many of the tens of thousands remaining Jews. Rauca was a part of the Gestapo Jewish Affairs Specialists for Einsatzkommando 3, Einsatzgruppe A and it was his responsibility to oversee the day-to-day operation of the elimination of the Jews of Kaunas. He was a man devoted to his cause; obedient and loyal when honouring the SS Party creed and prepared to be harsh and ruthless to perpetuate the master race philosophy. He planted informants in the ghetto, made final decisions on the setting of food rations and fuel, became a ruthless enforcer dealing harshly with all infractions and made unexpected visits to the Judenrat to instill fear into their ranks.

On the day Rauca arrived, the Judenrat was ordered to summon five hundred of the city's intelligentsia to organize the Lithuanian archives. Only three hundred volunteered. Not satisfied with the response, the Gestapo entered the houses looking for men to fill their quota. Batia was at the hospital and left Feiga and Faiva in their room. The door was broken open and soldiers entered and dragged Faiva out, leaving Feiga alone and frightened. She told Batia what happened. The two awaited the bad news, expecting to hear of Faiva's death. Twenty-four hours later Faiva returned unharmed. That day 534 Jews were executed.

Very few days passed without some form of German reprisal being carried out to the detriment of the Jews. The Judenrat Council attempted to defuse the situation with perseverance and logic, but the results were always the same – the Jews continued to be eliminated. On October 28, 1941, the Council received instructions to have the Jewish population of Kaunas assemble in the square for a roll call. They were warned that the order was mandatory for everyone, the old, the sick and the crippled, no exceptions and no excuses would be tolerated. Those not obeying would suffer the consequences for their disobedience. It was the judgement of the Council that they were being prepared for some impending disaster. The Judenrat agonized on how to let the people know that the directive was not theirs but the German authorities and it might be a prelude to another scenario of mass killings. Finally they issued the directive, wording it in such a way that they hoped the people would be aware to comply would be dangerous. Unfortunately, not complying meant anyone found outside the square would be shot. Almost everyone showed up and the Jews of Kaunas waited for the outcome.

Batia Schmidt wrote in her diary:

"In October of 1941, the Gestapo ordered that all the Jews in the ghetto, whether young or old, sick or invalid, assemble on a certain field as a population census was to be taken. That was only an excuse to get us all assembled, for on the field the Germans picked out 10,000 Jews and drove them four miles beyond the ghetto where in mass graves all were executed. There was not one family that day that had not lost at least one member, but again life went on. In a couple of days the children went back to school, people went to lectures and self-organized concerts – stubbornly wanting to live."

At eight in the morning on October 28, 1941, the 26,000 Jews of Kaunas assembled in Democracy Square. They were grouped in sections of their work brigade, many wearing arm bands marked with what they did in their work details. A troop carrier arrived and the soldiers positioned themselves around the square. Helmut Rauca marched into the square carrying his whip with an Alsatian dog at his heels.

Rauca stepped onto an earthen mound at the end of the square and ordered all Jews to pass by him. By late afternoon, all 26,000 Jews passed him on his review stand. On his right, Rauca had 2,007 men, 2,920 women and 4,272 children, a total of 9,200 Jews. It was these who would be marched to their deaths.

Feiga remembers . . . "My mother told me to get dressed in my good clothes in case we didn't come back. As usual,

Batia was preparing herself for the worst – being relocated. Batia was nervous. For the first time that I can remember, she seemed to have lost control of her normally reserved composure. She didn't know what to do and when she made a decision she changed her mind. I remember as if it was yesterday watching her in her confused state, and tugging at her sleeve. Batia looked down at me. 'Don't worry,' I said. 'It will be good.'

"The instructions were explicit, families had to stay close together. People were dragging the sick to the square in cots, on mattresses, even on planks of wood because no one could be left behind. When we arrived, Rauca was standing just outside of the square, holding a whip and whistling. He was wearing white gloves and there was a dog sitting next to him. He was an imposing figure; his arrogant face glared at the Jews as they passed, his back straight, shoulders back with contempt on his face. He shouted in German, left or right and the people confused by what was happening, obeyed his directive. There didn't appear to be any rhyme or system to his pointing until he had established two distinct groups.

"On the left, the majority were old, sickly or impaired in some obvious fashion. Those who looked healthy, presentable or well dressed were on the right side. I looked to see if there was anyone I knew in the other section, not knowing why we had been separated. My grandfather and my father's youngest sister, Chava, were looking at us from the left side, confused by the small but impenetrable gulf that separated us, while my grandmother, my mother, father and I could only stare back helplessly. Our side was ordered back to our homes. Those on the left were taken to what was called the Small Ghetto, an area accessible by footbridge on the opposite side of Paneriai Street.

"On October 29, 1941 those in the Small Ghetto were forced to line up, men in the front, women and children in the rear and ordered to march to Fort IX for relocation. We watched them going along the road toward the hills from our windows. Kaunas is in a little valley surrounded by high hills in which there are old forts overlooking the valley, built many years ago as a defence against foreign invasion. From where we stood, we could see the people, thousands and thousands of them shuffling up the road into the hills toward the forts. The old were helping the invalid while the soldiers screamed and hollered at them to move quickly, occasional striking someone who didn't abide the threat. My mother said she thought they were being resettled somewhere else to reduce the overcrowding, but we later learned otherwise.

"We heard their weapons firing and at first we didn't comprehend what was happening. As the shooting continued unabated, the realization of where our neighbours and family had gone, became painfully obvious. They were indeed being relocated, but to their graves. Later a few survivors returned to Kaunas, having escaped the march and they revealed what they had witnessed. The next day, more returned and told of the massacre.

"They ordered the Jews to remove their clothes and place them in a neat pile. In sections of 100 they were made to lie in an open pit, side by side until the diameter of the pit could hold no more people. The Germans then shot everyone with machine guns. A base of lime was poured over the bodies and the process was repeated again and again until the pit was full. Those who were wounded were buried alive.

"When the news spread to the Jews in the ghetto, everyone remained in their rooms awaiting the next day with fear and dread."

DURING THE LATTER PART OF 1941 AND EARLY 1942, FAIVA WAS put into a work brigade. Batia worked in the infirmary and Feiga remained with the children. To prevent the children from being kidnapped by the Germans, the parents hid them during the day.

Feiga studied and read books in a basement without windows, most times supervised by an adult. When the Schmidt's heard they were looking for volunteers to build an aerodrome, Batia applied for the family and they were accepted. Once more Batia was sent to the infirmary to care for the sick and injured prisoners. They were quartered in temporary barracks and given beds of bare board bunks, a blanket and a thin pillow.

Feiga remembers . . . "One Saturday, the Jewish prisoners were celebrating the Sabbath and I stayed up very late, singing with my friends. The next day, I was tired and did not want to get up from my bunk. Each morning, my mother left the barrack and joined the work detail, returning late in the night. She always went alone to the infirmary leaving me and my grandmother behind. Children were not allowed in the infirmary. This morning, she came for me and said, "You are coming with me." I complained of being too tired, but my mother insisted and as was always the case, she made me get out of the bunk, get dressed and go with her to the infirmary. I was very angry with her.

"At the end of the work day, we returned to the camp to find it empty. It was as quiet as death. There wasn't a soul anywhere and the only sound was the wind blowing into the empty barracks. We learned later, that after we had left, German soldiers arrived in trucks and took all the elderly and children away. My friends were gone and so was my grandmother – sent to Auschwitz. Sent to their deaths.

"We grieved for the loss of my grandmother, my father especially. A gentle man by nature, he took the loss of his mother very hard. Again, my mother's intuition had proven to be the saviour of my life. Why my mother felt that I must go with her to the infirmary that day of all days, she doesn't know. She remembers being compelled to be sure that I did not remain behind. For me, my thoughts were that we were still together; my mother, father and I were still a family. As long as I knew we were together, I could face the pain and the horror of the next day – even uncertainty could be confronted. There was comfort in knowing I was not alone. That week they closed the labour camp and the detail returned to the Kaunas ghetto.

"In Kaunas, food was scarce, Jews were being slowly starved to death. Tired and hungry, Batia always went to the infirmary, sometimes with clothes hidden on her person that belonged to Feiga and returned with smuggled food. In desperate times, many people took desperate risks. The punishment for being caught smuggling food was death. Many risked it. Many died.

"Nothing remained the same. To say that each day was identical would be true as well as misleading. There was no way to measure fear by comparison; to weigh hunger by degrees or the desire to live by quotas. Fear walked ahead, behind and beside everyone. It turned friend into suspicion, a Lithuanian into the reincarnation of the devil and a German into physical evil in human form. No day passed without pain. Each hour heightened the awareness of how short life could be. Each minute a sigh of survival and each second a desire for freedom. And always time inched forward.

"By March 1944, the population had been reduced to a third of its original size. That month, the Gestapo and the auxiliary police moved from house to house searching for children, while their parents were on a work detail. Many children were hidden in closets, basements, attics and in the drawers of dressers. Even those that did not make a sound were eventually discovered by dogs used to smell out their hiding places. A mother, when confronted with her two children being removed from her house was offered a choice to keep one. Unable to decide, she joined the children instead. The Gestapo returned for two days looking for more children but were unable to find them. Those that survived never went outside again. I was always at the infirmary with my mother."

THE ADVANCING RUSSIAN ARMY FORCED THE GESTAPO TO evacuate Kaunas. By July 1944, more than 27,000 Jews had been murdered; there were only 8,000 left. They were ordered to assemble in the square to be transported to a concentration camp. The ghetto was being liquidated but only 3,500 assembled, the Schmidt's among them. They were loaded into trucks and driven away, most knowing, not to a concentration camp, but to join the 27,000 who had already disappeared. The Germans set fire to the Kaunas ghetto to flush out more than 4,000 who were hidden. As the fire raged and people tried to escape, the Germans forced them back into the flames or shot them when they broke from cover. When it was over, the Germans were satisfied that no one survived – but eighty-four managed to live through the fire to tell the world of their ordeal.

In Batia's diary, she wrote:

"We were packed into freight trains like cattle and shipped to a concentration camp in Stutthof. There the men were separated from the women. They deported the men to Dachau and the women remained in Stutthof, putting an end to the chapter of the Kaunas ghetto."

Stutthof Concentration Camp was established in February 1940, twenty miles east of the Free City of Danzig. By 1944 it was being used to replace some of the camps already over-run by the Russians. Known for its brutality, it is estimated that only 3,000 women survived from over 30,000 that passed through in the nine months prior to being liberated. Stutthof operated under the most appalling sanitary conditions, poor nutrition and the imposition of unspeakable brutal punishment never before equalled in history.

Feiga remembers . . . being in a cattle car and squeezed into a corner. There were so many people that everyone bumped against each other. It wasn't long before the people were hungry and thirsty and many of the children could not stop crying. For two days they were in the cattle car and at no time were they fed or given water. The smell from their unwashed bodies filled the air and in time the odour of human excrement overpowered the sense of smell, nauseating and sickening those confined.

"We arrived at the new camp to unbearable conditions. The door of the car was opened, releasing the terrible odour that had been trapped inside for two days. An SS officer ordered the women and children out; the men were to remain inside. With the use of their rifle butts, the soldiers pushed the weakened and sick women and children out of the car, some barely able to stand. I clung to my father, begging him to come with us. Someone tore my hands away from him and as the last woman was removed, the door was slammed shut and the train moved away. I heard my father calling, but within seconds, the train was gone. He was gone . . . my father was gone.

"As we waited in line to be processed, word reached us that the Germans had intended to gas everyone but the ovens had broken down. They marched us to a barrack. To this day, I will never forget the mountain of shoes that stood outside. Every colour and shade, every size and style. Thousands and thousands of shoes, rising to a height that my mind finds difficult to comprehend. We were ordered to remove our filthy clothes and waited naked for the doctors to pass judgement on us. They examined just the adults in every crevasse and crease in their body, looking for hidden valuables. The children were not touched. In single lines, the thousands of women filed into a shower and were deloused. Afterwards, clean clothes belonging to earlier prisoners were given to us. I was ten years old and like any modest ten year old, I reached for anything that would cover my nakedness.

"My mother stopped me. The soldiers leered at everyone, but my mother did not care. As a nurse, she had seen many naked bodies and she chose to ignore their stares. Her mind was on our survival, not on our nakedness. She was not ashamed as much as angry.

"She rummaged through the clothes finding a skirt with a jacket. She selected a bra. At the age of ten, the only breasts I had were in my mind; I was flat as a board. She found some brown wrapping paper and crumpled them into a ball and filled both cups of the bra, giving my appearance a more adult look. The jacket accented the artificial bulge she had made. Next she went to the pile of shoes and found a pair that had higher heels than I was accustomed and increased my height. She turned me in all directions, staring intently at my appearance. I did not know how I looked, but my mother seemed satisfied. 'That's good,' she said and then looked for clothes for herself. When we left the barrack, the guard asked my age and my mother without hesitation said – 'twelve'. Twelve year-olds were sent to work. Ten year-olds were sent to their death.

"The barrack was no more than walls and a roof and layers of bunks. My mother went to the infirmary, while I was placed in a work detail. The sights my eyes saw were too horrible to accept. To breathe with pain, to move with pain, to taste it, smell it and lie in it became a nightmare for an adult and a unbelievable horror for a ten-year old. And then I got scarlet fever again. I was put into the infirmary, but to be diagnosed by a doctor would have meant my death. My mother moved me every time a Nazi doctor came to inspect the ward until I was able to return to my detail. Until then, my life depended on my mother's ingenuity and guile.

"When my mother heard that a work detail was being assembled to dig ditches in a labour camp, she volunteered. A premonition warned her to leave Stutthof. Again she lied about my age.

"We were put to work on a detail that was hard and cruel. People died of dysentery and typhoid fever every day. The guards were known German criminals, sadistic animals that thrived on human misery. Inflicting pain was their stimuli and we were the means of their pleasure. Not for our bodies, but for our misery, which they enjoyed.

Batia wrote:

"In Stutthof, 1,200 women were selected to go to a labour camp to dig trenches. Me and my small daughter included. We were glad to be selected for we wanted to leave Stutthof and its gas chambers where people were being gassed and burned every day. To save my daughter from being taken from me, I had to dress and disguise her to look like a big girl for only people that could work were taken. Under blows and curses, the Germans used to drive out the women onto the fields, give them a pick and a spade and lead them three kilometres from the camps to dig trenches. Inside my head, anger would scream out from the abuse I saw. Kill me, I screamed. Kill my daughter. Kill everyone, but enough pain. Enough torture. Kill us or let us go.

"Like this we lived in the tents till the snow covered the grounds and the earth froze. Our rations were a bit of watery soup, a piece of stale bread and black coffee. Later, I and my daughter got assigned to the hospital. The hospital was overflowing with sick women with swollen stomachs from hunger, dysentery and swollen feet. Even water we did not have enough. With the left-over coffee, we used to wash the hands and faces of the patients. When no one could hear me, I would cry."

The stench was overpowering. The women were in near-starvation condition, laying in their tents with glazed eyes and racked with pain. Without blankets, some stark naked on meagre bundles of straw, laying in their urine and excreta, their limbs covered from the bites of the lice that infected every tent. They waited to die – wanting to die – beyond help. With a twisted sense of pleasure, the guards shot only four women a day, allowing them to suffer as long as was possible, enjoying their torment.

Batia wrote:

"In January 1945, our guards started to feel a bit uneasy. Allied planes flew over us. We also heard shooting from the distance. We found out from our guards that the

Russians were pressing forward. What good music this was to our ears. Suddenly our guards received orders to move our camp further away from the front lines. We marched 50 kilometres in the rain, wind and sleet. One day, we were led into a camp to stay overnight. Later we found out that we were supposed to have been gassed there, but somehow the orders were not confirmed as the Nazis were too confused from the pressing allied advances.

"A whole day we marched till we reached a forest. Deep in the forest, we found abandoned huts. We were very happy to find any place to put our weary heads down, no matter what happened. That night, all that I lived through was vivid in my mind. Is it true, that my little girl is still with me? How quiet and peaceful everything is here with the snow covering everything. We are like a part of the bushes and broken down trees that protrude through the snow. The spruce and pine trees stand proudly covered with their evergreen branches. It appears to me that they hold themselves aloof being afraid of the armed two-legged animals.

"They laid mines all around the huts, in order to get rid of us. They never could fulfill this order for more and more shooting was heard. A loud shrill pierced the forest. That was the signal for our guards to abandon us – and they did."

Feiga remembers . . . "On January 25, 1945, the camp was evacuated and the death march began in the midst of a snowstorm and bitter cold wind. Stragglers were shot, while many prisoners simply dropped in the snow and froze to death. I pushed myself, willing my body to move. The snow made passage difficult and when I stumbled, my mother reached down and lifted me to my feet, dragging me until I could regain a hold on the snow. My feet froze and the pain made me cry. Again and again I stumbled only to feel my mother's hand on my collar. The Germans drove by, stopping to shoot any who had faltered. As we trudged forward, head down, we waited to be killed. When we rested, my mother rubbed my feet and put my cold shoes against her body to thaw out the cold. Death looked so inviting, but my mother never let me think of anything but life.

Batia wrote:

"They left immediately and in all the confusion, we thank God that we were forgotten – the guards were gone. We were left alone. The next morning, there was no one to awaken us. It seemed strange that we did not hear the shouts and curses of our guards. The living skeletons crawled out of their huts to see what was happening. Some of the stronger women went to the highway to find out what was going on.

"Suddenly they saw from far, uniformed men riding on horses. One woman yelled, 'I think those are Russian soldiers.' The other women stood frozen in their tracks. The riders advanced and stopped to ask the women who they were and what they're doing here. The captain of the group who was on a white horse, turned out to be Jewish. He told the women that the Russian infantry was marching a mile behind and that they were scouting the area. The women took the soldiers to see the rest of us.

"You cannot imagine our happiness as we saw the captain on the white horse riding toward us. The soldiers cried as they saw us, living skeletons, sunken eyes and grey faces. With all the strength they could muster, the women pulled down the captain from his horse and started to hug and kiss him. We nearly choked him to death had not his friends rescued him in time. The women were laughing and crying, some to the point of hysteria. Like angels from heaven, they had saved us from death. In reality, we still thought it was a dream.

"They gave us food and the starving women pushed the food into their mouths, fearing they would not get more. I ran around shouting, "don't eat a lot!" but many would not listen and some died because they ate too much. They had not eaten for so long, their bodies could not take the shock of so much food.

We marched backwards, in other words, we dragged ourselves onto the side of the roads, further away from the battlefield. Towards us were the Russian tanks and infantry, marching on the snowy highway. The whole world around is white and it seems that the sun is shining."

THE WAR WAS OVER AND BATIA AND FEIGA SCHMIDT MADE THEIR way back to Kaunas. They knew that all of their immediate family were dead, but hopefully they prayed they might find someone, but such was not to be. They journeyed to Lodz, Poland when they heard that someone thought they saw Faiva alive. With high expectations they read the bulletins that hung on the walls of the buildings. On one such list, they saw the name of Faiva Schmidt: died in Dachau. The realization that her father did not survive devastated Feiga and she collapsed under the stress of the news. They met other friends from Kaunas who told them the tragedy of Faiva's death.

Convinced that his wife and child were dead, he lost his will to live. When the train pulled away from Stutthof, his life had no further meaning and as the weeks and months passed, he became weaker and weaker, not as much from the lack of food, but the lack of hope. When the prisoners were force-marched from Dachau, he gave up entirely and died on the march. According to friends, he died the third week in January, the same week that Batia and Feiga were liberated.

They registered as refugees and were placed in a displaced persons camp in Badgastein, Austria, where Batia worked as a nurse. Feiga returned to school. Batia decided they had to build a new life but not in Europe. She located her sister in Montreal, Canada and they emigrated to a new life.

Batia arrived in Montreal on March 21, 1948, without proper accreditation for continuing as a nurse. Her previous experience, although impressive, was not recognized. She was angry. She returned to school to earn her nurses' certificate. In January 1952, at the age of forty, she completed her nurse's course at McGill University with the highest marks in her class and quickly rose to become the head nurse for the Jewish General Hospital in the paediatric wards until her retirement twenty-five years later.

Batia moved to Toronto to be near her daughter, Faigie Libman and her grandchildren and her great grandchildren. Batia found that at eighty-two, aging was not the blessing she anticipated. Unaccustomed to being dependent on others and unable to accept that her body could no longer fulfill the needs of her mind, she became difficult to handle. The very characteristics that were instrumental toward her survival were now to her detriment. The once proud and independent woman would not submit to age and the burden fell on Faigie to help.

FAIGIE LIBMAN DISCOVERED THAT LIFE COULD BE A WONDER OF God's miracles. In Montreal, she fell in love with a Polish survivor and became the mother of three boys and a girl. She excelled in school, graduating as an accountant. When her youngest was in kindergarten and she was there to help, the teacher said she should be a teacher because it was evident she was a natural the way she responded to the children's needs. The miracle of her survival had taught her many things and until that moment she was unaware what skills she possessed. She felt she could share what she had learned with pre-kindergarten children and decided to return to school at night for her certificate.

Her family moved to Toronto in 1972 and she continued to teach Junior Kindergarten for over twenty years at Associated Hebrew School. In that time, about one thousand children have been in her class, learning not what is in a book, but what is in a person. To understand themselves and who they are as well as who they must be. To love others and to be loved. To treat others with respect and to be treated with respect. She told them that Hitler came to power with one vote so it is important to vote. She stated that life goes on and it is important that they remember the bright side. Study! Vote! Be nice to each other.

Although Kaunas and Stutthof may be many years in the past, they are constantly on her mind. Her success is written in the hundreds of letters she received from the students and their parents, one of which she selected:

Dear Morah Faigie,

We wish to thank you very much for Elizabeth's most wonderful introduction to Associated. Her Junior Kindergarten year with you as her teacher has been one filled with warmth, caring and learning. Every day she was happy and excited both before and after school.

Thanks again!

Love Shari and Robert

* * *

"What is happening to my mother is sad." Faigie paused before she continued. "It's not that she saved my life that I feel beholden . . . that is a small part of it. Because of her, she made possible the lives of my children and my grandchildren and that is the miracle of my survival. There are thousands of people who knew my mother, but have never known her as I have. I and so many others are alive because of her. She affected our lives by the fact that we survived and only she is responsible.

My mother spent a lifetime being a nurse. On numerous occasions, her presence meant the difference between someone living or dying. During the war, she tried to ease the pain of the sick and dying. Afterwards, she was responsible for the birth of the living. She chose to work in paediatrics because it meant life and I chose to work with children because that gave me the opportunity to make children understand the meaning of life.

I have touched many children with my experience of horror, but my own children are testimony to the beauty that hell made. Many survivors will always carry their scars inside of them unable or afraid to remember and relive what they were forced to endure. And many, like myself, have been able to make a life for ourselves and our children, hoping that our experience will make them focus on the past as they build a better future. Sometimes, the seed that we give birth to may be the instrument of a better life for others.

One day my oldest son came to me with shocking news. "Mother. I've decided to make aliyah to Israel."

I paled with the impact of what he had said. "Why? Are you not happy here in this country?"

"Yes. But I'm a Jew and I belong in Israel."

"Where did you get this idea?"

"From you."

"From me? How?"

"From what you've been through. From what you have done with your life. From my upbringing. From the values you and my father have taught me, my brothers and sister. From the respect I have for myself that you instilled in me. From being your son."

He now lives in Israel. He is married and has children. He lives by the Book as does his whole family. He has returned to his roots, the roots that Hitler foolishly thought he could destroy. *I have planted an acorn from which has grown an oak and its leaves will bring shade and comfort for generation as yet unborn.*

Between Kaunas and Toronto, a lifetime has passed. It was made possible because of my mother's will and strength to survive. After my father was sent to Dachau, I became dependent on my mother, borrowing her strength and her courage. I have come to understand her better now that she is in the twilight of her life and I regret that aging is proving to be a hardship for her. She deserves better for what she has done. This is her hour of need. Never before would she allow me to carry some of her burden until now. It was her pride that gave her strength. It was her strength that gave her courage. And now aging is nibbling away at her pride. She was there for me, when I needed her strength. I am here for her, when she needs mine and I am grateful that I can at last repay a debt.

To some, they will say I have Jewish guilt, because I survived and others did not. To others it may appear to be an obligation that fell on my shoulders because there was no one else. In all probability there is a degree of truth in those explanations, but there is still one reason that should be added – it is respect.

In my mother's present mental confusion, I find myself holding her hand, and offering words of comfort. 'Don't worry . . . it will be good,' I say, and I pray it may be so.

1934
Batia and Feiga Schmidt
Kaunas, Lithuania

July, 1939
Krakinova, Lithuania

1936, Krakinova

1938 Kaunas, Lithuania

Feiga Schmidt (Libman) and her mother Batia Malamud

1997, Baycrest, Toronto.

7

SKETCHES FROM OUT OF THE DARKNESS

A sheet of paper in his hands,
a stub of a lead pencil hidden on his body
and an image before his eyes
that he wanted to capture.
When he finishes, what will he do with it?
Where does he hide his treasure?
Will anyone ever see what he saw?
Questions.
Questions without answers
because he waits in an extermination camp
and knows not whether tomorrow will ever come.
But he draws his image,
hoping that it will not be in vain.

Drawn by Yehuda Feld
Warsaw (1943)

In 1941, Stanislav Rozycki wrote in his diary:
"on the streets children are crying in vain, children are dying of hunger. They howl, beg, sing, moan, shiver with cold, without underwear, without clothes, without shoes, in rags, sacks, flannel which are bound in strips round their emaciated skeletons, children swollen with hunger, disfigured, half conscious, already completely grown-up at the age of five, gloomy and weary of life."

Excerpt from "TELL THEM: THE JEWS ARE FIGHTING IN WARSAW"
– *The Light After The Dark II*

Still not sure of what had taken place at the selection, she approached a woman to find out if she knew what had happened to her mother and where she might be.

"My name is Judit Schwartz, my family lived in Mezocsat and I was separated from my mother."

The woman's face showed no expression.

"Do you know where they took my mother?"

The woman pointed to the large chimney belching black smoke.

Excerpt from "THE MIRACLE OF MY SURVIVAL"
– *The Light After The Dark II*

Sketches From Out Of The Darkness

Drawn by Yehuda Feld
Birkenau (1944)

The camp was closed and everyone was put onto trucks and taken to Pionsk where we stayed only four days. We were told we were being exchanged for German prisoners and that we were going to Switzerland. The beatings which had been common in other camps almost ceased. We were given additional food as an act of good faith by the Germans. We lived in shacks not fit for humans and out on the field and we waited for the day we would be set free. They lied.

Excerpt from "Dare I Forget"
– *The Light After The Dark II*

Sketches From Out Of The Darkness

Drawn by Woznik (1936)

The cousin scoffed at Mordecai.
"There is nothing to fear. I am a farmer, not a politician.
I deal with everyone. They won't harm me.
They need farmers to grow their produce.
Don't panic.
They will take charge over the government,
change a few rules and then everything will return to
normal. Stay and you will see."
"You are wrong. We are not staying
and I am begging you to come with us," Mordechai
pleaded, but the cousin would not change his mind.
He gave them as much food as they could carry
and bid them to "Go with God."
Bags in their hands, they left the cousin's home
and again joined the stream of refugees heading east.
The last time they saw him, he was standing at his front
door watching them, waving goodbye. *(The cousin was
shot in front of his home by the Germans before he had a
chance to talk.)*

Excerpt from "THE JOURNEY"
— *The Light After The Dark II*

Sketches From Out Of The Darkness

Drawn by Yehuda Feld
Poland (1942)

Before the Germans completed the ghetto registration, my father applied for relocation to Piotrkow.
To my father's surprise, the authorities gave us permission, and we packed all the belongings we could carry, and journeyed to a community not too far from Lodz.
What we did not know was we were doing the Germans a service by going to an established ghetto.
We left everything that was a part of our past except our memories, and in due time, even our memories would be left behind.
Although the journey to Piotrkow was short, it was painful.
We were not alone on the road, but each of us had withdrawn into our thoughts where no one could enter.

Excerpt from "THE GLASS FACTORY"
– *The Light After The Dark II*

Sketches From Out Of The Darkness

Drawn by Yehuda Feld, Poland (1942)

"WHY, ZAIDA?"

Fiction or is it Fact?

AN OLD MAN AND A YOUNG BOY SAT CLOSE TOGETHER ON THE grass in a field. They were different in size, but they had a similarity of features; the shape of the head, the contour of the chin and the structure of the nose. A relationship of blood, but generations apart. There was silence between them as they listened to the rushing stream, the birds, the squirrels, the breeze and their thoughts.

The old man was troubled. He had passed his seventh decade and the last several years of his life revolved around his son and his grandson. He loved them both. They were his hold on a world he had built after surviving the war and the Holocaust. He had heard from his son that his grandson was asking questions. Questions that the old man would rather not answer.

The clear stream bumped its way down the slight incline, churning white froth against the partially submerged rocks. Multi-coloured leaves floated madly along the rapidly unstable water, moulding themselves to the highs and lows of the current. There were many sounds competing with the babbling of the stream; the screech of birds, the chatter of squirrels and the rustle of leaves as they fell, blanketing the ground with a collage of red, orange, yellow and brown.

Turning to the old man, the little boy asked, "Zaida. Birds have fathers and mothers don't they?"

The old man flipped a small pebble into the stream. They watched the waterspout it made and the ever-widening ripple until the current prevented any more from being formed. "Yes," he said.

A squirrel hopped in front of them, a chestnut in its mouth. He stopped, his teeth ground away at the morsel.

"Zaida. Squirrels have fathers and mothers too don't they?"

The old man squinted at the young boy, curiousity on his face. "Yes," he answered.

The little face looked up, a frown on his forehead. "How come, you never had a father or a mother?"

"That's not true, but why are you asking?"

"I never saw them. There are no pictures of them. Nobody talks about them. That's why."

The old man gazed at a branch, bobbing and dipping over each wave. Two rocks captured its flight. Stretched between them, the water that was taking the branch downstream had now become its prison pouring over it, locking it in place.

"It's hard to explain," he whispered.

"Why, Zaida? What's so hard?"

The old man gazed back at the stick, urging it to free itself. How can I tell him what I have been unable to tell anyone in fifty years? He won't understand at his age. I was his age when it all happened and I still don't understand. I'm like the stick, caught between the pain of the past and the uncertainty of the present. Trapped in my head are thoughts that I won't let out because I can't find the key to open the door.

A candy wrapper floated into view. It struck the stick as the current pushed it between the rocks, upsetting the equal balance that had forced the branch in place, and both floated free and out of sight. The old man stared at the two rocks with the water rushing freely between.

"Zaida?"

The old man looked down at his grandson, choking back his feelings before replying.

"They . . . they died when I was very young."

"Why?"

"Because."

"Daddy said because is not an answer. It's an excuse."

The old man grinned. "I know. I told him that."

"Why did they die? Were they sick?"

"No, they weren't sick."

A robin fluttered to the ground. It jabbed its head into the grass and a worm appeared, captured in its beak. They watched intently as the robin hopped about with the worm struggling and then the robin flew into the trees. "Did you see what the robin did?" the old man asked.

The boy nodded his head.

"Robins only put into their mouths what they can eat. Many years ago, a bad man started to eat. First, he ate things people didn't care about and a lot of people cheered. Then he ate people who caused problems and many liked that too. Afterwards, he ate good people and those who were left were confused. Then he ate everything and there was no one left who disagreed with what he ate."

"Is that what happened to your mother and father?"

"Yes. And many others. Everyone thought the bad man was either mad or a genius. Those who thought he was mad, ignored him and those who thought he was a genius followed him. He ate and ate, getting bigger and bigger and others ate with him and everything they ate, they destroyed."

"Why was he so hungry?"

"That's not easy to explain also."

"Why?"

"At first, he suffered from hate; then envy, greed and finally power. Each desire ate at him until all he saw was ugliness. There was no beauty in his life."

Just then the squirrel stopped eating and sat on his haunch. His head snapped in all directions in a quick, jerky motion. The old man touched the young boy on the shoulder and placed his finger to his lips for him to be quiet. "Watch," he said.

A dog had appeared at the top of the hill, and was barrelling down towards the squirrel, barking and yelping. The squirrel dropped the partially eaten chestnut, chattered a fraction of a second, then leaped towards the nearest tree, scampering up the trunk, into the branches above and out of sight. Barking and wagging its tail, the dog jumped against the trunk until accepting he had lost his prey and ran away to look for his next adventure.

The young boy laughed.

"The bad man picked on the weak. He did it to draw attention to himself. He jumped and barked, frightening those unable to help themselves. The dog was having fun, but the squirrel didn't know it. It was frightened."

The little boy dropped his head to his chest, his lips formed a pout. "I'm sorry zaida, I laughed. I thought it was funny. I wasn't thinking of the squirrel."

The old man placed his arm around the boy and gave him a hug. "I know. It was the same when the bad man was making fun of others and many joined him. But it wasn't funny for those who were his victims."

"What's a victim?" The little boy gazed up at the old man and noticed a tear on his cheek. "Are you crying zaida?"

The old man shook his head and smiled. "I was remembering."

"About what?"

"About my mother and father. They were victims. They didn't understand what the bad man was doing. They couldn't believe the stories they heard. One day they found out the truth."

"Daddy said, that the truth never hurts. It's when you don't tell the truth that it hurts."

"Yes, lies hurt . . . but the truth can also hurt. There were others who couldn't believe the truth and they closed their eyes to what they heard. One day, bad men came for my father and took him to a bad place. Then my mother understood the truth and gave me to a family to keep me safe. Later, they came for my mother."

"What happened to the bad man? Did he get punished?"

"I want you to look at the water and wait for a leaf to float down." They stared at the rushing stream in silence. The old man pointed, "there – do you see it?"

"Yes! Yes!" The little boy said excitedly. "It's like my sled when we go down the hill in the park."

"Watch what happens when it reaches those two rocks in front of us. Don't lose sight of it."

"I won't."

Being a big leaf, it slapped one rock and was momentarily pasted against its surface but the continuous rush of water under it lifted it free and it floated out of sight.

"For a little while it looked like the bad man might succeed, but those who were against him chipped away at his strength until he could not withstand them, and he was stopped. But it was too late for so many."

"Is that man still here?" the grandson asked.

The old man looked about before answering. "Do you see the grass?"

The young boy smiled, "Yes, zaida. It's everywhere."

"Yes, it's everywhere. Grass grows all over the world. In between the grass there are weeds. Sometimes they are in clumps and sometimes they are alone. Weeds are bad. They take, instead of giving to the soil. That bad man is gone, but others spring up all over the world and they cause ugliness wherever they appear."

"Why don't people stop them?"

"Some try, but most are afraid. They hope if they don't get involved, maybe they'll be left alone. But another weed grows beside the first and another until there is a clump and by then the good grass has been eaten and is gone."

A woman's voice called.

"It's your mother. It's time to eat. We had better get back." They stood and headed up the hill.

"Zaida."

"Yes."

"I'm sorry you lost your mother and father."

The old man placed his hand on the little boy's head and tousled his hair. As they neared the crest, the little boy slipped his hand into the old man's. Before they passed from the sound of the stream, the little boy said, "I love you zaida."

The squirrel came down from the tree and scampered around until he found the partially nibbled chestnut. It froze momentarily when he heard the yapping of the dog, but realized he was in no immediate danger and continued to chip away at his lunch. Meanwhile the birds hovered overhead and the stream continued to flow out of sight. Everything was as it was before. Nothing had changed – or had it?

Definitions

AKTION: A planned SS or Gestapo raid or round-up of prisoners of a specific category.

ALIYAH: Jewish immigration to the Land of Israel. Used either generally or in relation to a particular wave of immigration.

AMALEK: Ancient people mentioned several times in the Bible, almost always hostile to Israel. The name remains in rabbinic literature as a symbol of everlasting enmity to Israel.

ANTI-SEMITISM: A popular name for the prejudice against Jews. In ancient times, the Jews were charged for refusal to conform. In the Middle Ages, Jews were condemned as a religious minority. In modern times, anti-Semitism has been fostered by fascist states.

ARYAN: Nazi racial ideology for Nordic race; non-Jews.

BARBAROSSA: Code name for the German invasion of the Soviet Union (1941).

BAR MITZVAH: A boy becomes bar mitzvah at the age of thirteen. On the Sabbath closest to his birthday, he is called to the Bimah in a synagogue to read from the Torah, usually its concluding portion (*Maftir*) and from the Haftorah. The ceremony signifies that he has become of age to assume full religious responsibilities as a Jew.

BLITZKREIG: German term, literally meaning 'lightning war', used to describe the intensity and speed of German military onslaught against their enemies territory.

BLOOD: Drinking or any use of blood is prohibited under penalty of death (*Lev. 47:10*); reply to those who accuse Jews of using human blood.

BRIKHA: A group dedicated to the finding of Jewish children after the war and smuggling them to Palestine.

BUND: (*General Jewish Workers' Union*) a strong Jewish socialist movement founded in tsarist Russia in 1897. Committed to secular non-territorial nationalism, Jewish cultural and linguistic (*Yiddish*) autonomy and strongly antagonistic to Zionism.

COMMANDANT: Camp commander.

CONCENTRATION CAMP: Involved forced labour and the systematic use of terror, usually with a high percentage of Jews. Originally intended for detention for enemies of Germany, it eventually was used for everyone that were deemed unwanted.

DAVEN: Praying

DEATH CAMP: Maintained solely for the annihilation of its population. Most were located in Poland, but the notorious were also found in Czechoslovakia, Germany and Russia occupied territory.

DEATH MARCHES: The evaluation and forced marches of camp inmates during the latter stages of the war, when the Nazis felt threatened by the proximity of Allied troops. Tens of thousands of victims died while on these marches.

DEPORTATION: The term used by the Nazis when they removed undesireables from their normal place of residence to a labour, concentration or death camp.

DISPLACED PERSON: Millions of Europeans, Jews and non-Jews, who by the war's end had been forced out of their homes, both by the Nazi decrees and by the overall effect of the war.

EINSATZGRUPPEN: (*Killing squads*) Men committed to the National Socialist ideology and thoroughly imbued with the notion that Jews were Bolsheviks and mortal enemies of the German people and German state. They performed their special task of removing the Jews with staggering efficiency by combining guile, terror and systematic savagery.

EXTERMINATION CAMP: A camp for mass extermination of Jews and other targeted for death by Nazi ideology.

FINAL SOLUTION: (*Endlosung*) A term used by the Nazis for the annihilation of the Jews in Europe.

GESTAPO: Secret state police. Political police under Reich SS leader Heinrich Himmler that controlled admission and release of prisoners at Buchenwald.

GHETTO: Restricted areas within a city in which to confine a portion of the population. Used by the Nazis to separate the Jews from everyone else and then to remove them to other locations for final disposition.

GOY: Hebrew for "a people." Now the word is used to mean a gentile or non-Jew.

HAGANAH: Underground military force comprised of Jews from the Jewish community in Palestine under the British Mandate.

HITLER YOUTH: Founded in 1926 to teach German youth the racial, social and militaristic values of the Nazi philosophy.

HOLOCAUST: The slaughter of six million European Jews by the Nazi regime during World War II.

JERUSALEM: The religious and political centre of Israel and Judah. Taken by David from the Jebusites, he made it his capital and brought the Ark there. It was the centre of Jewish life until the destruction of the Temple in 70 C.E.

JEW: (*Yehudi*) originally the name for a member of the tribe of Judah. After the return from Babylonian Exile, the name for all Israelites became Jews (*Yehudim*).

JUDENRAT: Reference for a Jewish Council who were to provide the Nazis with administrative and supervisory assistance, including implementing Nazi decrees.

KADDISH: From the Aramaic for "holy." Doxology following study period, now recited also at death of parents and other relatives by sons. Recited at daily services for eleven months if for father or mother and also on anniversary of death.

KAPO: The origin of the word is unknown. According to one account, Italian men used kapo to address their foreman. Prisoners in Dachau picked up the slang. From there it spread to the other camps.

LABOUR CAMP: A place where slave labour was used to contribute for war-time production.

LEBENSRAUM: Literally 'living space'. The acquisition of additional Lebensraum to be colonized by the German people in the east was central to Hitler's racial vision of the future and therefore a key to his foreign policy and military preparations.

MENTSCH: A word referring to a person as a human being. More often it was a compliment extolling that the person exhibited the qualities of compassion, understanding and tzedakah. During the Holocaust period, it denoted a poor Jew who did the forced labour for the rich Jew for some form of compensation.

MIDRASH: A compilation of rabbinic sermons and stories interpreting the Scriptures. Such collections were made in different countries and at different periods.

MINYAN: Number or quorum. A minimum of ten men above the age of thirteen for public worship.

NUREMBERG LAWS: German racial laws of September and November 1935 under which Jews lost rights of citizenship. To be a Jew by definition, they had to have at least two Jewish grandparents.

PALESTINE: Name for the land of Israel. The name is a derivation from the word Philistine and was first used by the Greeks and later by the Romans (*Palestina*).

RABBI: (*my teacher*) The spiritual leader of a congregation ordained by a theological seminary or a Yeshiva. The rabbi is expected to be devoted to the principles of Judaism, to be a scholar and to lead an exemplary life.

SABBATH: (*Shabbot*) the weekly holy day of rest, the last day of the week. It begins Friday night at sundown and ends at sundown on Saturday evening. A day of rest and sanctification. It is ushered on Friday night with the lighting of the candles and the saying of Kiddush.

SHTETL: Yiddish for small town, but more than a small town, predominantly Jewish.

SHTIBL: a house used for religious purposes. Replacement for a synagogue.

SHIELD OF DAVID: (*Magen David*) a six-pointed star consisting of two interlaced triangles. In modern times the generally accepted symbol of Judaism.

SHOFAR: A ram's horn used in ancient times to signal an alarm or to assemble the people. Its stirring notes announce the New Year and a divine summons to repentance and improvement.

SHUTZSTAFFELN (SS): Created in 1925 to protect the Nazi Party. Originally known as 'Blackshirts', but became a paramilitary protection body after Hitler's rise to power and controlled all the concentration and death camps.

SYNAGOGUE: A Greek word meaning assembly or congregation. First used by the Jews of Egypt in the Third century B.C.E. to describe their houses of worship.

TALMUD: *(teaching)* The teaching covers both legal rulings and the balance of accumulated knowledge, ethics and legend.

TEFILLIN: Small leather boxes which contain four handwritten sections of the Torah and to which leather straps are attached. Traditionally, men and boys over thirteen place them on the head and left arm during daily morning prayers except on Sabbaths and holidays.

TORAH: The Five Books of Moses (*Genesis, Exodus, Leviticus, Numbers,* and *Deuteronomy*) which form the foundation of the Jewish tradition and faith.

TZEDAKAH: (*Charity*) The act of someone who is being righteous and charitable. The Jewish belief is based not on pity for the needy but on the principle of justice and the belief that all men are brothers.

WAILING WALL: (*Kotel Maaravi*) known also as the Western Wall. Remnant of the Temple on the Temple Mount in Jerusalem.

WEHRMACHT: German regular armed forces.

WORK DETAIL: SS terminology for a squad of prisoners assigned to labour duties.

YESHIVA: (*Academy*) originally a school of higher Jewish learning. In modern times, it refers to a Jewish elementary all-day school in which students receive a secular and Jewish education.

ZIONISM: Movement to re-establish State of Israel. Term used in 1886 by Nathan Birnbaum as a political movement, culminated in the establishment of the Jewish State in 1948.

Glossary

HISTORICAL PEOPLE REFERRED TO IN THIS BOOK:

THE GOOD GUYS

MORDECHAI ANIELEWICZ
Young Zionist activist who as the combined head of the Jewish combat Organization with Yitzhak Zukerman led the Warsaw Ghetto Uprising of April - May 1943.

ANNE FRANK
(1929-1945) A Jewish girl who lived in Amsterdam with her family. She kept a poignant diary of the war years 1942-1944, displaying great literary ability and psychological insight. Her diary was discovered after her death in the concentration camp of Bergen-Belsen and was later published and became world famous.

HERSCHL GRYNSZPAN
Seventeen-year-old Jew who assassinated a German official from the Paris embassy in November 1938. His action caused the Kristallnacht pogrom.

CHAIM KAPLAN
Polish writer who chronicled life in the Warsaw Ghetto until he was deported to Treblinka in September 1942.

THE BAD GUYS

ADOLF HITLER
(1889-1945) Austrian-born leader of the German National Socialist Party (*Nazi*), who became Chancellor of Germany. After serving in World War I, he built the party into a major force exploiting anti-Semitism. He was the personal embodiment of Nazi Germany and the evil that flowed from it, a charismatic demagogue who plunged Europe into a World conflict. For the people of the Allied

and conquered countries in World War II, Hitler was the real enemy. He was a strutting, shouting dictator with an obsession as a Jew-hater, who had to be stopped before he and his diabolic philosophy engulfed the world. He committed suicide as Russian troops advanced through Berlin.

SS LIEUTENANT-COLONEL KARL ADOLF EICHMANN

(1906-1962) Career bureaucrat in the SS, who became the head of the Jewish Office of the Gestapo from 1940 to 1945. He was directly in charge of the round-up of Jews in occupied Europe and their transport to death camps. So fierce was his dedication to this task that, despite shortage of transport and the approach of the Allied troops, he almost succeeded in wiping out European Jewry. In 1945, he went into hiding to Argentina. In 1960, he was captured by Israeli agents and flown to Israel and charged with crimes against humanity. After a lengthy trial, he was found guilty and hung at Ramlah Prison on May 31, 1962. His body was cremated and his ashes scattered into the sea.

SS OBERGRUPPENFUHRER REINHARD HEYDRICH

(1904-1942) Leader of the Einsatzgruppen or special action squads, whose responsibility was the extermination of the Jewish populations of Poland, the Baltic states and the Soviet Union. Co-responsible with Heinrich Himmler for the creation of the Nazi police state and the concentration camps. Thirty-four years of age, blond, blue-eyed, Heydrich was the epitome of the Aryan stereotype so beloved by the Nazis; nick-named the "Blond Beast" and known as "The Hangman." He is regarded as the real engineer of the Final Solution. On May 27, 1942, two Czech agents ambushed Heydrich's car near Prague and fatally wounded him.

SS REICHSFUHRER HEINRICH HIMMLER

(1900-1945) Minister of the Interior. Head of the SS and Nazi police apparatus, with overall responsibility for eliminating all enemies of Hitler's new order. Chief architect of the concentration camp system and prime mover and organizer of the Final Solution. Committed suicide in May 1945.

HANS FRANK, GOVERNOR OF SOUTHERN POLAND

(1900-1946) German Nazi leader, who became Bavarian minister of justice in 1933 and Reich minister without portfolio in 1934. As governor-general in Poland, he was responsible for the deportation and massacre of 2.5 million Jews from the ghettos and death camps for slave labour, ensuring their removal through starvation, expulsion and extermination. Was executed with the verdict of the Nuremberg tribunal.

SS HAUPTSCHARFUHRER HELMUT RAUCA

Jewish Affairs specialist who controlled the destiny of the Jewish population in Kaunas, Lithuania on a day-to-day basis. Rauca appeared at the ghetto gates, made surprise visits to Jewish Community headquarters, planted informants in ghetto workshops, approved or disapproved the delivery of food and fuel to the ghetto and decided which of the ghetto's residents should live and which should die. On Thursday, June 17, 1982, he was arrested by the Royal Canadian Mounted Police in Toronto, Canada and extradited to Frankfurt, Germany on May 17, 1983. On September 28, 1983, he was charged with the murder of 11,500 Lithuanians, but died of natural causes on Saturday, October 28, 1983 before going to trial.

HISTORICAL PLACES REFERRED TO IN THIS BOOK:

TREBLINKA CONCENTRATION CAMP, POLAND

(*Treblinka*) Located in Treblinka village about fifty miles north of Warsaw, it originally began as a labour camp but evolved into a liquidation camp to accommodate the Final Solution. It was the only death camp that had a major revolt by prisoners. The revolt started on August 3, 1943, killing 20 guards. About 600 managed to reach the nearby forest. Estimates of those who died overall exceed 700,000. When liberated in 1945, only 40 prisoners were found alive.

STUTTHOF CONCENTRATION CAMP, POLAND

Built in September 21, 1939 in the village of Stutthof, twelve miles east of Danzig in Poland. On April 25, 1945, just days before the end of the war, 200 Jewish women were executed. From 1,500 women being evacuated by barges across the Baltic Sea, half drowned or were killed by the Germans. In the early part of the war, Jews were deported to Dachau from Stutthof.

THE BEREZNE GHETTO, UKRAINE

A section of Berezne was designated as a ghetto run by a Judenrat that was corrupt in its responsibilities. The edict of the Germans were upheld by Jewish policemen whose motives were self-serving and for personal gain. The ghetto was entirely liquidated shortly after its establishment.

KAUNAS GHETTO, LITHUANIA

Established July 15, 1941 in the suburb of Vilijampole in the district of Slobodka. This neglected suburb, tucked in a bend of the Vilija River had no sewers, no running water and few paved streets. Prior to the war, it had a population of 7,000 people, half being Christians who were ordered to leave to make way for 30,000 Jews. When the ghetto was liberated, there were only 84 survivors.

References

Historical information to substantiate the stories in this book and to accurately describe places and incidents referred.

Atlas of the World. (Revised Edition) National Geographical Society (1995).

Cavendish, Marshall *The War Years 1939-1945 Eyewitness Accounts.* Coles Book Stores, Toronto, Canada (1994).

Comay, Joan. *Who's Who in Jewish History: After the Period of the Old Testament.* David McKay Company, Inc., New York, U.S.A. (1974).

Dawidowicz, Lucy S. *The War Against the Jews 1933-1945.* Holt, Rinehart and Winston, New York, U.S.A. (1975).

Fogelman, Eva. *Conscience & Courage: Rescuers of Jews During the Holocaust.* Anchor Books, New York, U.S.A. (1994).

Gilbert, Martin. *The Holocaust: A History of the Jews of Europe During the Second World War.* Henry Holt and Company, New York, U.S.A. (1985).

Herzog, Chaim Major-General. *The War of Atonement: October 1973.* Little, Brown and Company, Boston, U.S.A. (1975).

Kuchler-Silverman, Lena *My Hundred Children.* Dell Publishing, New York, U.S.A. (1961).

Landau, Ronnie S. *The Nazi Holocaust.* Ivan R. Dee Inc., Chicago, U.S.A. (1992).

Lawliss, Charles *. . . and God Cried: The Holocaust Remembered.* JG Press, Massachusetts, U.S.A. (1994).

Littman, Sol *War Criminals on Trial: The Rauca Trial.* Lester and Orphen Dennys, Toronto, Canada (1983).

Posner, Raphael, Rabbi Dr. *Junior Judaica: Encyclopaedia Judaica for Youth.* Keter Publishing House Jerusalem Ltd., Jerusalem, Israel (1982).

Roth, Cecil, B.Litt., M.A., D. Phil., and Wigoder, Geoffrey,

D.Phil., Editor-in-chief; *The New Standard Jewish Encyclopedia*: Doubleday & Company, Inc., New York, U.S.A. (1970).

Runes, Dagobert D. *Dictionary of Judaism*. Citadel Press, New York, U.S.A. (1959).

Schiff, Zeev. *A History of the Israeli Army (1870-1974)*. Straight Arrow Books, California, U.S.A. (1974).

Shirer, William L. *The Rise and Fall of the Third Reich: A History of Nazi Germany*. Simon and Shuster, New York, U.S.A. (1960).

Suhl, Yuri. *They Fought Back: The Story of the Jewish Resistance in Nazi Europe*. Schocken Books, New York, U.S.A. (1967).

Szydlowiecz Benevolent Society, *Szydlowiecz Memorial Book*. New York, U.S.A. (1989)

Taylor, A. J. P. Editor-in-Chief *History of the Twentieth Century*. Purnell BPC Publishing Ltd., London, England (1968).

The Oxford Companion to World War II. Oxford University Press, New York, U.S.A. (1995).

Trunk, Isaiah. *Judenrat: The Jewish Councils in Eastern Europe under Nazi Occupation*. The Macmillan Company, New York, U.S.A. (1972).

Yahil, Leni. *The Holocaust: The Fate of European Jewry*. Oxford University Press, New York, U.S.A. (1990).